Hiking the Grand Canyon

The Sierra Club Totebooks®

The Best About Backpacking
Bitterroot to Beartooth
The Climber's Guide to the High Sierra
Climber's Guide to Yosemite Valley
Climbing and Hiking in the Wind River Mountains
Cooking for Camp and Trail
Fieldbook of Nature Photography
Food for Knapsackers
Footloose in the Swiss Alps
Hiker's Guide to the Smokies
Hiking the Bigfoot Country
Hiking the Grand Canyon
Hiking the Great Basin
Hiking the North Cascades
Hiking the Old Dominion
Hiking the Southwest
Hiking the Teton Backcountry
Hiking the Yellowstone Backcountry
Hut Hopping in the Austrian Alps
Starr's Guide to the John Muir Trail and the High Sierra Region
Timberline Country
To Walk With a Quiet Mind
Words for the Wild

A Sierra Club Totebook®

Hiking the Grand Canyon

by John Annerino

SIERRA CLUB BOOKS
SAN FRANCISCO

The Sierra Club, founded in 1892 by John Muir, has devoted itself to the study and protection of the earth's scenic and ecological resources – mountains, wetlands, woodlands, wild shores and rivers, deserts and plains. The publishing program of the Sierra Club offers books to the public as a nonprofit educational service in the hope that they may enlarge the public's understanding of the Club's basic concerns. The point of view expressed in each book, however, does not necessarily represent that of the Club. The Sierra Club has some sixty chapters coast to coast, in Canada, Hawaii, and Alaska. For information about how you may participate in its program to preserve wilderness and the quality of life, please address inquiries to Sierra Club, 730 Polk Street, San Francisco, CA 94109.

Library of Congress Cataloging in Publication Data

Annerino, John.
Hiking the Grand Canyon.

Bibliography: p. 319
Includes index.
1. Hiking—Arizona—Grand Canyon National Park.
2. Hiking—Arizona—Grand Canyon National Park—Guidebooks. 3. Grand Canyon National Park (Ariz.)—Guidebooks. I. Title.
GV199.42.A72G7334 1986 917.91'32 85-18450
ISBN 0-87156-755-5

Book design by Merrill Peterson, Matrix Productions
Interior photographs by George H. H. Huey
Cover design by Bonnie Smetts
Cover photograph by Joseph Holmes
Printed in the United States of America on acid-free paper containing a minimum of 50% recovered waste paper, of which at least 10% is post-consumer waste
10 9 8 7 6

*To Harvey Butchart,
who somehow heard the silent
footsteps of the Canyon's ancient
masters and who subsequently plotted
the course through this labyrinthine
maze for future generations of
canyoneers who will eagerly
follow in his footsteps.*

Contents

Acknowledgments

The trouble with acknowledgments is that you think you're going to incur someone's wrath if you forget to include his or her name, and with *any* kind of work on the beloved Grand Canyon that can become a Sisyphean task, primarily because the work of many people ultimately contributed to the successful completion of this guide. But let me be the first to confess that I am absolutely the worst person in the world when it comes to remembering names—though I'll never forget your face. So if for some reason I have failed to include your name, please accept my apologies and my gratitude for your help.

In the meantime, I would like to thank those friends and talented professionals whose names I do readily remember: my Grand Canyon climbing partners—Dave Ganci, who first suggested I do this book, and George Bain, whose wit and perspective on the modern gunslingers who still ride the Canyon's romantic trails provided me with the necessary levity to keep this project rolling in high gear; Kimmie Johnson, who tirelessly ran down elusive answers to sometimes odd questions fired at her at all hours of the day and night; and the National Park Service professionals who shined as people when I asked for their assistance—Robert C. Euler, Butch Farabee, Pam Bell, Chuck Lundy, Ken Phillips, and, of course, the "booch" himself, Dave Bucello. I'd also like to thank Norm Tessman, Curator, Sharlot Hall Museum, for his patient research assistance over the years; Rex Tilousi, Vice-Chairman of the Havasupai Indian Tribe, for his assistance; Jim Ohlman, Grand Canyon Trail Guides; Dorothy House, Librarian, Museum of N.A.; and the two prescient-minded editors at Sierra Club Books who picked up this ball and ran with it—Diana Landau and Jim Cohee.

This guide wouldn't have the breadth it needed if it weren't for its contributors, who eagerly lent their individual expertise: Jan Balsom, for her "Native Americans in the Grand Canyon"; Larry Stevens, for his overview on the Canyon's natural history; George Huey, for his striking black & white photography; and Michael Young, for his work on the geology of the Grand Canyon—and for his patience in trying to pound some "rock sense" into this Paleolithic skull.

I'd also like to thank those friends whose shared experiences with me in the Grand Canyon had more to do with the completion of this guide than they'll ever know: sweet Suzanne Jordan, who taught me everything I thought I knew about running the Colorado River; Tim Ganey, Chris Keith, Craig Hudson, Ginny Taylor, Tony Mangine, Chris May, Randy Mulkey, and Bob Farrell who supported me during my three trans-Canyon runs; and my backpacking and wilderness survival students from Scottsdale Community College who first helped me learn the secrets of canyoneering 15 years ago.

Lastly, I'm indebted to the Old Man for taking this frail city boy off the streets of Chicago and steering him in this sunny direction, and to my dear mom for her prayers, her belief in me, and for somehow saying "no, absolutely not" when surgeons quite literally wanted to shunt my canyoneering career before it really got started.

Thank you.

About the Author

John Annerino graduated from Prescott College in 1975 with a B.A. in Creative Writing/Wilderness Leadership, and has 15 years of professional experience as a wilderness guide, instructor, and boatman. Annerino presently divides his time between photojournalism and wilderness exploration. Some of his present work is being handled by Gamma-Liaison/NY and Marka/Italy, while some of his past photo-features on the Grand Canyon and man and the Southwest have appeared in *Arizona Highways*, Germany's *Bunte*, *GEO*, *Fortune*, Italy's *Panorama Mese*, Denmark's *Ifot*, *Inside Kung-Fu*, *Life Magazine*, England's *Mountain*, *The Navajo Times*, *Runner's World*, Sierra Club Books, *Survive*, *TW Norway*, *Ultrasport*, and numerous other publications. His Grand Canyon experience is extensive and includes a half-dozen technical first ascents of Canyon temples, 18½ trips as a Colorado River boatman, 68 overnight canyoneering trips as a guide, and running the length of the Grand Canyon by three different routes in order to prove his Hopi travel theories: 1980, a six-day 170-mile run below the

South Rim; 1981, a seven-day 210-mile run along the ancient Hopi/Havasuapi trade route atop the South Rim; and 1982, an eight-and-a-half-day, 250-mile run below the seldom-explored North Rim.

PART ONE

WELCOME TO THE GRAND CANYON

CHAPTER 1

About This Guide

Hiking the Grand Canyon is a guidebook to one of the most sublime and awesome natural arenas on Earth, and being just a guide it can only be an outline for your own journeys; in this case, it focuses primarily on those areas within or immediately adjacent to the old Grand Canyon National Park boundaries. And while the entire guide was compiled and written with painstaking care, particularly detailed attention was devoted to the preparatory sections, so that your canyoneering experience will be as sage and rewarding as possible. To ensure the accuracy and credibility of the trail sections, the author has described only those areas he's personally hiked, trekked, or run; those descriptions were compiled from his map and field notes and (when possible and appropriate) cross-referenced against those on file at the BRO (Backcountry Reservations Office).

What these trail and route descriptions are not, however, are lead-me-by-the-hand, step-by-step, switchback-by-switchback blueprints; they can't be, because everyone's impressions are different—in particular when it comes to attempting to generically interpret the fantastic and finite details of someplace like the Grand Canyon. They're the author's impressions, sketches if you will, which may very well differ from your own once you're in the Canyon; but even if they could be more than just sketches, the author wouldn't want them to be. Because one of the inherent attractions of canyoneering is the adventure of discovering for yourself some of its mysteries, the rewards of piecing together another part of the puzzle on your own, and using your skills and judgment to plot your way through the Great Unknown from Point A to Point B. And the author wouldn't want to dilute that experience for anybody. So while the trail and route descriptions *will* guide you, they don't provide all the answers, nor do they eliminate the potential hazards of trekking their peculiar courses. You will still have to think, and you'll still have to make your own judgment calls, however you use this guide, because the Canyon will ultimately be seen and experienced through your eyes.

IN DEFENSE OF THIS GUIDE

Mention the word "guidebook" and the heads of purists turn. Suddenly *you're* wearing the black hat for giving away the family jewels. Well, the Grand Canyon—its trails and routes, rapids, vistas, hidden corners, and now its airways—has never been the best-kept secret, as evidenced by the publication of a single, exhaustive, and scholarly work titled *Bibliography of the Grand Canyon and the Lower Colorado River 1540–1980*—not to mention the 2½ million people who visit it each year.

But, yes, writing a guidebook *is* a two-edged sword, just as any outdoor-related profession or activity is; while introducing new people to an area or activity, you subsequently advertise it. And if the Grand Canyon itself doesn't feel the direct results of outdoor enthusiasts and tourists being introduced to the area through active or passive activities, some other fragile ecosystem will.

That's the downside, of course. But what about the future of our remaining roadless, wilderness, and natural areas if we don't descend from our lofty perches and build a large enough conservation constituency to prevent the entire planet from being bulldozed, clearcut, or strip-mined, and jammed down the evolutionary trash compactor? I mean, "they" are still actively pursuing the Bridge City area around Mile 237 on the Colorado River in order to build another dam in the Grand Canyon. And why is another dam still being considered in the Grand Canyon? Directly or indirectly, it has to do with "us." In the simplest of terms, there's still not enough of us who know or care, and one can't help but wonder and agree with the farsighted words of Yosemite climber Warren Harding when he said: "Elitists will argue that it is necessary to discourage the masses from the mountain areas. No doubt this would work quite well in a feudal system where a small nobility had complete control of the peasantry. But such is not the case—theoretically, at least, this country operates as a democracy . . . All, worthy or not, have equal right to public lands. Again, theoretically, the use and preservation of our mountain areas would seem to depend on the vote of the masses. How then can we expect support of the average citizen in conservation if he is told the mountains are too good for him, that they should be reserved for the minority of self-styled good guys?"

That puts each of us in the classic lizard-and-the-tail dilemma: like the playful cat that has both front paws on the lizard, do we chance letting go of the entire lizard in order to toy with that single, tantalizing tail; or do we accept a minor loss in order to save the whole? Well, I'm one of those folks who'd rather see more smiling and exhausted faces in the Grand Canyon discovering its secrets for themselves than see those same people water-skiing across it. And if the publication of this guide in any way contributes to building a grassroots political base that will prevent this Sistine Chapel from being flooded, that's good enough for me.

John Annerino
Groom Creek, Arizona
March 21, 1986

CHAPTER 2

Native Americans in the Grand Canyon

by Janet R. Balsom

The cultural history of the Grand Canyon began between 3,000 and 4,000 years ago with the makers of split-twig figurines. These figurines, made of either willow or cottonwood, have been found in caches in caves in the Mississippian Redwall Formation. The makers of the figurines are thought to have followed a hunting-and-gathering lifestyle known as Archaic. It is thought that the figurines may have been made by people of the Pinto Basin period Desert Culture for purposes of imitative hunting magic. Projectile points characteristic of the Desert Culture have been found in the vicinity of Grand Canyon, but never in direct association with the figurines.

Further evidence of Archaic manifestations at Grand Canyon is primarily limited to the South Rim and far western reaches of the North Rim, although recent information gathered from the inner Canyon suggests limited occupation of the Canyon itself. Adaptation most likely involved reliance on a hunting-and-gathering subsistence base. In general, subsistence would have adjusted to the environment based on the seasonal exploitation of various plant and animal resources in areas of high resource variability.

For many years it was thought that the Canyon was abandoned between the Archaic occupation and later Anasazi occupation. Recent research suggests that limited occupation continued from Archaic times until sometime around A.D. 700 to 800, when the Anasazi tradition was fully recognized. At that time population began to rise, and the Kayenta Anasazi established themselves in the eastern reaches of the Canyon while a group called the Cohonina became established in the western South Rim areas. The Anasazi were utilizing and expanding in both the South Rim and inner Canyon areas until around A.D. 1050, when they expanded to the North Rim. Evidence from research conducted on Unkar Delta and Walhalla Glades indicates that population had increased to a point where utilization of one area was not adequate for the population. Movement onto the North Rim provided an additional area that could be exploited for farming. Walhalla Glades supported a farming community for about 100 years, from A.D. 1050 until 1150. Mineralogic evidence from the ceramics found on both Unkar Delta and Walhalla Glades suggests that these two communities were comprised of the same people, utilizing the inner

Canyon most of the year and the North Rim to supplement the Canyon resources during the summer. A gradual decline in population occurred after A.D. 1100 until around A.D. 1150, during which time most areas of Grand Canyon were abandoned. Information recently gathered suggests that abandonment of some areas of the eastern inner Canyon was not until sometime after A.D. 1150. Along the eastern South Rim there is evidence to suggest that the population remained until after A.D. 1200 to 1225. It is thought that abandonment after A.D. 1150 was due to climatic changes on the Colorado Plateau.

The Anasazi lifestyle was marked by a number of cultural traits. The earliest Anasazi lived in pithouses characterized by upright rock slabs and a semi-subterranean floor. These early Anasazi did not make pottery. Instead they made and used baskets, usually of yucca. Because of this trait, this period of time is referred to as Basketmaker. It lasted from around A.D. 1 until A.D. 800. The economy at this time was primarily a hunting-and-gathering one. There is very little evidence of Basketmaker people in Grand Canyon.

Around A.D. 800 the Anasazi started to build coursed masonry structures. This is the beginning of the Pueblo period, the word *pueblo* coming from the Spanish word for town. The Pueblo period is divided into stages, beginning with Pueblo I (PI) dated to around A.D. 800–900, Pueblo II (PII) dated approximately A.D. 950–1150, Pueblo III (PIII) A.D. 1150–1300, and Pueblo IV (PIV) dated A.D. 1300–1540. Most occupation in the Grand

Canyon occurred during the PII period. At the beginning of the Pueblo period the Anasazi started to produce pottery. Early Anasazi pottery consisted of crude gray vessels. As time progressed, designs were added until a very sophisticated ceramic tradition existed. The different designs of black-on-white, black-on-red, and the corrugated-style pottery were characteristic of the PII periods in Grand Canyon. Of the 2,500 sites recorded in Grand Canyon so far, around 1,500 date to this time period.

Subsistence during PII times was characterized by a mixed hunting/gathering and agricultural economy. In an environment as marginal as the Grand Canyon, people must rely on a number of strategies in order to be successful. Evidence for agriculture on the South Rim is limited, but evidence in the inner Canyon and on the North Rim is extensive. Agricultural features such as check dams, terraces, and grid gardens can be found in a number of areas in the inner Canyon (e.g., Unkar Delta) and on the North Rim (e.g., Walhalla Glades).

At the same time that the Anasazi were utilizing the eastern areas of the Canyon, a group known as the Cohonina were utilizing the western South Rim, the Esplanade, and Havasu Canyon from around A.D. 700 until A.D. 1150. The lifestyle of the Cohonina was very different from the neighboring Anasazi, although it appears that the two groups did maintain close relations. On most sites found on the South Rim and on the neighboring Kaibab National Forest, artifacts will be comprised of both

The ruins at Nankoweap. *Photo by George H. H. Huey.*

Kayenta Anasazi and Cohonina ceramics. The Cohonina are poorly understood at this time.

Environmental conditions in the western Canyon areas would not allow an economy relying on agriculture like that of the Anasazi. Instead, Cohonina occupation was seasonal, relying primarily on hunting and gathering. Agave was of particular importance. Roasting pits can be found in many areas occupied by the Cohonina. Abandonment by the Cohonina around A.D. 1150 was probably due to the same climatic changes that drove the Anasazi from the Grand Canyon.

Reoccupation of the Grand Canyon did not occur until sometime after A.D. 1300 with the presence of the Southern Paiute and Cerbat. This later group is thought to be ancestral to the Pai (Hualapai and Havasupai) and to have occupied the same area as the Cohonina and the modern Pai. Another view suggests that the Cohonina were the direct ancestors of the Havasupai.

The Hualapai and Havasupai, Southern Paiute, Navajo, and Hopi represent the five tribes that live in and around the Grand Canyon today. Of these, only the Havasupai live within the Grand Canyon itself. They occupy a 160,000-acre reservation bordered by Grand Canyon National Park. The word Havasupai, which means "people of the blue-green water," refers to the color of the water of Havasu Creek, which runs through the side-canyon they inhabit. The Havasupai are primarily farmers, utilizing the Canyon for agriculture in the summer months and the rim and its resources of game and wild plants for food in the winter to supplement the food they grow. Their lifestyle is essentially unchanged since their ancestors first settled Havasu Creek around A.D. 1300.

Neighboring both the Havasupai and Grand Canyon National Park are the Hualapai, a group closely related to the Havasupai. "Hualapai" means "people of the pine trees," which refers to the tall pine trees that grow in the upper elevations of their reservation. Many changes have taken place since their ancestors first inhabited the area. The Hualapai were often at war with neighboring Yuman peoples, most notably the Yavapai. With the expansion of white settlers onto Hualapai land, hostilities began with the Anglos. In 1866, Anglos killed one of the Hualapai leaders. Retaliation was swift, but the poorly equipped Hualapai were no match for the white soldiers. By 1869, the war was over. The Hualapai were moved in 1874 to a portion of the Colorado River Indian Reservation. In 1875 they returned to their homeland. By 1883 a reservation was established, allocating the tribe approximately 1 million acres of land encompassing areas along the Colorado River and the rim.

Economically, the Hualapai relied on a subsistence pattern utilizing the many wild plant and animal resources. Today they rely on support from Anglo interests, namely tourism and river rafting.

The Southern Paiute inhabit areas on the North Rim of the Grand Canyon on the Kaibab Reservation. These people are descendants of Shoshonean groups and did not move into the Grand Canyon region until around

A.D. 1300. Their utilization of the Canyon was limited to the North Rim and some areas of the inner Canyon on the north side of the river in the west end of the Canyon. They were primarily hunters and gatherers, but they also practiced agriculture. They relied heavily upon the agave or century plant. Evidence for this is the number of mescal pits (agave roasting pits) found in the areas they inhabited.

The Hopi can trace their ancestry to the Anasazi who once inhabited Grand Canyon. It is thought that when the Anasazi abandoned Grand Canyon, they moved east and established the Hopi Mesas. The town of Old Oraibi on Third Mesa is the oldest continually inhabited community in the United States. It was established by A.D. 1200.

The Grand Canyon is very important to the Hopi. It is a symbolic place, the place where human beings and animals emerged from the underworld and the place where the dead returned. The Sipapu, or place of emergence, is located within the Grand Canyon, near the confluence of the Colorado and Little Colorado rivers. According to Hopi belief, the Hopi lived in a number of worlds below this one. They emerged through the Sipapu into this world.

The Hopi also used the Grand Canyon for salt. Salt deposits are found along the Colorado River near the confluence with the Little Colorado. These salt mines are sacred to the Hopi and have been placed off-limits to non-

Hopi by the National Park Service. Into historic times the Hopi have been known to make the 100-mile pilgrimage along the Salt Trail. The last documented trip was made in the 1960s.

The Hopi today are farmers. They practice a type of agriculture known as dry farming. By planting deep in the sandy soil, they have managed to farm desert areas thought by many to be unproductive. They also rely on the tourist trade. Hopi pottery, jewelry, and basketry command an ever-increasing market.

The Navajo are relative newcomers to the Grand Canyon region. Migrating from Canada, the Navajo are an Athapaskan people closely related to the Apache. The Navajo refer to themselves as "Dineh,"which means "the People." Opinions as to when the Navajo migrated vary widely with the earliest dates around A.D. 1000 and later dates around A.D. 1525. The Navajo were established at least by 1680, the time of the Pueblo Revolt that drove the Spanish from Hopi. The Navajo settled areas surrounding the Hopi lands. Many land disputes have arisen between the two tribes that are still unsettled.

The Navajo Nation is the largest Native American tribe in the United States. More than 200,000 people are considered to be Navajo, and their reservation encompasses more than 2 million acres of land in northern Arizona, New Mexico, and southern Utah. A portion of their reservation has rich deposits of coal, which have been mined by Peabody Coal Company. Revenue from the sale of the minerals is an important part of the Navajo economy, which includes farming, herding, jewelry and rugmaking, and tourism.

None of the tribes living in the Grand Canyon region today is isolated. Each has, in historic times, established trade relations with other groups in the region. Hopi and Havasupai established trade in the 1300s. Navajo and Hopi have traded since the Navajo migrated into the area. Hualapai and Havasupai trade freely and were not recognized as separate groups until 1776 or possibly later. The tribes today co-exist with each other and with the Anglo-Americans who have moved onto their lands.

JANET R. BALSOM is a graduate of Arizona State University. She is currently the archaeologist for Grand Canyon National Park.

CHAPTER 3

Natural History

by Lawrence E. Stevens

INTRODUCTION

The first observations on Canyon biology were recorded by Edgar Mearns in 1884, and the first purely biological expedition in the area was mounted by C. Hart Merriam and Vernon Bailey of the U.S. Biological Survey staff in 1889. Merriam studied distinctive zones of vegetation that he encountered from the 2,400 foot floor of Grand Canyon to the 12,600 foot top of the nearby San Francisco Peaks. He formulated his Life Zone Concept (see below), ascribing vegetational zonation to temperature and precipitation norms at different elevations. Biological interest in the Canyon was nominal until 1919 when Grand Canyon became a national park. Ranger-naturalists such as G.E. Sturdevant, E.D. McKee, and Lewis Schellbach observed, collected and identified the Canyon's biota. A biological expedition to Shiva Temple led by Harold Anthony in 1937 attracted national interest, but yielded no novel animal species on that isolated "sky island." Botanists Elzada Clover and Lois Jotter collected and reported on the vegetation of the Colorado River corridor from the first commercial river trip with Norm Nevills in 1938. By the 1960s river running made access to the inner Canyon easier, and detailed biological research began in earnest. Biological surveys sponsored by the National Park Service in the 1970s and, recently, by the Bureau of Reclamation, have added greatly to our knowledge of Grand Canyon biology.

This chapter discusses the structure and development of biological communities in the Grand Canyon region on a broad scale. The story of vegetation communities in Grand Canyon National Park, Holocene climatic changes, biogeography, and human impacts on Grand Canyon biology are complex and well worth telling. Space does not permit inclusion of exhaustive species lists here, and we have not tried to recount the life histories of individual species; however, checklists of the various taxa present in the park are available from the Grand Canyon Natural History Association at the South Rim and selected references are included at the end of this section.

LIFE ZONES AND VEGETATION

The Grand Canyon provides more than 7,000 feet of vertical relief and a diverse climate. From its rims down to the Colorado River, gradients of temperature, precipitation, and exposure regulate the occurrence of plant and animal species. Precipitation, much of it as snow, exceeds 25 inches per year at the highest elevations on the North Rim and may be less than 4 inches per year at Phantom Ranch. Exposure is an important determinant of growing conditions: north-facing slopes are cooler and more moist and harbor different plant species than south-facing slopes. In his Life Zone Concept Merriam described several zones of boreal vegetation which on the North Rim include Hudsonian and Canadian forests of spruce, fir, some pine, and aspen interspersed with marshy, open meadows. More notable vertebrates of the North Rim include turkeys, goshawks, various woodpeckers, kinglets, nuthatches, Townsend's solitares, Kaibab squirrels, chipmunks, deer mice, mule deer, black bear, and bobcats. On the South Rim, the Transition Zone ponderosa pine forest is mixed with stands of aspen, pinyon pine and juniper woodland, and open expanses of grassland, sagebrush and rabbitbrush. Common South Rim animals include golden eagles, mountain chickadees, pinyon jays, common ravens, robins, mule deer, coyotes and rock squirrels. At and below the Canyon's rims, deciduous and evergreen shrubs predominate, including serviceberry, skunkbush, New Mexico locust, cliff rose, manzanita and scrub and Gambel's oak. Douglas fir occupies cooler, north-facing ravines at higher elevations where rufous-sided towhees are likely to be encountered. As one descends to the Tonto Platform, increasing aridity causes tree species to be replaced by low shrubs, such as blackbrush, century plants, barberry, and prickly pear. Here the common vertebrates include collared lizards, side-blotched lizards, and western whiptail lizards, rock and canyon wrens, rock squirrels, mule deer, and desert bighorn sheep. Water courses, such as Garden Creek at Indian Gardens, provide sufficient moisture to support Fremont's cottonwood, velvet ash, hoptree, redbud, and willow. The vegetation of the dry Inner Gorge is comprised of Sonoran desertscrub plants, including prickly pear, hedgehog, tiny fishhook, and barrel cacti, desert sunflowers, century plants, banana and narrowleaf yucca, other low shrubs and desert grasses. Black collared lizards, side-blotched lizards, chuckwallas, black-throated sparrows, rock and canyon wrens, rock squirrels, and cactus and canyon mice become increasingly abundant at lower elevations. Riverside vegetation is dominated by tamarisk, mesquite, acacia, coyote willow, brickellia and seepwillow, and more than 1,000 plant species, 250 families of insects, 28 species of reptiles and amphibians, and 215 species of birds, as well as lizards, mice, beavers, small carnivores, mule deer and bighorn sheep have been reported from this biologically rich riparian zone.

THREE DESERTS

Three of North America's four desert ecosystems converge in the Grand Canyon region. The rims and higher elevations of the eastern Grand Canyon support the low shrub species characteristic of the cold Great Basin Desert of Nevada and Utah. Bigtooth sage and rabbitbrush occupy open valleys between stands of pine and juniper, and shadscale occurs along the upper Colorado River. The hot Sonoran Desert occupies central and southern Arizona and northwestern Mexico. Honey mesquite, catclaw acacia and other vegetation characteristic of the Sonoran Desert reaches upstream into Marble Canyon in the river corridor. Mohave Desert vegetation in the western Grand Canyon includes creosote bush, chollas, and ocotillo (also found in the Sonoran Desert), and blackbrush at higher elevations.

HOLOCENE CLIMATIC CHANGES

The climate of the Grand Canyon region has changed dramatically since the last ice age. From 23,000 to 15,000 years ago conditions were cooler, more humid and more moist. Glaciers developed on the San Francisco Peaks 70 miles south of Grand Canyon. At that time the Canyon floor was occupied by junipers and ash trees, and the vegetation zones extended as much as 2,700 feet lower in elevation. Pleistocene mammoths, bison, camels, horses, tapir, and giant ground sloths roamed the Colorado Plateau, and Harrington's mountain goats were common in the Canyon. Condors and Merriam's teratorn (a bird with a wingspan of more than 12 feet) soared the skies and roosted in Grand Canyon caves. With the retreat of the Canadian ice sheets from 15,000 to 10,000 years ago, the climate dried out and these magnificent Pleistocene beasts became extinct. Early humans in the region may have played a role in these extinctions. By 8,500 years ago desertification allowed lower elevation and more southerly plant and animal species to extend their ranges northward and elevationally upward. Likewise, boreal species retreated northward and farther upslope. Today the flora of the North Rim is dominated by vegetation characteristic of northern coniferous forests, while the plant, insect, and animal life on the Canyon floor is derived from desert populations found farther to the south. The Grand Canyon has been a meeting place for diverse groups of species in time as well as in space.

BIOGEOGRAPHY

Biogeography is the study of how and why living things are distributed as they are. Biogeographically, the topography of Grand Canyon exerts a powerful influence on the distribution of species, but this influence depends on a plant or animal's habitat requirements, mobility, and its mode of travel. For several plant and animal species, the Grand Canyon is not an important topographic obstacle: one-seed junipers, common ravens, violet-green swallows, deer mice, rock squirrels, least chipmunks, packrats, bobcats, coyotes, and desert mule deer are relatively ubiquitous throughout the Canyon. But for most species and populations, Grand Canyon serves as either a barrier, as a corridor, or as a refugium.

The Barrier Effect

As a barrier, Grand Canyon prevents north-south dispersal by terrestrial organisms. The Kaibab squirrel occurs on the North Rim and has been evolutionarily isolated from other races of the tassel-eared squirrel by the erosion of the Canyon and recent climatic changes. Similarly, numerous reptiles such as western skinks, sagebrush lizards, and fence lizards are prevented from spreading southward by harsh desert conditions of the inner Canyon. Southern plateau lizards and other species are prevented from northward population expansion. In the Canyon itself, rock pocket mice are found almost exclusively on the south side of the Colorado River, while their congeners, long-tailed pocket mice, are found on the north side.

The barrier effect also operates at the end of the Grand Canyon. Steep talus slopes and other habitat differences have prevented Joshua trees, desert iguanas, gopher tortoises, and other Mohave and Sonoran desert species from moving upstream into the Canyon from the region west of the Grand Wash Cliffs. Because of its turbulence and silty waters the Colorado River has also proved to be a barrier to upstream dispersal of Sonora mud turtles and exotic spiny soft-shelled turtles.

The Corridor Effect

As a corridor, the path of the Colorado River provides a route for low desert species to move from the western

Black collared lizard. *Photo by George H. H. Huey.*

Arizona desert into southern Utah. Desert riparian plants such as Gooddings willow, netleaf hackberry, tamarisk, seepwillow, and arrowweed occupy the banks of the Colorado River throughout Grand Canyon. Desert animal species whose ranges extend through the river corridor include the following species: the migratory monarch butterfly; speckled dace and other fish; red-spotted toads, rocky mountain toads, and canyon treefrogs; yellow-backed spiny lizards, black collared lizards, western whiptail lizards, side-blotched lizards, and banded geckos; migratory waterfowl, raptorial birds, song birds and other avifaunae; and mammals such as pocket mice, beaver, mule deer, desert bighorn sheep, ringtail cats, and, formerly, river otters.

This corridor effect is incomplete for many species because habitat availability and climate change gradually with distance downstream. Low desert species from the west, whose ranges extend only partway up through the Canyon, include crucifixion thorn, creosote bush, Herbert's giant water bug, gila monster, zebra-tailed lizard. The ranges of honey mesquite and catclaw acacia extend upriver into Marble Canyon. Leopard frog, white-tailed antelope, and ground squirrel populations extend southward into the Canyon from the Four Corners region. The corridor effect also operates at intermediate elevations in Grand Canyon. Through geologic time the range of black-brush, a Mohave Desert shrub, has extended into the Four Corners region via a corridor at intermediate elevation through the Canyon that includes the Tonto Platform. Scrub oak is also found at intermediate elevations through the national park.

The Grand Canyon as a Refuge

The Grand Canyon serves as a *refugium*, harboring plants and animals which are either *endemic* (occurring only in one locality) or are extremely isolated. As an island of habitat, the North Rim's boreal forest supports an endemic population of Kaibab squirrel. The Canyon itself harbors several endemic species. McDougall's ragweed occurs only in several small tributaries of the Colorado River in western Grand Canyon. *Octerus rotundus* is a small semi-aquatic water bug that has been found only in Grand Canyon and in the mountains of central Mexico. The rare and endangered hump-back chub is now restricted to the Colorado River in Grand Canyon and apparently only breeds at the mouth of the Little Colorado River. The Grand Canyon rattlesnake, *Crotalus viridis abyssus*, occurs only in the Canyon.

The Grand Canyon provides an abundance of several specific microhabitats that support locally common but highly isolated populations. For example, desert seeps and springs host populations of maidenhair ferns, horsetail, cardinal monkeyflowers, helleborine orchids, and other aquatic and semi-aquatic plants and insects. Cave entrances provide another specific microhabitat for endemic and isolated arthropods, such as harvestmen and spiders.

HUMAN IMPACTS ON GRAND CANYON

Human activity has exerted a profound influence on the biology of Grand Canyon. Although 2½ million visitors see the Canyon every year, including nearly 40,000 hikers and 15,000 river runners, impacts from visitation are generally localized and are well managed by the National Park Service. Of greater consequence have been the impacts of animal control and introduction programs, and regulation of the Colorado River.

Predator Control on the North Rim

When Teddy Roosevelt proclaimed the North Rim a National Game Preserve in 1906, he secured protection only for game animals, and an intensive predator elimination program began. One bounty hunter, James T. Owens, killed more than 530 mountain lions on the North Rim. A large pack of wolves and thousands of bobcats and coyotes were also killed. Because of predator control, lumbering, cessation of livestock grazing and other factors, the North Rim deer herd increased from about 4,000 head in 1906 to more than 30,000 head in 1924. A roundup was attempted that year in which 125 men tried to drive 8,000 deer down the Nankoweap Trail and across the river to the Tanner area. Weather and confusion turned against the men and the drive failed completely. The deer remained on the North Rim where starvation and a general population collapse soon followed.

Introduced Species

A large number of plant and animal species have been accidentally or intentionally introduced to the Grand Canyon region. Exotic rodents, rock doves, house sparrows, and European starlings have reached inhabited areas, and tamarisk, camel thorn, tumbleweed, sweet clover, red brome and other grasses have invaded the Colorado River riparian zone. The National Park Service unsuccessfully introduced the pronghorn antelope to the Tonto Platform in the late 1920s. Introductions of Gambel's quail and ring-necked pheasants in the inner Canyon were unsuccessful, but turkeys and chukar were successfully planted on the North Rim. The Roosevelt elk that occasionally reach the South Rim were introduced to the Flagstaff area following extirpation of native Merriam's elk.

Feral Burros

Burros were released in the Canyon by prospectors such as William Bass around the turn of the century, and over the years the burro population gradually increased. The National Park Service unsuccessfully tried to remove the herd in some areas by shooting in the 1940s. In the mid and late 1970s researchers concluded that burros were severely damaging native vegetation in the central and western portions of the park, and control measures were undertaken. Cleveland Amory, president of the Fund for Animals, sponsored a humane and highly effective removal program. By the end of 1981 he and his staff had rounded up 580 burros, which were driven out of the Canyon on trails, flown out by helicopter, and floated out on pontoon rafts. The animals were given to concerned citizens and a large portion of the herd was placed on a ranch in Texas. A few burros still roam the Diamond Creek drainage on the Hualapai Indian Reservation, but the burro herd has been eliminated in the park.

Regulation of the Colorado River

Glen Canyon Dam has been man's most significant impact on Grand Canyon. Located near the end of Glen Canyon, 15½ miles upstream from Lees Ferry, Arizona, this massive gravity arch dam was completed in 1963. It has influenced the Colorado River corridor in Grand Canyon by preventing floods, by trapping sediments and by decreasing the river's water temperature.

Glen Canyon Dam largely eliminated annual spring floods that scoured away riparian (streamside) vegetation along the river. By preventing floods, the dam has permitted plant life to invade once-barren riverside beaches. The initial plant invader in the river corridor was tamarisk, a widespread exotic shrub accidentally introduced to the Southwest from the Mideast before the turn of the century. After two decades of flood control, native plants such as coyote willow, honey mesquite, seepwillow, arrowweed, and numerous herbaceous species have also gained a foothold in the riparian zone. This profusion of plant life provides food and habitat for numerous species of insects, amphibians, reptiles, birds, and mammals, and is now an extremely valuable, naturalized habitat.

Another change wrought on the Colorado River by Glen Canyon Dam involves sediment trapping by Lake Powell. Prior to the dam, the Colorado River carried as much as 500 million tons of sediment per year through the Canyon. Now these sediments settle out in Lake Powell and the river runs clear green during much of the year. This clear water has permitted a profuse growth of filamentous green *Cladophora* and other algae in the river channel and this plant life, in turn, supports aquatic arthropods that serve as food for fish, wildfowl and other vertebrates.

Glen Canyon Dam has also significantly decreased the river's water temperature. Prior to the dam, the water ranged from near freezing in the winter to more than 80°F in the summer. Eight species of native fish dominated the pre-dam river, including the Colorado squawfish which grew to five feet in length and more than 70 pounds in weight. Now the river's water is released from deep in Lake Powell and ranges between 47°F and 65°F. Cooler, less variable water temperatures have extirpated four of the Canyon's native fish species by preventing them from breeding, and has allowed introduced carp and trout to proliferate.

Has Glen Canyon Dam been beneficial or detrimental to the Colorado River corridor in Grand Canyon? The dam produces much-needed hydroelectric power and has, by accident, allowed a lush growth of valuable riparian vegetation to spring up on formerly bare riverbanks. It has greatly increased the value of the river for white water recreationists and has produced the best trout fishery in the Southwest. Unfortunately, the dam has eliminated half of the native fish species, endangered another, and may have been responsible for the disappearance of the native river otter. Thus the dam has been a mixed blessing for this system. Heretofore it has been operated without much concern for the newly established ecosystem in Grand Canyon, but the Bureau of Reclamation has recently begun to consider how the dam affects this ecosystem, and may eventually consider operational modifications that will rectify some of these detrimental effects.

The Grand Canyon exerts a powerful influence on the organisms that live in and around it. Here, as everywhere, we must try to honor all living things and respect their right to an undisturbed existence. The inner Canyon's plant and animal life are somewhat less conspicuous than at other national parks: desert plants flower rarely and most desert creatures are crepuscular or nocturnal, and are not usually observed by humans. This means that seeing the life of the Canyon may take a little more time and attention than elsewhere, but one's patience is rewarded with a deeper appreciation for the ability of living beings to survive and proliferate in this harsh and topographically diverse environment.

LARRY STEVENS has been studying the biology of northern Arizona for 15 years. He currently resides in Flagstaff where he is pursuing doctoral studies in ecology. Stevens has been a commercial white water guide on the Colorado River in Grand Canyon for 12 years and has worked for the National Park Service and the Museum of Northern Arizona. He received a bachelor's degree from Prescott College and a master's degree from Northern Arizona University. He has written a book and several scientific and popular articles on the natural history of the Grand Canyon, and is currently at work on a book on the Great Basin Desert.

CHAPTER 4

Geology

by Michael Young

This discussion of the geology of the Grand Canyon is divided into two sections. The first concerns the evolution of the Grand Canyon region and may be subdivided into four topic areas: 1) age of oldest and youngest rock layers, 2) varieties of sediment, 3) discussion of geologic process as it applies to Canyon rock layers taken in ascending order from the oldest to youngest, layers as the hiker will encounter them moving from the bottom of the Canyon to the top, and 4) an introduction to the geologic time scale.

The second section is composed of the descriptions of the individual rock layers. These layers are reviewed in descending order as the hiker will encounter them moving down from the rim. Each layer is described on the basis of five categories: 1) chronologic placement in the geologic time scale, 2) thickness of Grand Canyon exposure, 3) color, 4) character—origin (sedimentary, volcanic, igneous), and 5) prominent features recognizable from the trail.

There is then a brief discussion of recent geologic events.

The mileages refer to river miles measured from Lees Ferry. River guides are available at the South Rim Visitor Center.

You will find it helpful to read this chapter with the *Geological Map of the Grand Canyon National Park* (published by the Grand Canyon Natural History Association, P.O. Box 399, Grand Canyon, AZ 86023). And don't forget to put it in your pack when you hike the Grand Canyon. Learning the rock layers of the Canyon is one of the great joys of being there.

EVOLUTION OF THE GRAND CANYON

The rock layers of the Grand Canyon bracket a time period that represents fully one-third of the life of the planet. The most ancient rock in the Grand Canyon, in the Vishnu Group, is 1.7 billion years old; the youngest, the Kaibab Limestone, is 250 million years old.

Varieties of sediment—boulders, breccias, cobbles, gravel, sand, silt, mud, clay, organic chards, chemical precipitates—are found in the stone walls of the Grand Canyon. Examination of these sediments reveals their place of origin, direction of travel, and previous form.

The intensely deformed Vishnu Group, for example, with its mineral migrations, crenulations, and intrusions, was originally a combination of deposited sediments and volcanics. Those sediments were laid down in water and transported by water to Proterozoic seas as, more recently (until damming), the Colorado built its delta on our continental margin. From ancestral mountains came the sediment to be left in a subsiding (sinking) catchment offshore. Possibly disinterred, intruded, or covered by volcanics, these sediments were finally reinterred to depths of 60,000 feet at 700 degrees Celsius where under pressure approaching 75,000 pounds per square inch these volcanics, sands, shales, and limestone lenses were metamorphosed. This is the initial recognizable geologic event in the Grand Canyon. With the onset of this event came the emplacement of igneous plutons (magma that cooled below the earth's surface), the Zoroaster Granites. The metamorphosis of these intrusive igneous bodies gave birth to the foliated Zoroaster Gneiss.

This event lasted for up to 100 million years, and was followed by a second episode of metamorphism—and then a third, where low-grade deformation occurred and zones of intensive shearing developed in this Precambrian complex. These shear zones (i.e., the major faults) in the Vishnu Group were in place before the deposition of the Bass Formation and may have been a response to collision of peregrine plates.

For 450 million years there is no sedimentary record to decipher. The Bass Formation is the next datable rock unit, at 1,250 million years old. That 450-million-year gap, equaling one-tenth of the earth's history, is called the "Greatest Unconformity." (An unconformity is a block of time when the land was above sea level and therefore under attack by atmospheric agents: heat, cold, water, and wind.)

Somewhere in this unconformity emerged an altered terrain to be attacked and worn smooth by the erosive forces of the planet's surface. From the west came the seas, and from the east, sediments—the Unkar Group: Bass Formation, Hakatai Shale, Shinumo Quartzite, Dox Sandstone, Cardenas Basalts. Deposited from approximately 1,250 million to 1,100 million years ago, rock types vary from oxidized continental sands, silts, and muds to intertidal dolomites and evaporites.

The Cardenas Basalts, deposits up to 1,200 feet thick, were followed by a separate and distinct suite of intrusive events perforating all Unkar sediments with diabase dikes and sills. The Unkar terrane, exhumed following Cardenas time and exposed to weathering, shows the atmosphere's cumulative effects to a depth of 30 feet. For how long were the lavas naked before the elements? Ten million years? Twenty? Onward rush the waters with Nankoweap Sandstones—ripple marks, mudcracks—over 300 feet of sediment, and the sea was gone once more.

The Chuar Group—Galeros, Kwagunt, Sixtymile Formations, reclining on the mildly undulating weathered surface of the Nankoweap—fully 6,000 feet thick, show shallow-water sedimentation with intermittent desiccation—shales, altered limestones, continental sands. Then the Proterozoic, characterized by fossils of filamentous algae, stromatolites (clump algae), and finally megaplankton (floating plant life), came to a close with a major tectonic event. The more than 13,000 feet of material comprising the Grand Canyon Supergroup, emplaced during a 400-million-year moment in earth history, were exhumed from their subsiding home. Thrust skyward as much as 10,000 feet, the blocks of tortured Vishnu with their layered burden were exposed to the ravages of 250 million years. The Great Unconformity is the name of this 250 million years that built a range of north-south-trending fault-block mountains 15,000 feet high, then wore them down to a surface that was regular except for some resistant islands of Shinumo Quartzite. The seas from the west—with animals this time, not just plants—inundated the remnants of Precambrian time, and the Paleozoic was on.

To the west lay the open seaway, and what is now the western Grand Canyon was then the continental margin. In multiple pulses the sea covered the Precambrian landscape with the sandstone, mudstone, limestone sequence of the Cambrian Tapeats, Bright Angel, Muav. Nearshore sands, offshore muds, abyssal limes, these layers all thicker in the west, flick their tongues to the east. "Each of the three Cambrian formations is older to the west than it is to the east. This important discovery clinched the case for a marine transgression. It also illustrates that a formation need not be the same age from place to place. The formation is simply a mapable, recognizable unit indicative of a past environment of sedimentation" (David Rahm, *Reading the Rocks*).

Unconformity—125–150 Million Years

The erosional surface of the Muav accepted sediments of the Temple Butte Limestone that represent channel fill in the east and a hypersaline lagoonal environ in the west.

Unconformity—25 or 30 Million Years

Virtually pure carbonate sediments are deposited in shallow Mississippian Redwall Limestone seas during three cycles of marine advance and retreat.

Unconformity—20 Million Years

The redbeds of the Pennsylvanian-Permian were deposited in a warm, humid, tropical clime on top of the Karst topography that had been eroded into the surface of the Redwall during the preceding unconformity. Sediments in the Supai become increasingly limey and dolomitized to the west and southwest—more shale and sand components to the east. Four unconformities are found within the redbed sequence, one marking the boundary of each of the formations of the Supai Group and one at the basal boundary of the Hermit Shale. The change from marine to continental sediments during Supai time is indicated by the decrease of limey sediment.

As the semitropical climate that authored the Hermit redbeds changed to a truly desert environ, a dune field carried by north winds engulfed the northern half of Arizona. The Coconino, thickening from a razor edge near the Utah–Arizona line in the north to 50 feet at the upper end of Marble Canyon and 65 feet in the western part of the Grand Canyon, reached a maximum depth approaching 1,000 feet at the Mogollon Rim, the truncated southern limit of the Colorado Plateau.

Again from the seaway in the cordilleran geosyncline to the west, the Toroweap and the Kaibab formations encroached upon this wedge of dune sand. Both formations represent episodic marine transgression, maximum advance and retreat. However, there is an unconformity separating these two formations—hiatus between Toroweap retreat and Kaibab advance. To the east, Kaibab rests on the surface of the Coconino—Toroweap is absent.

A time-change continuum: land, sea, mountain building, liquid eruptions, metamorphic mobilization of minerals, facies changes; and interspersed within this frame, the unconformities-erosive events. (Any formation may differ substantially from one location to another; e.g., a given formation might be sandy nearshore and limey offshore. These differences in character within a single formation are called facies changes.)

Current data show that, at present rates of deposition, shallow marine environs may produce a meter of sand in 1,500 years, shales in 3,000, and carbonates in 7,500 years. At that rate the entire sequence of Mississippian Redwall could have been emplaced in 1.5 million years. What of the balance of time? From Precambrian through Permian, more than 50 percent of the time cannot be documented—900 million years of unconformity!

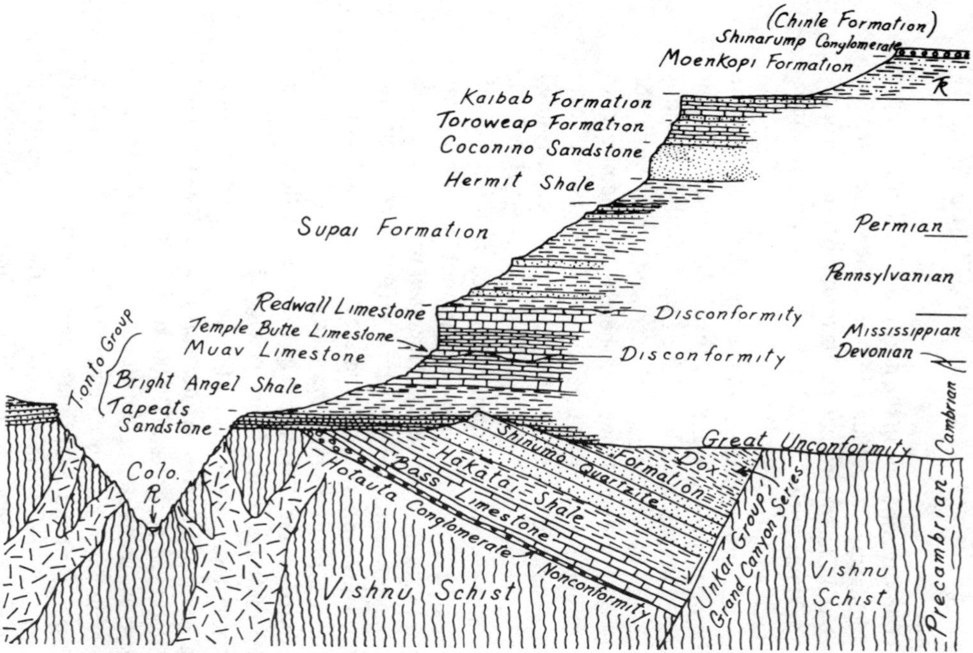

Principal rock layers of the Grand Canyon

GRAND CANYON ROCK FORMATIONS

The Paleozoic

Kaibab Formation—Middle Permian—250 m.y.a. (Million Years Ago)—300 feet

Cream to tan sands and light-gray limestone make up the Kaibab Formation. Three internal divisions of the Kaibab, called members, can be recognized. From top to bottom they are (1) Alpha, (2) Beta, and (3) Gamma. The Alpha member is composed of a mixture of redbeds, thin limestones, and some gypsum ($CaSO_4$) beds. The Beta member is massive and forms the cliff that is the Canyon rim. This layer is well expressed within the park but grades from limestone in the west to sandstone in the east (a facies change). There are abundant chert (a silica precipitate) concretions throughout this member. The basal member (Gamma) is a slope-forming unit with thin alternating beds of sandy, silty, and limey muds indicative of a mobile shoreline in an equatorial sea. East of the park, the Kaibab rests unconformably on the Coconino Sandstone. Marine invertebrate fossils are abundant throughout this formation and include brachiopods, bryzoans, cephalopods, corals, crinoids, crustaceans, fish, gastropods, and pelecypods.

Toroweap Formation—Middle Permian—260 m.y.a.—to 200 feet

Tan sands and light-to-dark-gray limestones form the

Toroweap, and three members can be recognized within the formation. They are identified with the nomenclature adopted in the Kaibab Formation—(1) Alpha, (2) Beta, and (3) Gamma—and represent a succession of depositional events very similar to those of the Kaibab. The Toroweap cliff, massive in the west, pinches out to the east in Marble Canyon. The Beta member becomes progressively magnesian or dolomitic in the east, indicating a coastal environ cut off from normal oceanic circulation. The gypsum found in concert with continental sediments may represent evaporite deposits from lagoonal environs.

Coconino Sandstone—Early Permian—270 m.y.a.—50 to 300 feet

The cream, tan, and ivory sandstones of the Coconino thin to nearly 50 feet both east and west from its maximum Canyon thickness of 300 feet in the vicinity of Bright Angel Creek. A prominent cliff, the Coconino, represents eolian origin—sand dunes blown from the north. This pure quartz sand is composed of well-sorted grains frosted by myriad impacts as they traveled southward. Transverse-type dunes frozen in the rock, some 70 feet long, produce cross-beds that dip as much as 34 degrees in the paleo-windward direction. Laminae in these high-angle beds are graded by wind velocity. Fossil skeletons have yet to be found, though invertebrate tracks and burrows are common.

Rock Island near the Coconino Overlook on the North Kaibab Trail. *Photo by George H. H. Huey.*

Hermit Shale—Early Permian—280 m.y.a.—300 feet

The red shales and siltstones of the Hermit thicken greatly: from 300 feet in the Grand Canyon Village area to more than 1,000 feet in the west. This sequence of redbeds indicates a source in highlands to the north. Easily eroded, the Hermit forms an almost continuous slope throughout its exposure. In the west (Grand Canyon National Monument) these soft shales have undermined the Coconino cliff, causing its retreat, and have been largely removed from the surface of the underlying sandstone, the Esplanade Formation of the Supai Group. This broad expanse is termed "The Esplanade". The Hermit was deposited in a climate that was at least seasonably wet. Mudcracks and raindrop prints are evident. Fossils from the early Permian flora can be found.

Supai Group—Pennsylvanian—Permian—300 m.y.a.—600 to 700 feet

Deep-red shaley siltstones and buff sandstones that are stained red on exposed surfaces comprise the Supai Group. The Supai Group has been broken into four formations that represent changes in depositional conditions: from top to bottom, 1) Esplanade Sandstone, 2) Wescogame, 3) Manakacha, and 4) Watahomigi. Both sand facies and shale-siltstone facies become increasingly calcareous to the south and west, indicating that marine conditions existed in those directions. Each formation outlines a cycle of shale-siltstone events capped by a sandstone facies. Continental redbeds diminish to the west and are replaced by more resistant limes that form a more prominent cliff. A dearth of fossils exists in the Supai within the park; however, fern prints and some amphibian tracks attest to a terrestrial origin. A distinctive conglomerate (to 30 feet) at the base of the Esplanade Sandstone is a good marker bed for hikers.

Redwall Limestone—Mississippian—330 m.y.a.—400 to 500 feet

Light-gray limestones with somewhat darker dolomites and white (opaque) lenses of chert form the Redwall Limestone. The Redwall gets its name from the stain of iron oxide on its weathered surface (chert weathers to dark brown). More than any other rock unit, the Redwall is a barrier to hikers in the Canyon. Because it is not weathered to a slope in any area, traversing the Redwall depends on fault-controlled joints or constructed trails.

Appearing as a single unbroken facade, the Redwall has been divided into four members (top to bottom—Horseshoe Mesa, Mooney Falls, Thunder Springs, Whitmore Wash), each representing a separate depositional cycle. There are seven different identifiable sedimentary structures—recrystallized, aphanitic, limestone conglomerate, oolitic, peloidal, and skeletal—which include horizons of both clastic (fragmented) and unbroken fossils, all virtually pure carbonate. Bedding planes are numerous and vary from 2 feet to 20 feet or more. Some beds are highly fossiliferous, while others are void of any fossils, having formed through chemical precipitation of carbonates. Chert lenses are abundant in the Thunder Springs Member and are evident to a lesser degree near the top of the section in the Horseshoe Mesa Member. The Horseshoe Mesa Member, having been exposed to the atmosphere for an extended period prior to deposition of Supai sediment, is honeycombed with solution structures that form a Karst topography (e.g., caves on the west side of Horseshoe Mesa on the Grandview Trail, Vasey's Paradise, Redwall Caverns in Marble Canyon, natural arches, springs and Cheyava Falls in the Clear Creek drainage). Fossil types to be found in the Redwall are numerous—foraminifers, brachiopods, corals, crinoids, bryzoans, gastropods, pelecypods, cephalopods, fish, trilobites, and algae.

Temple Butte Limestone—Late Devonian—370 m.y.a—100 to 1,000 feet

Named for exposures near Temple Butte about three miles downstream from the confluence of the Colorado and the Little Colorado rivers, the Temple Butte Limestone represents somewhat of an anomaly. In the eastern Canyon this Devonian interval is represented by freshwater limestone lenses which fill channels eroded into the surface of the underlying Muav Limestone. These channels can be as large as 400 feet wide and 40 to 50 feet deep with a basal pink-to-purple conglomerate layer. Flanking these channels, the Redwall rests directly on the Muav.

Thickening greatly to the west, the limestone becomes dolomitized and is expressed in a well-bedded cliff. These dolomites can run from gray to a distinctive tan-yellow-white combination and thereby constitute a marker bed. A marine fossil assemblage is expressed in the west but to the east there are bony plates identified as belonging to freshwater fish. This Devonian chapter represents the intertonguing of both fresh and saline coastal waters.

TONTO GROUP

Muav Limestone—Middle Cambrian—530 m.y.a.—150 to 800 feet

The Muav is the youngest of the tripartite Cambrian sequence termed the Tonto Group. These sediments thicken markedly from east to west. The Muav is a series of gray limestone beds separated by greenish-gray beds of micaceous shaley mudstones and micaceous siltstones. The upper and lower members of the formation are cliff-forming units, with the basal unit less massive. These are separated by a thinly bedded sequence of calcareous siltstones. Some of these narrow beds are a limestone conglomerate possibly formed by wave action on relatively unconsolidated sediments in shallow seas. Red-brown dolomites in the west trace the marine retreat that left the Muav exposed to Cambrian weather. The erosional surface between the Muav and either Temple Butte or the Redwall exhibits some stream channelization and various solution features. Fossils in the Muav are found primarily in the thin shale-silt beds and include trilobites, brachiopods, algal structures, and ripple marks.

Like the Redwall, the Muav is easily dissolved by flowing groundwater. Waters percolating through the layers above the Muav are halted in their downward movement by the relatively impermeable shales of the Bright Angel which form numerous seeps and several perennial springs, e.g., Thunder River, which flows into Tapeats Creek (Mile 134), and Deer Creek Spring, which flows into Deer Creek (Mile 136).

Bright Angel Shale—Early/Middle Cambrian—540 m.y.a.—200 to 450 feet

Composed predominantly of mudstone and fine-grained sandstones, the Bright Angel Shale can be identified readily by its many hues. The mudstones are light green; siltstones are generally gray with brown spots; sandstones range from magenta to pale green to tan; glauconite is bright green; and of course there are gradational changes in color.

The erosion of Bright Angel Shale is the controlling mechanism for the retreat of the Canyon rim. The broad bench eroded into this friable (soft) sediment of the Bright Angel and onto the surface of the underlying Tapeats Sandstone is called the Tonto Platform. Located about 3,000 feet below the Canyon's South Rim, it is the main east-west route through the Canyon. This terrace thins markedly to the west as the Bright Angel becomes more sandy and less easily eroded. Representing a mildly active, nearshore coastal environ, the Bright Angel is the central episode in the tripartite advance of Cambrian seas. Fossils to be found are trilobites, brachiopods, casts of worm burrows, and pteropods (Hyolithes).

Tapeats Sandstone—Early Cambrian—550 m.y.a.—100 to 300 feet

Following the 250-million-year hiatus in deposition termed the Great Unconformity, advancing Cambrian seas covered the existing landscape. The Tapeats sands overlie every Precambrian sedimentary formation and the crystalline metamorphic basement complex. There are several locales where this blanket of sand is pierced (to 800 feet) by islands of Shinumo Quartzite (near Clemente Powell Butte) that were later covered by Bright Angel muds. These islands are surrounded by blocks of quartzite that fell from island cliffs after being undercut by incessant battering of ocean waves.

The quartzose sands are medium- to coarse-grained and are typically a deep red-brown. Weathered surfaces are dark brown, but fresh surfaces are much lighter. The texture becomes finer as the Tapeats grades upward into the Bright Angel. Fossil types include brachiopods, trilobites, and trilobite trails (cruziana). Ripple marks are common in the top of the section where sands grade into the muds of the Bright Angel. West-dipping cross-bedding in the lower sand units indicates marine advance from the west on a north–south-trending coast. Tapeats forms the ramparts that guard the shadowed depths of the Inner Gorge and make cross-Canyon travel impossible except through fault-controlled drainages.

The Young Precambrian

Younger Precambrian rock was laid down between 800 and 1,250 m.y.a. Deposits are visible only on the west side of the Butte Fault, named by Charles Walcott "on account of its connection with the origin and development of the six great buttes" that flank the fault on the east from Nankoweap Creek to Tanner Canyon Rapid.

Chuar Group—825–1,000 m.y.a.—6,400 Feet

Sixtymile Formation—120 feet

The only exposures of the Sixtymile Formation are in Awatubi and Sixtymile canyons and where it caps Nankoweap Butte. Composed of pebbly sandstones, breccias, and slump structures deposited in a kinetic environ, the Sixtymile joins the balance of the Chuar terrane in filling a drag syncline, a structure associated with movement along the Butte Fault.

Kwagunt Formation—approximately 2,100 feet

The Kwagunt is divided into three members: Carbon Butte, Awatubi, and Walcott. The basal layer in the Carbon Butte is a massive red sandstone (an excellent marker bed) on the slopes of Carbon Butte. Resting on this sand stone are red-to-purple mudstones, which comprise the bulk of this member.

The Awatubi is dominantly shales and mudstones, but again the bottom of the member has a marker unit. This unit consists of a massive biohermal (algal) layer with domelike structures in a dolomitic matrix. A fossiferous layer of black shale is located near the top of this member.

The Walcott Member in ascending order consists of a flaky dolomite, black shales, and thick-bedded dolomites, all exhibiting algal structures.

Galeros Formation—approximately 4,200 feet

The Galeros is divided into four members: Tanner, Jupiter, Carbon Canyon, and Duppa. A dark-gray basal marker bed of massive (40–80 feet) dolomite identifies the Tanner Member and therefore the Galeros as a whole. The balance of the member (580 feet) is almost entirely shale. The Jupiter Member repeats the carbonate-shale scenario with thin siltstone-sandstone horizons. The shales are colorful, showing red to purple, blue-black and light green to brown-yellow in various layers.

The Carbon Canyon Member exhibits the triplet of limestone, shale, and sandstone throughout the member. Mudcracks and ripple marks are common on the upper surface of the beds. The Duppa Member is primarily argillaceous with scattered limestones and sandstones.

Nankoweap Formation—1,050 m.y.a.—300 to 600 feet

The Nankoweap is classified separately from both the Chuar and the Unkar groups. Bounded by unconformities, Nankoweap exposures are visible from Basalt Canyon to near the mouth of Carbon Canyon and in Comanche Creek, Tanner Canyon, and neighboring drainages. Ripple marks, crossbeds, and mudcracks are evidenced in the white-brown-purple sandstones.

UNKAR GROUP—1,100–1,250 M.Y.A.—APPROXIMATELY 6,700 FEET

Cardenas Basalts and Intrusives—740 to 1,380 feet

Due to the 10–15-degree NE dip of the fault blocks that they ride, the Cardenas Lavas outcrop only in a section from Unkar Creek (Mile 72.5) to Chuar Lava Hill (Mile 65). There is an isolated outcrop at the north end of the trail that follows the Butte Fault 4 km from the Colorado River in the Nankoweap drainage. To date, 14 separate flows have been mapped. These are delineated by vesicular zones and thin sandstone layers. The structures found within the flows are described by Ford and Breed (1976): "Scattered throughout are vesicular horizons, occasional ropy lavas, massive lavas with columnar and fan jointing, and ash layers with bombs. The pillow and sandstone horizons indicate that much of the lava was erupted into shallow water, while the vesicular, ropy, and ash layers suggest temporary emergence." The dark brown to black basalt cliffs of the upper flows grade into a greenish slope at the base of the formation.

Outcrops of the intrusives are more widespread, being visible opposite the mouth of Red Canyon at Hance Rapids, up Clear Creek in Ottoman Amphitheater, along Bright Angel Creek north of Phantom Ranch, up Crystal Creek and along the river in two sections from Bass through Shinumo to Hakatai creeks and from Bedrock through Galloway to Tapeats creeks. The sills range from 60 feet to almost 700 feet in thickness; their composition is primarily medium- to coarse-grained diabase.

Perforating all of the Unkar sediments, the sills (horizontal) and dikes (vertical) are predominantly located in the Bass and Hakatai formations. Flanking the sills are zones of contact metamorphism where surrounding rock was baked following the injection of hot magma. This phenomenon produced local alteration of minerals and accounts for deposits of chrysotile asbestos in the Bass Formation above Hance Rapids and in Hakatai Canyon. William Bass's mine at the contact of the Bass Formation and a diabase sill in Hakatai Canyon (Mile 111) produced asbestos that was shipped to Europe and used in the manufacture of fireproof theater curtains. John Hance's asbestos mine was located in a similar zone of contact metamorphism opposite Red Canyon (Mile 76.5). Hakatai shales were baked to slates in zones up to 15 feet from the contact. These intrusives are fine-grained at their margins due to rapid cooling. Current research indicates that while the intrusives and the lavas are not the same age, they most probably represent successive events with a common parent magma.

Dox Formation—approximately 1,190 m.y.a.—to 3,100 feet

The principal exposure of the Dox is in the eastern Canyon between Seventy Five Mile and Escalante creeks. This section illustrates the markedly different responses to weathering and erosion exhibited by the resistant Paleozoic strata of Marble Canyon, the extremely resistant metamorphic complex of the Inner Gorge, and the nonresistant, easily weathered Unkar sediments of the Dox. These gently sloping hills are traversed south of the river when hiking the Beamer Trail.

The Dox is tentatively divided into four members: Lower, Lower Middle, Upper Middle, and Upper. The Lower and Upper Middle are arenaceous (derived from sand) while the Lower Middle and Upper are argillaceous (composed of clays). The cyclic alternation of sediment types—sands, silts, muds—indicates a tidal, deltaic, mudflat sequence for deposition. The Dox consists of oxidized maroon-red-orange mudstones, siltstones, and quartz sandstones, with the exception of a basal sandstone layer (800 feet) that is light tan to greenish-brown. The formation is overlain by 400 feet of dark brown to green shales and mudstones. Fossils are restricted to stromatolites, filamentous algae, and abundant ripple marks, green reduction spots, mudcracks, and salt casts. Some structures indicative of deformation prior to lithification include load casts and slumped bedding. Small-scale crossbeds indicate sediment was transported from the west.

Shinumo Quartzite—approximately 1,200 m.y.a.—1,100 to 1,350 feet

Evident only between Papago Creek at the entrance to the Inner Gorge in the east and Tapeats Creek in the west, the Shinumo is not a true quartzite, never having been metamorphosed. The exposures of Shinumo sandstones are not continuous but are expressed intermittently. The eroded upper surface of this cliff-forming unit retains resistant "islands" that pierce the Great Unconformity and may continue up-section as far as the Bright Angel Shale. Beds within the Shinumo vary in thickness and character. Well-cemented sands range from poorly sorted to well sorted and coarse to fine. The result of this varied assemblage of sands is an inconsistent cliff with ledgy intervals. Colors found are tan, purple, deep red, rusty brown, and white. The top 400 feet of the formation is a marbled purple and white that can be recognized easily. Load casts and deformed bedding planes (slumped bedding) characterize this upper member. These predominantly quartz sands imply a shallow, high-energy nearshore or shoreline environment for deposition. Crossbeds are abundant throughout; ripple marks, mudcracks, and clay galls are common at specific horizons.

Hakatai Shale—approximately 1,200 m.y.a.—550 to 950 feet

The Spanish Fathers named the river Colorado for the red of its muds; the Havasupai tribe had a name for the Colorado before they came—it was Hakatai. It is most appropriate that the formation with the most exposure of all Unkar Group sediments should be the most brilliantly colored—vibrant orange, red and purple—and lend its name to the river that carved the Canyon.

Similar to the Dox in color and form, the Hakatai is below the Shinumo. Predominantly argillaceous, capped with a thick (200–300 feet) bed of poorly consolidated purple sandstone, this formation yields a sloping topography. Whereas the lower contact with the Bass may be difficult to discern because of a transitional environ that interfingers sandstones and conglomerates on top of Bass dolomites, the contact with the overlying Shinumo is sharp and distinct. This basal zone contains interbedded arkosic sand and conglomerates containing metamorphic and volcanic fragments.

The majority of the Hakatai is red (weathered to orange) mudstone and shale, with the color (hematite) a product of oxidation of iron-bearing minerals. The mudstone and shale units are highly fractured. V. Stephen Reed describes this Precambrian time: " . . . the Hakatai Shale was deposited in shallow water with periods of emergence in an arid climate. The mudstones are probably mudflat deposits formed as the sea retreated after deposition of the Bass Formation. The upper sandstones appear to be shallow water deposits laid down shoreward of the mudstones, where energy was sufficient for winnowing."

Bass Formation—approximately 1,250 m.y.a.— 180 to 330 feet

Named for William Wallace Bass, the Bass Formation outcrops above Hance Rapids in the east and thence intermittently to the west until Tapeats Creek. The Bass Cliff rests unconformably on the crystalline metamorphic complex of the Vishnu Schist and the Zoroaster complex of intrusives. In the Grand Canyon this break in the record encompasses approximately 450 million years. As the sea encroached upon the stream-cut surface of the Vishnu, waves reworked accumulated gravels and may account for a discontinuous layer of Hotauta Conglomerate, which outcrops primarily in the east and sporadically in the west. The Hotauta Conglomerate (formerly considered a separate formation but now tentatively included in the Bass) consists of a mix of chards from the metamorphics that support it. Thicker in the west, the beds of lime mud, later altered to dolomite by magnesium replacement of calcium, were left by the advancing sea. Marine retreat to the west left shales and muds and possibly some gypsum casts now filled by collapse breccias. Some sands are also seen in the Bass and complete the cycle of depositional environ—from high-energy stream-transported conglomerates, through wave-sorted shore sands and calm offshore waters precipitating lime muds, to the evaporating brine of stagnant lagoons leaving gypsum. Stromatolites are common in the brown to gray dolomites and typically are preserved as chert. Argillite units vary from red to blue and exhibit mudcracks and ripple marks.

The Old Precambrian

Vishnu Group and Zoroaster Plutonic Complex—1,700–2,000 m.y.a.—to 1,300 feet

Named for the Hindu god, the Preserver, the Vishnu Group outcrops in Granite Park and in the upper, middle, and lower granite gorges. It is composed of a mix of metamorphosed sediments (sandstone, siltstone, shales, and minor amounts of limestone) with metamorphosed mafic flows (volcanics) and intrusives (dikes and sills). The metamorphic history of these Vishnu metasediments and metavolcanics is extremely complex.

After deposition in a subsiding (sinking) basin these sediments were buried by additional sediment to a depth of aproximately 12 miles. At this depth, force was applied from what would now be the west. This directed force may have originated from the collision with or subduction of a wandering plate. Whatever the exact mode for application, these deeply interred sediments were folded tightly, perpendicular to this force. The original clay minerals and quartz sand grains, no longer able to survive in their original form at this depth with temperatures that rise 35 degrees C/km of burial, responding to intense pressure, were released from their chemical bondage. Mobilized in such manner, the minerals reoriented themselves in parallel planes. This layering of minerals, termed foliation, is characteristic of metamorphic rocks such as schist and gneiss. This orogenic deformation through-prints to the surface with the birth and maturation of mountains. Mountaintops are bent and broken but not metamorphically altered as are the roots. Relict crossbeds from the original sandstones are preserved in these schists. The mafic flows (basalt) and intrusive dikes and sills (diabase) metamorphose to amphibolite and are widely evident in the Vishnu Group as black to dark green bands in an otherwise layered dark gray to gray-green mica-schist with concordant (parallel) white quartz-rich veins.

The Zoroaster Plutonic Complex includes numerous dikes and sills that alternately pinch and swell along their length, plus a series of ten large plutons varying from white to pink in color. These plutons—named for Pluto, Greek god of the underworld—invaded the realm of Vishnu, being emplaced during and after metamorphosis of the schists. Ranging from quartz-monzonite to quartz-diorite, they are termed "granitic" here. The plutons intruded during the metamorphosis of the Vishnu sediments were further altered to gneiss, while new intrusives remained granitic and nonfoliated. Some of the dikes and sills are pegmatite (coarse-grained), while others are primarily aplite (fine-grained). Large potassium feldspar crystals in the pegmatites are up to 50 cm long and indicate a protracted cooling period for the hydrothermal fluids from which they crystallized. These pegmatites may make up from 0 to 100 percent of the total volume of rock, but commonly represent 40 to 50 percent in the zones of most intense metamorphism.

RECENT GEOLOGIC EVENTS

The Grand Canyon continues to enlarge both laterally and vertically. The Colorado Plateau continues to inch skyward, propelled by forces within the planet, aiding the liquid saw of the river in its quest for the base of the Vishnu. But what of the mechanisms that continuously widen the Canyon? "The processes of slab-failure, rock avalanche, rock fall, talus slide, mudflow, landslide, gravity faulting and solution are at present very active in enlarging the Grand Canyon, and there is some evidence that they have at times been even more active in the past" (Ford, Huntoon, Billingsly, and Breed, 1976).

Large-scale rotational landslides have been described as "Toreva block" slides by Reiche (1937). There are five within the Canyon; however, only two affect foot travel—these are in Surprise Valley and Tanner Canyon. The Surprise Valley landslide involves a terrane of approximately three to four square miles and approximately one cubic mile of shattered rock. The trail to Thunder River crosses the slide. This landslide is developed on the Bright Angel Shale at the base of the Muav Limestone. The Muav carries a large volume of water within its boundaries. This water lubricates the shales below and provides a plastic medium that will no longer support the strata above. In this case, approximately 2,000 feet of rock (to the Esplanade Sandstone) broke loose from the supporting cliff. As the blocks slid downhill they rotated backward toward the new cliff face. A similar structure exists adjacent to Tanner Trail.

Due to the profusion of lime deposits ($CaCO_3$, $CaMg(CO_3)_2$) in the Canyon and the resultant amount of salts in solution in ground and surface waters, there are many travertine deposits in the Canyon. Numerous examples may be found near the base of the Muav (e.g., near the confluence of the Colorado and the Little Colorado) and throughout the Redwall exposures. Recent river gravels are cemented by these same compounds (e.g., opposite the mouth of Nankoweap Creek).

Keep your eyes open for faults while you walk. They are plentiful in the Canyon and control most of the drainages and certainly all the major geologic features of the plateau surface.

MICHAEL YOUNG was adopted by the Colorado Plateau 20 years ago. He has rowed the Plateau rivers for eight years watching the multiple expressions of the rock face and measuring with the yardstick of geologic time. Currently, he is teaching geology and mathematics at Yavapai College in Prescott, Arizona.

CHAPTER 5

Above the Rim

People come from all over the world to visit the Grand Canyon, and during the peak season of spring, summer, and fall, they come in droves. During 1984, interpretative rangers at the Grand Canyon Visitor Center met face-to-face with more than two million people.

You can make your visit more enjoyable, and their job a little easier, if you write in advance for a detailed list of visitor services offered at the Grand Canyon. These include campground and trailer sites, transportation, service stations and garages, propane dealers, a pharmacy, dental and medical clinics, a U.S. magistrate, a telegraph office, a U.S. Post Office, bank, a grocery store, showers and laundry, beauty and barber shops, curio and gift shops, kennels, and religious services. Write: Chief of Interpretation, Visitor Center, Grand Canyon National Park, AZ 86023.

Once there, you can drive around the Grand Canyon, raft through it, hike into it, or just stand and stare at it. But the first thing you should do before planning your trip is decide how much time you can afford to spend at the Canyon and whether or not you want to spend all your time above the rim, below the rim, or a combination of the two.

Remember, spring, summer, and fall campground and hotel accommodations are reserved months in advance—so don't wait until the last minute to make reservations.

CAMPING

Camping at the Grand Canyon is permitted only in designated campsites.

At the South Rim, there are two: Mather Campground, located in Grand Canyon Village; and Desert View, located 25 miles east along the East Rim Drive. Trailer sites and hookups are located at Trailer Village, adjacent to Mather Campground. Permits are $5 per night. For reservations write: National Park Service, 1115 North First Street, Phoenix, AZ, or Ticketron Reservation Office, P.O. Box 2715, San Francisco, CA 94126. Or make reservations in person at either Desert View or Mather campgrounds.

At the North Rim, there is one designated campsite: North Rim Campground near Bright Angel Point, which operates on a first-come, first-served basis. Permits are $5 per night. Group reservations can be made in advance for the summer season (closed in winter) by writing: Group Reservations, North Rim, Grand Canyon National Park, Grand Canyon, AZ 86023.

Late Arrivals. If you've failed to make advance reservations and the campgrounds are full, try your luck at the U.S. Forest Service Ten X Campground 10 miles south of the South Rim Entrance Station; the Jacob Lake Campground at the junction of U.S. 89A and Arizona 67, 32 miles from the North Rim Entrance Station; or De Motte Campground, 5 miles from the North Rim Entrance Station.

LODGING

At the South Rim, there are seven different lodges offering everything from rustic cabins to deluxe accommodations. They are Bright Angel Lodge, El Tovar Hotel, Kachina Lodge, Maswik Lodge, Thunderbird Lodge, and Yavapai Lodge. Prices range from $30–110 for a standard double occupancy per night. For further information and advance reservations, write: Grand Canyon National Park Lodges, Grand Canyon, AZ 86023. Or call (602) 638-2631.

Outside the park, three other lodges are located 8 miles south of the South Rim Entrance Station on Highway 64. Grand Canyon Squire Inn, phone (602) 638-2681; Moqui Lodge, (602) 638-2424; and Red Feather Lodge, (602) 638-2637. Rates vary from $40–60. Call for advance reservations.

At the North Rim, there is the Grand Canyon Lodge. Write: T.W.A. Services, 4045 South Spencer Street, Las Vegas, NV 89109, or call (800) 634-6951.

Outside the park, there are four lodges near the North Rim. Starting at the Marble Canyon Bridge on U.S. 89A, they are: Marble Canyon Lodge, (602) 355-2225; Cliff Dwellers Lodge, (602) 355-2228; Jacobs Lake Inn at the junction of U.S. 89A and Arizona 67, (602) 643-7232; and Kaibab Lodge, located 5 miles north of the North Rim Entrance Station, (602) 638-2389. Accommodations outside the park are also available at Kanab, Utah, and at Fredonia and Page in Arizona.

ORIENTATION

One of the first things you'll want to do after arranging for your campsite or accommodations is to stop at the Visitor Center located three miles north of the South Rim Entrance Station. The emphasis is on the human history and ecology of the Grand Canyon. Interpretative rangers can answer most of the questions you might have about the Canyon, visitor services, and programs. The center is open from 7 a.m. to 7 p.m. daily, in summer.

At the North Rim, the Visitor Information Desk is located in the Grand Canyon Lodge at Bright Angel Point. Hours are 7 a.m. to 7 p.m. daily, in summer.

MUSEUMS

There are two museums located at the South Rim. The Yavapai Museum is located at Yavapai Point, just east of the Visitor Center, and features the geological history of the Grand Canyon. It's open from 8 a.m. to 7 p.m. daily, in summer. The Tusayan Museum is located a few miles west of Desert View on the East Rim Drive and features the archaeological history of the Canyon. Don't miss the Hopi House a few hundred yards east of the El Tovar Hotel or the Fred Harvey History Room in the Bright Angel Lodge.

GUIDED WALKS, TALKS, AND SLIDE SHOWS

The National Park Service offers a series of informative and entertaining programs for the visitor every day. They include the hour-and-a-half long Sunrise Walk; the Cedar Ridge Hike, a 3½ hour hike in and out of the Canyon guided by a park ranger; the Junior Ranger Program, ideal for 7–13–year–olds interested in nature; the 1½ hour long History Walk through Grand Canyon Village; Geology Talks and Walks; Lunch with a Ranger; Rim Walks; and Canyon Talks; "Through the Eyes of Many," a walk which features the impressions of Grand Canyon poets and writers. And if you've yet to discover the celestial world, the Astronomy Talk is a must. The hour long Evening Program offers something new and different each evening. Programs change from season to season. For further details, contact the Visitor Center.

SOUTH RIM SCENIC VISTAS

If a person does not fear to look into the Canyon and see distance such as he has never seen elsewhere, depth such as he has never dreamt of, and if he becomes lost in shades of gentian and cherry and trout-like silver, watches the unceasing change of hue and form in depth, distance, and color, he will have feelings that do not well go into words and are perhaps more real on that account.

—Haniel Long

Once you've gotten your bearings at the Visitor Center, you have to take another look at the Canyon—a long one. And take a copy of Hamblin and Murphy's *Grand Canyon Perspectives* or Nancy Loving's *Along the Rim* to help plot your course through this visual wilderness.

There are 15 established panoramic viewpoints on the South Rim, and each offers something different.

Mather Point (7,120′)—2 miles from the South Rim Entrance Station.

Yavapai Point (7,040′)—3 miles from the South Rim Entrance Station.

Along the East and West Rim drives, there are markers identifying all the scenic vistas.

East Rim Drive

Yaki Point (7,260′)—at the head of the South Kaibab Trail.

Grandview Point (7,406′)—at the head of the Grandview Trail.
Moran Point (7,157′)—overlooking the New Hance Trail.
Lipan Point (7,360′)—at the head of the Tanner Trail.
Navajo Point (7,498′, the highest point on the South Rim)—near Desert View.
Desert View (7,438′)—Desert View Watch Tower.

West Rim Drive

Trailviews I & II (6,960′).
Maricopa Point (7,000′)—overlooking the Bright Angel Trail.
Hopi Point (7,071′).
Mohave Point (6,974′).
The Abyss (6,883′).
Pima Point (6,720′).
Hermits Rest (6,640′)—at the head of the Hermit, Dripping Springs, and Boucher trails.

Ways to Visit South Rim Scenic Vistas

Hiking. The paved 3½-mile-long South Rim Nature Trail links Yavapai Point and the Yavapai Museum with Maricopa Point west of Bright Angel Lodge. The views en route are exhilarating. You can start this hike at either of these points, or pick up the trail at the Visitor Center near the Shrine of Ages.

West from Maricopa Point, there is a 5-mile-long dirt trail that skirts the very lip of the South Rim and ties together the Major John Wesley Powell Memorial at

The view from Lipan Point. *Photo by George H. H. Huey.*

Powell Point with Hopi Point, Mojave Point, the Abyss, Pima Point, and Hermits Rest.

Sneakers or lightweight walking shoes are more than adequate for either of these trails. If you're not walking off breakfast or dinner, take a snack and a quart of water, and catch the West Rim shuttle bus back to the village.

Bicycles are also an excellent way to visit the scenic vistas along both rims during the summer. But get on the road at daybreak, before the shuttle and tour buses crank out their exhaust fumes.

Shuttle Bus. A free shuttle bus leaves the depot every 15 minutes during the summer, starting a 50-minute loop through Grand Canyon Village and making 14 scheduled stops at well-marked bus stops en route, including Yavapai Point. Leave the driving to them and get an informative tour of the village at the same time. Hours are 6:00 a.m. to 10:00 p.m. daily. For the Village Loop shuttle bus schedule, write: Grand Canyon National Park Lodges.

West Rim Shuttle. Leaves the West Rim interchange at the head of the Bright Angel Trail every 15 minutes from 7:30 a.m. to 7:00 p.m. each day throughout the summer. It is free, stops at all the scenic vistas along the West Rim, and takes 1½ hours roundtrip.

Hiker's Special. Leaves the West Rim interchange every day during the summer at 6:00 a.m. and goes directly to the Hermit, Dripping Springs, and Boucher trailheads at Hermits Rest. After you hike out of the Canyon, you can catch this West Rim shuttle back to Grand Canyon Village.

Bus Tours. Grand Canyon National Park Lodges offers guided tours of both the East and West Rim drives twice daily. Call the Bright Angel Transportation Desk (602) 638-2631 for current schedules and fares, or write Grand Canyon National Park Lodges.

NORTH RIM SCENIC VISTAS

Due to the relatively pristine and undeveloped nature of the North Rim, there are only four established panoramic viewpoints there.

Cape Royal (7,865′)—22 miles from Grand Canyon Lodge.

Vista Encantada (8,000′ +)—on the Cape Royal Road en route to Cape Royal.

Point Imperial (8,803′)—3 miles off the Cape Royal Road.

Bright Angel Point (8,255′)—a third of a mile by paved footpath from Grand Canyon Lodge.

(There are also several remote scenic vistas, which are described under "Rim Trails" in Chapter 9.)

Ways to Visit North Rim Scenic Vistas

Hiking. Once at Cape Royal, you can take the half-mile Cape Royal Trail to both Angel's Window and the tip

Mt. Hayden from Point Imperial, North Rim. *Photo by George H. H. Huey.*

of Cape Royal; or the mile-long Cliff Springs Trail, which starts opposite the Angel's Window Overlook and ends at Cliff Springs. The short Bright Angel Point Trail leaves the veranda at Grand Canyon Lodge and ends at the terminus of Bright Angel Point; it makes a fine evening walk.

Bus Tours. During the summertime, a commercial bus leaves Grand Canyon Lodge each afternoon and motors out to both Point Imperial and Cape Royal. The trip concludes with a "rock talk." Check the Transportation Desk at Grand Canyon Lodge for fares and schedules, or write: T.W.A. Services, 4045 South Spencer Street, Las Vegas, NV 89109; (800) 634-6951.

SCENIC VISTA PHOTO TIPS

Some of the most celebrated color photos of the Grand Canyon have been taken from the established scenic vistas. By exploring each, you'll be able to get the feel of what the photo opportunities are.

For best results, professional photographers usually shoot in the early morning or late afternoon on clear or relatively cloudless days; that's usually when the colors and moods are the most dramatic. If you're shooting just before or after midafternoon, summer thunderstorms will also produce some excellent images.

A 35mm (or larger-format) camera, stabilized with a tripod, is best. A polarizing filter is good for reducing or eliminating glare and haze. And you'll want to use at least a 28mm wide-angle lens if you're trying to capture the breadth of the Canyon.

But don't get so excited about what you're doing that you wander too close to the edge! Grand Canyon rock is dangerously crumbly. Keep an eye on toddlers, and resist the temptation to climb over the guardrails.

Finally, please don't throw your film wrappers on the ground.

CHAPTER 6

Below the Rim

What applies above the rim during the peak spring, summer, and fall season generally holds true below the rim when it comes to making reservations for developed or designated campsites, or accommodations at Phantom Ranch. Again, don't wait till the last minute to make reservations.

CAMPING

Camping below the rim is by permit only; these are obtained at the Backcountry Reservations Office.

Below the South Rim are Indian Gardens and Bright Angel, two developed campgrounds with staffed NPS ranger stations, privies, emergency phones, and purified water.

Below the North Rim there is one such campground: Cottonwood.

Designated campsites and at-large camping will be listed below under each trail and/or route description.

LODGING

Below the North and South rims, Phantom Ranch provides the only lodging services for saddle-weary dudes and hikers. Rooms in segregated male and female dormitories—each consisting of 10 bunkbeds, with restroom and shower—go for $11 each night, while private cabins go for $54.15 for one person or $69.80 for two each night. For breakfast and dinner menus and prices, beer hall hours, and reservations, write: Reservation Department, Grand Canyon National Park Lodges, P.O. Box 699, Grand Canyon, AZ 86023. Or call (602) 638-2401.

GUIDED HIKES

Whether it's a brief morning hike down the South Kaibab Trail, or a weeklong backpack across a seldom-explored section of the park, there is perhaps no better way to see and experience the vastness of what some park rangers refer to as "the ditch" than by taking a walk below the rim. For it's your hiking, switchback after switchback, that will enable you to meet the Grand Canyon on her own terms—the musical pitter-patter of trickling water, the soft fragrance of spring flowers, the sweat streaming down your salt-crusted cheeks, the unforgettable sight of a desert bighorn bounding across craggy sandstone ledges.

The Sierra Club

The Sierra Club's Outing Department offers weeklong treks into remote areas of Grand Canyon National Park. For information on trip dates, fees, and hiking areas, write: Sierra Club Outing Department, 730 Polk Street, San Francisco, CA 94109. Or call (415) 981-8634.

Grand Canyon Trail Guides

This is the only commercial hiking concession currently sanctioned by Grand Canyon National Park, under the provisions of Public Law 89-249, the Concessions Policy Act of October 9, 1965. The concession is owned and operated by Gaylord Stavely, who also owns and ramrods a Grand Canyon river outfit called Canyoneers. His highly experienced guides, headed by Jim Ohlman, offer guided day hikes and half-day hikes; overnight hikes; extended hikes; and hiking–river-running combinations. Write: Grand Canyon Trail Guides, P.O. Box 2997, E. Flagstaff, AZ 86003; (602) 526-0924.

Noncommercial Guided Hiking Groups

Educational institutions, government entities, civic organizations, conservation organizations, and the Boy Scouts and Girl Scouts are generally considered noncommercial so long as the leaders' or instructors' salaries are not collected "directly through fees contributed by members of the guided party." If you have any questions regarding the commercial status of your group, contact the Backcountry Reservations Office. Commercial groups need to apply for a one-time Commercial Use License.

RIVER RUNNING

> It has, however, been the good fortune of but a few to be able to journey at the bottom of these canyons, along the only path that is open to man—the raging waters of the river itself—and to look up at the beauties and wonders that nature has formed, piled one upon the other, seemingly to the blue of the sky above; or to live among the stupendous gorges and caverns that have been cut out of the very bowells of the earth, as this mightiest of rivers has carved itself a pathway to the sea.
>
> —*Robert Brewster Stanton, 1890*

More than 15,000 river runners navigate the Colorado River through the Grand Canyon each year. They come from all over the world to experience the wonders and adventures Stanton described and Major John Wesley Powell—some river historians think it was a prospector named James White—pioneered. If you have your own river-running gear and the expertise, a private trip through the Grand Canyon is the way to go. But first you must apply to the River Sub-District at Grand Canyon National Park for a permit, and the waiting list for those permits is not a short one. Still, if you have the patience, it's worth the wait.

If you're like most folks, however, you probably don't own the expensive gear or have the time to coordinate the food, logistics, and everything else required to put together a successful private river trip—let alone have the patience to wait 3 or 4 years for a permit. So you might consider booking passage with one of the 21 commercial river-running companies currently sanctioned by Grand Canyon National Park to offer trips down the Colorado River. The trip is not a difficult one, and has a safety record that's impressive. Outfitters offer every kind of trip imaginable: from 3½-day-long motorized trips in giant baloney boats to 18-day-long trips in oar-powered wooden dories.

Whether oar, paddle, or motorized, these trips are led and navigated by experienced boatmen and -women who wear a variety of different hats in their roles as river guides. A good boatman is part naturalist, historian, geologist, cook, and court jester. And his or her job is to see that you have a safe and rewarding whitewater experience.

The adventuresome should definitely try a paddle trip; the only outfit regularly offering paddle trips is Arizona Raft Adventures (see listing), which also offers oar and motor trips. Paddle trips are captained by experienced guides, but passengers actively participate in both propelling and navigating the small boat. And it's the one surefire way to experience the power and excitement of the Colorado River.

Whatever type of river trip you might ultimately choose to take, there really is nothing like a two-week-long river trip to engage your soul and rekindle your sense of awe and wonder.

Contact far in advance for information and reservations:

ARIZONA RAFT ADVENTURES, INC.
P.O. Box 697, Flagstaff, AZ 86002
(602) 526-8200. Paddle, Oar, and Motorized trips.

ARIZONA RIVER RUNNERS
P.O. Box 2021, Marble Canyon, AZ 86036
(602) 355-2223/4. Motor trips only.

CANYONEERS, INC.
P.O. Box 2997, Flagstaff, AZ 86003
(602) 526-0924. Primarily Motor trips, some Oar.

COLORADO RIVER & TRAIL EXPEDITIONS, INC.
P.O. Box 7575, Salt Lake City, UT 84107
(801) 261-1789. Primarily Motor trips, some Oar.

CROSS TOURS & EXPLORATIONS, INC.
274 W. 1400 S., Orem, UT 84057
(801) 225-0849. Motor trips only.

DIAMOND RIVER ADVENTURES
P.O. Box 1316, Page, AZ 86040
(602) 645-8866. Primarily Motor trips, some Oar.

GEORGIE'S ROYAL RIVER RATS
P.O. Box 12057, Las Vegas, NV 89112
(702) 451-5588. Motor trips and Oars, triple rigs.

GRAND CANYON DORIES, INC.
P.O. Box 3029, Stanford, CA 94305
(415) 851-0411. Oars only, dories!

GRAND CANYON EXPEDITIONS, INC.
P.O. Box O, Dept. NPS, Kanab, UT 84741
(801) 644-2691. Primarily Motor trips, some Oars.

GRAND CANYON YOUTH EXPEDITIONS, INC.
Rt. 4, Box 755, Flagstaff, AZ 86001
(602) 774-8176. Oars only.

HATCH RIVER EXPEDITIONS, INC.
Box A.F., Vernal, UT 84078
(801) 789-3814. Motors only, in G.C.

HUALPAI TRIBAL RIVER BOATS
P.O. Box 246, Peach Springs, AZ 86434
(602) 769-2216. Primarily Motors, some Oars.

MARK SLEIGHT EXPEDITIONS
P.O. Box 118, LaVerkin, UT 84745
(801) 635-2177. Primarily Oars, some Motor trips.

MOKI MAC RIVER EXPEDITIONS
6829 Bella Vista Drive, Salt Lake City, UT 84121
(801) 943-6707. Oars only.

O.A.R.S. INCORPORATED
P.O. Box 67, Angels Camp, CA 95222
(209) 736-2924. Oars only.

OUTDOORS UNLIMITED
P.O. Box 22513, Sacramento, CA 95822
(916) 452-1081. Oars only.

TOUR WEST, INC.
P.O. Box 333, Orem, UT 84057
(801) 225-7600. Primarily Motors, some Oars.

WESTERN RIVER EXPEDITIONS, INC.
7258 Racquet Club Drive, Salt Lake City, UT 84121
(801) 942-6669. Motors only.

WHITE WATER RIVER EXPEDITIONS, INC.
P.O. Box 1249, Turlock, CA 95381
(209) 667-7714. Motors only.

WILDERNESS RIVER ADVENTURES
P.O. Box 717, Page, AZ 86040
(602) 645-3296. Primarily Motors, some Oars.

WILDERNESS WORLD
P.O. Box 310, Flagstaff, AZ 86002
(602) 774-6468. Oars only.

PACK ANIMALS

Horses

Probably the most colorful tale of horseback riding in the Grand Canyon is the one that stems from an unconfirmed National Park Service memorandum dated January 11, 1944. About a hundred years ago, the story goes, a ragtag bunch of horse thieves rode from the slickrock canyons of Utah, across sprawling Houserock Valley, to Saddle Mountain near the head of Nankoweap Canyon; there they'd peer into the very depths of the Canyon before spurring their mounts on a daring ride across the fluted terrain of the eastern Grand Canyon to the Colorado River. After swimming their steeds across the wild river, they'd take an old Indian route up Tanner Canyon to the South Rim, then head across the pinyon/juniper country to Flagstaff, 60 miles distant. There they'd raid some unsuspecting pilgrim, then ride hell-for-leather with their stolen stock all the way back across the Grand Canyon to the Utah badlands before turning around and doing it again. Onetime Colorado miner Peter D. Berry "claimed that after the gang had 'shot it out with the sheriff,' one wounded man reached his [Berry's] place at Grand Canyon. Before he died he confided that a copper kettle at the foot of the Tanner Trail contained the gold collected for the horses."

Whether or not this tale can be verified, both horses and mules played an integral part in the early exploration and history of the Grand Canyon area. Major John Wesley Powell favored the back of a horse when not sitting in the captain's chair of the *Emma Dean*. So did government bounty hunter Jim Owens, who shot over 400 mounatin lions on the North Rim at the turn of the century—compromising forever the tenuous ecological balance between the North Kaibab deer population and the mountain lions. Likewise geologist Charles Doolittle Walcott, who spent the fierce winter of 1882 studying Grand Canyon rock layers, which he discovered were much older than had been thought. Horses were favored by a number of prospectors-turned-dude-ranchers who guided most of the Canyon's first tourists into its far reaches on the backs of these sure-footed animals.

If you prefer saddle leather to Vibram, you can ride your horse into the Grand Canyon, but private stock use is permitted only in a handful of designated areas and requires a Backcountry Use Permit for both day and overnight use. Contact the Backcountry Reservations Office regarding permit guidelines, written regulations, and pretrip oral briefings before you put the cart before the horse.

Mules

> We are the first, and will doubtless be the last, party of whites to visit this profitless locality.
>
> —*Lieutenant Joseph C. Ives, 1858*

More than 60 million people have visited the Canyon since Ives's proclamation, and more than 14,000 of them each year experience the Canyon the way Ives did, from the back of a mule.

Below the South Rim, Grand Canyon National Park Lodges offers one-day trips to Plateau Point and back, and two-day overnight trips to Phantom Ranch and back. Both trips are physically demanding, but are safe and rewarding. One-day trips start at 8:15 a.m. every day and arrive back at the South Rim between 2:30 and 4:30 p.m. This trip includes a box lunch. The two-day trip includes overnight accommodations at Phantom Ranch, a box lunch, hearty dinner, and cowboy breakfast. For further information write or call: Reservation Department, Grand Canyon National Park Lodges, P.O. Box 699, Grand Canyon, AZ 86023, (602) 638-2410.

Below the North Rim, muleskinners lead dudes and pack-strings down the North Kaibab Trail to Roaring Springs, 9 miles roundtrip. For further information and reservations write: Grand Canyon Scenic Rides, Kanab, UT 84741; or check the Transportation Desk at Grand Canyon Lodge.

AIRCRAFT

Man began flying in the Grand Canyon for the sheer excitement of it as early as the 1920s. In fact, the first successful landing of any kind of aircraft in the Grand Canyon took place one summer day in 1922 when Commander R.V. Thomas of the British Royal Flying Corps voluntarily landed an airplane on the Tonto Platfrom near Plateau Point. A. Gaylord writes:

> The motor slows down. Thomas waves his hand to the people gathered along the rim high above him. The nose of the plane shoots up. One wing drops. Then the nose topples over and the plane shoots down. The tail wiggles and twists. Down, down, down; five hundred feet, eight hundred feet, one thousand feet—the plane is plunging and whirling to the bottom at a terrifying speed.
>
> Suddenly the motor begins to roar again. The plane has straightened out and now is flying on level course.

> The most dangerous and yet useful stunt known to aviators has been executed for the first time in the very bowels of the earth! . . . stopping about fifty feet from the edge of an 1,800-foot gorge.

What was stomach-in-your-throat excitement for the old barnstormer spelled death over 30 years later for 128 commercial airline passengers, who perished in one of aviation's worst disasters. According to the July 16, 1956, issue of *Life* magazine, " . . . a Trans World Airlines Super Constellation with 70 aboard and a United Airlines DC-7 with 58 aboard had taken off from Los Angeles three minutes apart on June 30. Approaching the Painted Desert, where their scheduled routes were known to cross, they had collided and plummeted over three miles into the Canyon. After both planes had been unreported for several hours, an aerial searcher found two charred and still smouldering smudges high on buff-colored buttes, less than a mile apart near the eastern end of Grand Canyon National Park. It was unlikely that all the victims would ever be found."

Another two decades later, veteran climber and Grand Canyon boatman George Bain was making a remarkable, one-day solo ascent of 7,529′ Vishnu Temple from the river when he discovered—and removed—a .50 caliber copper-jacketed tracer bullet near the bottom of Vishnu's lofty Coconino Sandstone Formation. In the past, pilots from Nevada's Nellis Air Force Base have been spotted flying swept-wing jets through the inner Canyon. (Military aircraft are still seen flying west out South Canyon and other areas in G.C.N.P.). Bain, who has a degree in mechanical engineering, thinks the shot came from the direction of either Rama Shrine or Lipan Point—evidence that at least one of the Canyon's hundred-odd rock temples proved too tempting a target to pass up. Perhaps Dept. of Defense ballistic experts could shed some additional light on this rare metallic fossil. In the meantime, canyoneers are herewith advised to sport flak jackets before climbing over Vishnu's needle-tipped summit.

Flying over the Grand Canyon has literally come a long way from the days of the first barnstormers, and now over 40 airtour operators carry approximately 300,000 people over and into the Grand Canyon each year. And now it is the rule, rather than the exception, for hikers to see and hear Bell Ranger jet helicopters and twin-engine Cessnas swarming over the inner Canyon's otherwise stone-silent bays and amphitheaters in general, and places like Thunder River, Havasu Creek, and the Corridor trails in particular. How these commercial flights affect the backcountry hiker is presently being studied by Grand Canyon National Park, which has conducted several Backcountry Visitor Surveys. And while air- and rotorcraft have unquestionably played an invaluable role in search-and-rescue operations, as well as contributing to scientific research like helicopter archaeology, what has to be decided once the G.C.N.P. Aircraft Management Plan has been completed for public review is whether or not commercial airplanes and helicopters provide a viable way for visitors to see and experience this natural wonder. The outcome of this issue will perhaps set an irreversible precedent for future generations and their national parks and wilderness areas. Shall we still use President Theodore Roosevelt's inspired words as guidelines? "Leave it as it is. You cannot improve on it. The ages have been at work on it, and man can only mar it. What you can do is keep it for your children, your children's children, and for all who come after you, as the one great sight every American . . . should see." Or should we administer it as just another city park, so that every man, woman, and child on the planet can go *into* the one and only Grand Canyon—regardless of their age or disposition and the long-range consequences to both this fragile ecosystem and man's atavistic relationship to it. If we do decide every tourist has an inalienable right to visit the inner Canyon, however they do it, perhaps we should salute the intrepid promoter and engineer Robert Brewster Stanton who proposed building a railroad through the length of the inner Canyon in 1889.

If you have an opinion on this issue write: Richard Marks: Superintendent, Grand Canyon National Park, AZ 86023.

CLIMBING

> Many of the buttes have never, so far is known, been climbed . . .
>
> —*Joseph Wood Krutch*

The official National Park Service brochure for Grand Canyon National Park says: "*Climbing in the Canyon is dangerous*; technical experts won't attempt it, so unskilled climbers shouldn't either." Nevertheless, man has been climbing in the Grand Canyon since prehistoric times, and the little-known history of Grand Canyon climbing is as exciting and colorful as that of Yosemite Valley's. To the inner-Canyon hiker and trekker this history is important whether they do any technical climbing in the Grand Canyon or not. The 100-odd named temples, spires, towers, castles, crests, and buttes—and 40 to 50 unnamed ones—not only provide significant orientation points for inner-Canyon travel but provide a certain dimension and perspective to the Canyon's seemingly mindboggling spatial dimensions.

Many of the more remote inner-Canyon routes were first pioneered by the prehistoric, historic, and modern climbers, and this history merits a brief overview.

Archaeological evidence indicates that climbing in the Grand Canyon began approximately a thousand years ago; that's about the time Pueblo Indians, using only their hands and feet, negotiated the descent across the bay from Tiyo Point on the North Rim and succeeded in climbing to the mesatop summit of 7,570′ Shiva Temple. The Pueblos scrambled up Shiva, it is believed, for the flint they thought to be embedded in the Kaibab Limestone that caps many of the Canyon's "islands in the sky." This fact was later confirmed by the American Museum of Natural History's expedition to Shiva Temple in 1937. Led by the museum's curator of animals, Dr. Harold Anthony, and accompanied by American Geographic Society mountaineers, the expedition discovered atop Shiva pieces of pottery, crude hand tools, and ruins hundreds of years old. They also couldn't help noticing rock cairns left by the late Emory Kolb, one-time Canyon explorer, lecturer, and photographer, who made both the first and second non-Indian ascent of Shiva Temple several weeks prior to the American Museum's much-ballyhooed first ascent. The Museum had rebuffed Kolb as a possible expedition member.

But Dr. Anthony and crew weren't out looking for arrowheads or pot shards, nor were they primarily out to bag a summit. Expedition scientists had a theory about the bushy-tailed Kaibab squirrel and its dependence on the ponderosa pine. The Kaibab squirrel is peculiar only to the North Rim primarily because it's been physically cut off from the South. Expedition scientists wondered if perhaps "sidetracked descendants, somewhat different from the mammals living today" didn't exist on Shiva. Their findings were inconclusive, but in the search they made what they believed to be the first non-Indian ascent of 7,633′ Wotan's Throne.

In addition to Shiva Temple and Wotan's Throne, evidence was discovered by canyoneers Harvey Butchart and Donald Davis that the Pueblos also succeeded in climbing 7,420′ Elaine Castle and 7,257′ Guinevere Castle, two Coconino Sandstone temples overlooking the North Rim's Modred Abyss. And who's to say how many other temples the Pueblos or the Anasazi climbed, whether in search of flint, making a spiritual rite of passage, or escaping marauding enemies?

Certainly not the scores of prospectors who arrived at the South Rim during the late 1800s. Responsible for constructing the 84 or more trails that once dotted the inner Canyon and many of the accompanying gloryholes, these argonauts were too busy poking around the Canyon in search of the Mother Lode in the form of gold, silver, copper, asbestos—*some* kind of paydirt.

Once the asbestos mines played out, it was generally thought that the Grand Canyon was devoid of any significant mineral wealth. Miners like Captain John Hance and William Wallace Bass then took up the more profitable profession of guest ranching and even guiding tourists down their hand-tooled trails. With this influx of the Canyon's first tourists came the first recorded ascents of Canyon temples. Bass and an unidentified tourist climbed 6,275′ Mt. Huethawli, near the junction of the S. Bass and Apache trails, sometime before 1900; an unnamed Hance guest scaled 7,108′ Coronado Butte, situated between the New and Old Hance trails, in the late 1890s. Several other temples were climbed about the same time by both prospectors and tourists. These are thought to be: 6,000′+ Apollo Temple overlooking Basalt Creek in the trailless eastern Grand Canyon; 4,538′ Cope Butte at the junction of the Hermit and Tonto trails; 5,030′ Dana Butte above the Tonto Trail at Horn Creek, a few miles west from the Bright Angel Trail; 5,160′ Sumner Butte, where climbers generally cache water above the Redwall on the Zoroaster approach; 7,344′ Sinking Ship, overlooking the Old Hance (or "Red Canyon") Trail; and the twin summits of 6,529′ Escalante and 6,269′ Cardenas buttes above the Esplanade Formation a few miles down the Tanner Trail. (Though the Hopi or Anasazi should probably be credited with the first ascents of both Cardenas and Escalante. There's a prehistoric Indian route Harvey Butchart found that goes over the pass between the two buttes; and it is no more than a half-hour scramble up the east side of either Escalante or Cardenas for the excellent vantage that both provide.)

No matter how you look at it, though, the first postmortem ascent of a Canyon temple has to go to W.W. Bass. After his death in 1933, his ashes were scattered from an airplane over 6,703′ Holy Grail Temple; sometimes called Bass's Tomb, Holy Grail Temple is perched high above the Shinumo, or N. Bass, Trail.

But that was the *very* beginning of climbing in the Grand Canyon. Things didn't really get serious until a math professor from Northern Arizona University came along in the fall of 1945 and took his first hike into the Canyon. Little did he know at the time that there before him stood waiting a lifetime of adventure. His name, and it's one that you shouldn't forget, is J. Harvey Butchart. He is, undisputedly, the father of canyoneering. Since his first hike down the Kaibab Trail, Butchart has spent well over 1,029 days in the Grand Canyon; in the process he's logged what he estimates to be over 12,000 miles of hiking in the Canyon—most of it off-trail; discovered 108 rim-to-river routes (in 1882 noted geologist Clarence Dutton proclaimed there were only two, each within a day's journey of the next); pioneered 164 breaks through the Redwall Formation, the most formidable and dangerous of the Canyon's half-dozen major barriers; and climbed—either alone or with partners—to the summits of 83 temples; close to 30 of them were first ascents.

Butchart had a predecessor, though, and that was Merrell Clubb, a former professor of Old English (specializing in *Beowulf*) at the University of Kansas. Before Butchart climbed Shiva Temple in 1957, his first, Clubb had already climbed ten temples and was laying the groundwork for numerous other first ascents, like 5,392′ Cheops Pyramid, 7,326′ King Arthur's Castle, and others. The most important of these was probably 7,529′ Vishnu Temple, the largest and highest detached mountain in the Grand Canyon.

But these were what some modern Grand Canyon rock climbers refer to as the "dirt piles." Nobody really got into ropes and ironmongery until September 1959. Enter Dave Ganci, a onetime adventurer who'd worked his way on a tuna boat all the way to Valparaiso so he could climb Peru's 20,000′ Nevada Laredo. When the giants of Yosemite rock climbing like Warren Harding, Royal Robbins, and Yvon Chounard were putting up the Valley's first multiday routes on the glacier-polished granite walls of El Capitan, Half Dome, and Sentinel Rock, Ganci was exploring the Grand Canyon. He thought if he could adapt the rock-climbing techniques he learned in Yosemite to sandstone climbing, and use the Alpine-style climbing tactics he'd used to climb 20,000-foot peaks in Peru's Cordillera Blanca, it might be possible to do the Canyon's "first real rock climb." His objective was the one temple that's greeted everyone who's ever peered over the lip of the South Rim, the then-unclimbed 7,128′ Zoroaster.

But the actual rock climb would only be half the problem. At the time, not even Butchart had discovered the key to getting through that unrelenting, sometimes overhanging Redwall barrier. Ganci and his partner, Rick Tidrick, did much groping, backtracking, and reascending, and used most of their precious water supply pioneering what is now the standard 4th Class approach through the Redwall. That was a remarkable accomplishment taken by itself, considering the loads they were carrying and the month. Even in September, the climb up to Zoroaster's base is not considered one of your more pleasant Canyon treks. Sunrise to sunset, the entire route burns under a relentless sun; in the Zoroaster Amphitheater late summer, that means 100+ degrees.

Once atop the Redwall, Ganci and Tidrick were faced with vertical and overhanging sections of Supai Sandstone to pick their way through—eventually arriving exhausted at Zoroaster's base at the end of day 2. The following morning, still suffering from the approach march, they quickly picked out what they thought to be Zoroaster's weakest line, on its north side. With marginal climbing gear and a quart of water apiece, Ganci and Tidrick climbed through the heat of the day and into the late afternoon of day 3. Still three full pitches below the summit, the dynamic duo came to grips with the Big Decision: to retreat, or to bivouac where they were and try to finish the climb the next morning. They were out of water and possibly, just possibly, the quart of water each of them had remaining in their packs several hundred feet below would get them all the way back down to Phantom Ranch, where they could drown themselves in the beer hall that evening.

Knowing others were "standing in line to do Zoro," Ganci and Tidrick decided to burn their bridges.

Their summer of skulking around Phoenix's Sonoran Desert in training paid off. At 11:05 a.m. on September 11, 1959, Dave Ganci and Rick Tidrick completed the first ascent of what is now regarded as the classic Grand Canyon climb.

Once Butchart and Clubb had pioneered many of the Redwall notches and 3rd and 4th Class temples, and Ganci and Tidrick demonstrated technical climbing techniques in the Grand Canyon, the temples started to fall. One by one, both technical and nontechnical, over 40 temples were climbed for the "first" time by the likes of Clubb, Donald Davis, Butchart, Allyn Cureton (who set the record for running the 20.6 miles from the North Rim to the South Rim in 3 hours and 56 minutes), and others. Butchart established yet another climbing record by topping out on five different temples in six days during July 1965: 3,945′ Chuar Lava Hill, 6,000′+ Espejo Butte, 4,242′ Lava Butte, 6,000′+ Apollo Temple, and 6,257′ Venus Temple on the Canyon's east end.

During this same period Ganci and Hughes Airwest pilot Jerry Robertson were making plans for yet another technical first ascent; this time it was 5,434′ Mt. Sinyala, which looms over heavily traveled Havasu Creek on the Canyon's west end (now a part of the Havasupai Indian's Traditional Use Area off-limits to non-Indians, because it is revered by traditional Havasupai as a sacred mountain). After three separate attempts, spread over a period of five months during the first half of 1969, Ganci and Robertson finally reached the summit of this truly majestic temple, only to discover a four-foot-high cairn and a note: "UCLA 1958." They were not amused.

Nor was that the last time temple climbers discovered summit cairns while pulling down a "first ascent." As late as 1977, climbers have found human artifacts atop several Canyon temples. After several prior attempts by experienced Flagstaff climbers, Jim Ohlman and party eventually succeeded in climbing Dana Butte, a less-than-solid Redwall Limestone temple situated 2,000 feet below the South Rim's Hopi Point. Once on the 5,030′ summit of Dana, the Ohlman party discovered large pieces of weathered hemp rope. Harvey Butchart said, "In 1919, one of the Canyon's more ambitious entrepreneurs wanted to build a scenic tramway across the Canyon . . . from Hopi Point down to Dana, across the river to the Tower of Set, and back up to Tiyo Point." A cross-Canyon Tyrolean traverse!

Led by Larry Trieber, one of Arizona's most prolific rock climbers, the 1970s in the Grand Canyon turned into a mad scramble for anything that hadn't already been climbed. Close to 50 temples were climbed for the first time, with Trieber and crew doing high-standard first ascents of 5,584′ Malgosa Crest, 8,107′ Brady Peak, 6,703′ Holy Grail Temple, and 7,200′ + Wolf Pinnacle—all at the 5.8 level or above; Butchart claiming nine 4th Class ascents; and the latest tornado on the scene, Jim Ohlman, pulling down nine 4th and 5th Class temples for a total of 61 temples during this period.

Ganci, accompanied by fellow Phoenix climber Chuck Graff, displayed his usual tenacity and inherent reptilian qualities by doing the first ascent of the difficult-to-reach-from-either-rim 6,400′ + Angel's Gate in April 1972.

In the 70s few climbers from outside the immediate Southwest had actually climbed in the Grand Canyon—the known exceptions being a group of British Columbia climbers who did the first ascent of 6,072′ O'Neil Butte, at the end of Cedar Ridge on the South Kaibab Trail, and Englishmen Pat Littlejohn and John Mothersele, who put up the difficult (5.10) Book of Genesis, also immediately off the South Rim.

Larry Trieber best capsulizes why a growing number of rock climbers are seeking out the Grand Canyon today. "The problems of climbing temples in the Grand Canyon are as complex as those found in remote mountain ranges. Only the climbs are located in a vast canyon, and are on desert mountains." When doing the first ascent of Holy Grail Temple with Bruce Grubbs in 1977, Trieber came *this* close to christening Bass Tomb as the official North

Rim boneyard. While leading Holy Grail's final pitch, Trieber pulled on a large rock that happened to be the keystone for the tons of loose rock behind it. Straddling the funnel (5.8) with a hand and foot on each wall, Trieber watched in horror as an avalanche of sandstone debris and rubble cascaded between his legs—expecting at any moment to be swept to his death.

Trieber survived that maelstrom to complete the last major first ascent up 6,377′ Kwagunt (overlooking the "Horsethief Trail") with Dennis Abbink, Jim Haggert, and Bruce Grubbs in March of 1979.

With first ascents of all but a handful of temples having been recorded, climbers soon began doing new routes on Canyon temples, primarily on the Coconino Sandstone plums like 8,372′ Mt. Hayden, the southwest face of Zoroaster, 7,203′ Buddha Temple, and others. An exception to these Coconino temples was the first ascent of 6,800′ Comanche Point Pinnacle, the Lost Arrow Spire of the Grand Canyon, done by Trieber and Grubbs. These climbs, along with George Bain's lightly equipped, one-day solo ascents of equally remote temples like Sinyala and 5,251′ Mt. Akaba, have set the tone and style for climbing in the Grand Canyon during the 1980s.

Access and Resources

Because the North Rim is eroded back from the river three to four times farther than the South Rim, most temples are situated on the north side of the Colorado River; the majority of these are located within the Vishnu and Bright

Angel quadrangles. Many temples are best approached from the South Rim, while others can only be approached from the North. All demand careful logistical planning; preplanned water caches; a strong degree of competence in inner-Canyon route finding; and grace under pressure when it comes to moving over exposed ground and trailless terrain with a heavy pack.

Be prepared for long and difficult approaches. What often looks like a feasible route on your map is often barred by at least one of the Big Five formations, frequently more: Kaibab Limestone, Cococino Sandstone, Supai Sandstone, Hermit Shale, Redwall/Temple Butte/Muav limestones, and the G.C. Series (Tapeats and Archaen). Lastly, be careful not to burn your bridges: The inner Canyon can be as unforgiving as any high-altitude objective.

It is worth noting that the North Rim is usually buried under a half-dozen feet of snow from December through April. So unless your objective can be reached from the South Rim—necessitating a river hitchhike or tenuous mattress float through dangerous currents and breath-stopping 40-degree water if your route doesn't cross the Kaibab Suspension Bridge—be prepared to wait until the snow melts or to make a 40 mile ski-tour one way from Jacob Lake.

Permits are no longer required for climbing in the Grand Canyon; however, you must still get a Backcountry Use Permit for overnight trips.

The list of Grand Canyon temples in the appendix includes each temple's name, quadrangle maps it's located on, the predominant kind of rock it's composed of, its elevation, and the name and (when known) the date of the first-known ascent party. An excellent way to familiarize yourself with these key features of Grand Canyon topography for backcountry travel is to get a copy of Hamblin and Murphy's *Grand Canyon Perspectives: A Guide to the Canyon Scenery by Interpretive Panoramas* and the appropriate topographical map. That way, once you're in the field the terrain and the Canyon's scale will be far more comprehensible to you.

CAVING

> A necklace of Grand Canyon caves, swallowed by sheer cliffs, have kept a secret about 12,000 years old: These were the dining nooks of carrion-eating condors.
>
> —*Carle Hodge, Arizona Republic*

In 1984 the National Geographic Society funded a scientific expedition into the Grand Canyon. The party was led by zoologist Steve Emslie, who believed caves in the Redwall Limestone might have been Pleistocene nesting areas for prehistoric condors. Emslie's scientific hunch was right. According to Carle Hodge, the expedition spent 35 days in the Canyon, climbing up to and rappelling into dozens of caves—discovering in no less than seven of them remains of condors that Emslie believed may be related to the modern California condors.

The fact that Emslie and his crew were able to discover and collect well-preserved remnants of this ancient bird can be attributed not only to his scientific skills but in large part to "the remoteness and aridity" of these caves, as well as to the undisturbed nature of their interiors. This is one of the primary reasons caving, or spelunking, in the Grand Canyon requires special permission from the Resources Management Division and a Backcountry Use Permit. For further information, call or write: Chief, Resources Management Division, P.O. Box 129, Grand Canyon National Park, AZ 86023; (602) 638-2411, extension 7751.

CHAPTER 7
Hiking the Grand Canyon

Hiking in and out of the Grand Canyon is, from an ecological standpoint, the equivalent of traveling from central coastal Mexico to central Canada. More often than not it's a journey that's done in a single day: first through the Lower Sonoran Life Zone, from river level up to the Tonto Plateau; then, as you climb higher, the Upper Sonoran, which generally includes that area from the Tonto Plateau up to both rims; the Transition Zone atop both rims, comprised of ponderosa pine forests; and the Canadian and Hudsonian zones beginning at around 8,000′ atop the North Rim.

What was it like for the Canyon's ancient inhabitants to make that hike, the rim-to-river-and-back hikes most people do in the Grand Canyon today? Nobody knows for sure. But one thing is certain, the days of the Anasazi are over, and with them has gone the mode of traveling simply, efficiently, and in harmony with the natural rhythms of the Canyon. And no one is more disheartened by that fact than myself, but the signs are everywhere: from the trampled shallows of Elves Chasm on the west end of the Grand Canyon to the garbage dumps of Mt. McKinley.

We expand our horizons and seek out that one spot where no one else has stood before. But someone *has* been there and left archaeological remnants: toilet paper hanging on trees and shrubbery, a fire ring the size of an Anasazi ruin, space-age Mylar soup packages, # 10 institutional food cans, dead trout in a stream full of biodegradable soap.

The list of affronts against Mother Nature is endless because too many backcountry users feel that it's some sort of omnipotent garbage disposal capable of digesting the swill and artifacts of modern humanity. It is not. Gone are the days when you could pitch camp with little regard for the environment or those who'll follow in your footsteps. Our once-vast planet has become a global village, and that fact is no more evident than in our nation's wilderness areas and national park backcountry areas. "In 1975, by the best estimate, Americans spent some forty-two million days hiking in the nation's wild and semi-wild places—a sixteenfold increase since 1945," writes John Hart in *Walking Softly in the Wilderness*. In the Grand Canyon in 1984, a total of 33,771 people spent 75,067 user-days hiking and camping overnight on the Canyon's corridor and wilderness trails. Unfortunately, we are part of the problem, and unless we exercise more care the pristine oases dotting the inner Canyon will become further inundated by a tumultous avalance of litter and noise.

But nobody wants to flee the harness of civilization only to have their wilderness experience restricted by government regulations: not you, and certainly not me. But we are, as boatman and conservationist Rod Nash said in the July 1978 issue of *National Geographic*, at the point of "loving the Grand Canyon to death. We must protect it from its friends." This sentiment was echoed by W.E. Garrett in the same issue when he wrote: " . . . the children's children for whom [Theodore] Roosevelt wanted to save the canyon are here. We're hiking and boating through the park with a Malthusian vigor that Roosevelt couldn't have anticipated. We wear heavily on the trails, the ecology, and each other's tempers."

Subsequently, several patient and prescient rangers and administrators at Grand Canyon National Park have been forced to establish and enforce a list of Backcountry Use Regulations to both lessen and redistribute our impact on this fragile ecosystem.

A WORD ABOUT BACKCOUNTRY RANGERS

Of all the National Park Service jobs at the Grand Canyon, perhaps none is more stressful than that of the backcountry ranger. Most people think these chosen few get paid to hike all over the Grand Canyon, trumpeting the call of the wild. Their responsibility, however, is twofold:

to protect both the Canyon, a nonrenewable resource, and your well-being, while at the same time maintaining the wilderness experience you seek.

Unfortunately for these rangers, most of their hiking time is spent in an overcrowded cubbyhole called the BRO (Backcountry Reservations Office). Sitting there listening to the phone ring off the hook, the squawking of the NPS radio, and the questions of hikers lined up 20-deep, reminded me of watching frantic air-traffic controllers trying to bring down seven jumbo jets on a foggy, rain-slickened runway—or waiting at the local travel agency while they try to book rooms, transportation, and lodging the week before the Super Bowl. During the peak spring hiking season, the pace inside the BRO is no less frantic, because the Grand Canyon *is* the Super Bowl of America's national parks.

Of the 2.5 million people who visited the Grand Canyon in 1984, 2.1 million walked into the Visitor Information Center. Who knows how many of them walked up to the Backcountry Reservations Office a half mile away to ask about "taking the mulies down the stairs," or to find out where they could find a trailer hookup or camping space. The job of the Backcountry Reservations Office is to orient you about the hazards, peculiarities, and rewards of hiking in the Grand Canyon, and to issue permits. But the sheer numbers the backcountry rangers are forced to deal with would make most people cave in from the pressure. At last count 33,771 people spent 75,067 nights in the Canyon during 1984.

On any given day, these patient rangers—and there are real human beings inside those Smokey the Bear outfits—will field hundreds of questions in German, Japanese, French and English. Many of these are the same tired old questions, because people didn't take the time to read the information that was sent or handed out to them or to study the informative, four-color photo display on backcountry travel in the BRO. Rangers answered 30.2 letters and 26.9 phone calls per day in 1984, which tallied out at the end of the year to 11,029 answered letters and 9,827 phone calls; that doesn't include the 11,596 permits they issued. Now if they had a presidential-sized campaign staff, that'd be one thing. But this work has to be done by two or three rangers who, like you and me, would rather be hiking in the Canyon than dealing with some macho who's seen too many Camel cigarette ads and thinks he can hike to Phantom Ranch and back with five hours of daylight left.

Why then, would someone choose so stressful a job? Fortunately, in an age of passivity there remain people who are dedicated to protecting this incomparable resource and to seeing that hikers don't unknowingly get in over their heads. And when the pace slows down to a modest hum, this glamorous job always affords these rangers the opportunity to patrol the backcountry to pack out other people's trash, clean the toilet-paper streamers out of the brush, or zip somebody up in a body bag.

So the next time you walk into the Backcountry Reservations Office all riled up because *you* didn't believe the rangers when they tried to explain how difficult hiking in and *out* of the Grand Canyon is, or because you've been waiting since sunup with 55 other backpackers who didn't make advance reservations, smile.

These fine people deserve that much. It's because of them that your hike in the Grand Canyon is still a rewarding wilderness experience.

The Backcountry Reservations Office is centrally located in the South Rim village, adjacent to Camper Services within walking distance of the Visitor Center. It is open seven days a week, 7 a.m. to 5 p.m. Mountain Standard Time (MST) in summer and 8 a.m. to 5 p.m. MST in winter.

BACKCOUNTRY PERMITS

A BACKCOUNTRY USE PERMIT IS REQUIRED FOR ALL OVERNIGHT BACKCOUNTRY USE. YOUR PERMIT *MUST* BE IN YOUR POSSESSION WHILE IN THE BACKCOUNTRY. 36 CFR 2.10(b)8.

"But why do I have to get a permit, when the Canyon's so big?" is a frequently muttered question.

In the words of Grand Canyon boatman and climber George Bain: "Before the Park Service enforced regulations for river running, beaches were being trashed out from garbage and porta-potties (20 tons of human feces a year!). Before the Park Service enforced hiking permits, people were delimbing trees and shitting in creeks. So, many of their regulations were a response to overuse and abuse—born more out of people's ignorance than anything else. What would you do if trailhead limitations were lifted and you went for a hike down the South Bass expecting solitude, only to discover 45 other hikers down there with you?"

There are presently two ways to obtain a Backcountry Use Permit: either by mail, or in person at the Backcountry Reservations Office on the South Rim. To make that office's job a little easier, and to ensure that you and your group get to hike where and when you want, I strongly recommend you use the *Advance Reservation System*. Write for the Reservation Request Form and Backcountry Trip Planner: Backcountry Reservations Office, Grand Canyon National Park, P.O. Box 129, Grand Canyon, AZ 86023. This material will detail all information necessary to reserving and obtaining a Backcountry Use Permit.

PLANNING YOUR TRIP

Once you've received your Backcountry Reservation Request Form, there are a number of things you should consider before filling it out and mailing it back in—not the least of which is where and when to go. To help you determine where to go, you should familiarize yourself with the Backcountry Zoning and Use Areas, Use Area Limits and Length of Stay, and Area Closures detailed on the Backcountry Trip Planner and Reservation Request Form.

When planning your hike into the Grand Canyon, there are two other considerations you should take into account: backcountry visitation figures, which will give you some indication as to the availability of permits for specific trails and routes, and what kind of solitude you can expect; and, of course, the Weather.

Weather

Ask any farmer who's knee-deep in bills—and that's most of them, unfortunately—what he thinks of weather predictions. Or ask a Bureau of Reclamation hydrologist why, with all the scientific weather data being beamed out of orbiting satellites, no one was prepared for the record precipitation of 1982–83—precipitation that ultimately spilled over the top of Glen Canyon Dam.

There may be recognizable weather patterns and cycles the Grand Canyon hiker can use as general guidelines, but the weather itself is always subject to change. And trying to predict the weather in the Grand Canyon is no easy matter. In hiking down any rim-to-river trail or route, you're dealing with the climatic equivalent of hiking from the north woods of Canada to the Arizona desert in a day.

Mid-February on the Bright Angel Trail can mean postholing through snowdrifts, or slipping on ice near the top of the switchbacks; rain at Indian Gardens in the early afternoon; and maybe shirtsleeve weather by the time you reach Phantom Ranch. What happens if you reverse the scenario? You're lying on a picnic table at Bright Angel Campground, basking in the warm winter sun, reading John Nichol's *Milagro Beanfield War*, and it's getting to be about time to hike out. Assuming the weather holds—something you really can't predict from the bot-

Backcountry Visitation Figures

	Annual Summary of Number of Parties: 1982–1984		
Travel Zones	*1982*	*1983*	*1984*
North Rim			
Inner Canyon:			
South Canyon	77	56	67
Nankoweap	94	168	145
Clear Creek	1,212	1,038	708
North Bass	120	109	122
Upper Tapeats	248	273	252
South Rim			
Inner Canyon:			
Tanner	815	670	522
Horseshoe	480	422	491
Monument	596	564	579
Hermit Creek	937	1,016	661
Boucher	920	741	553
South Bass	218	236	190

Monthly Area Information: 1984 Number of Parties

	JAN	FEB	MAR	APR	MAY	JUN	JUL	AUG	SEP	OCT	NOV	DEC	Year Totals
North Rim													
Inner Canyon:													
South Canyon	10	13	5	14	2	1	0	0	1	7	3	11	67
Nankoweap	1	6	34	20	37	12	9	6	2	11	7	0	145
Clear Creek	58	44	69	94	92	10	31	31	59	73	33	24	708
North Bass	0	0	4	15	25	22	13	10	21	11	1	0	122
Upper Tapeats	0	3	2	34	59	40	16	18	41	33	6	0	252
South Rim													
Inner Canyon:													
Tanner	31	39	110	95	77	18	4	6	16	53	64	9	522
Horseshoe	16	23	97	90	71	28	20	16	26	54	44	6	491
Monument	20	29	104	94	90	41	18	13	42	70	40	18	579
Hermit Creek	32	33	92	82	83	63	46	30	35	76	57	32	661
Boucher	27	33	110	99	93	21	23	16	20	50	41	20	553
South Bass	2	4	51	44	35	6	0	1	13	20	11	3	190

tom of the inner Canyon (so check the bulletin board at Phantom Ranch Ranger Station)—you'll be hiking from this oasis to the top of a 7,000′ mountain in winter conditions. If the weather closes in on the inner Canyon, which it does every two or three years, the snowline will go all the way down to Phantom Ranch, midway between Indian Gardens and the top of the Bright Angel Trail.

Now let's hike down the same trail in late July/early August. You can be wearing a jacket at the top of the Bright Angel Trail; be drenched by a summer rain and/or have your hair stand on end from St. Elmo's fire a few hundred yards out from Indian Gardens; and be stripped to your skivvies, *burning* your way through some heat-induced desert mirage, by the time you drag yourself through the sand to the Phantom Ranch beer hall. Going out that same trail the next day, you can be doused by a violent squall at Phantom Ranch; be walking across the Tonto in your swimsuit trying to catch a few rays; and be pelted by hail or drilled by lightning by the time you reach the top of the switchbacks.

Weatherwise, the best rule of thumb is to hope for the best, but be prepared for the worst.

The following table and synopsis are taken from averages at GCNP and should be used only as guidelines.

Weather Synopsis

South Rim. March can be cold and windy. April, especially late April/early May, seems to be the most fickle time of year for Canyon weather, no matter where you're

Temperatures and Precipitation (Fahrenheit and Inches)

	South Rim			*North Rim*			*Inner Gorge*		
Average:	*Max*	*Min*	*Precip*	*Max*	*Min*	*Precip*	*Max*	*Min*	*Precip*
January	41	18	1.32	37	16	3.17	56	36	.68
February	45	21	1.55	39	18	3.22	62	42	.75
March	51	25	1.38	44	21	2.63	71	48	.79
April	60	32	.93	53	29	1.73	82	56	.47
May	70	39	.66	62	34	1.17	92	63	.36
June	81	47	.42	73	40	.86	101	72	.30
July	84	54	1.81	77	46	1.93	106	78	.84
August	82	53	2.25	75	45	2.85	103	75	1.40
September	76	47	1.56	69	39	1.99	97	69	.97
October	65	36	1.10	59	31	1.38	84	58	.65
November	52	27	.94	46	24	1.48	68	46	.43
December	43	20	1.62	40	20	2.83	57	37	.87

hiking in the park. (I've been snowed on, sunburned, and snowed on again all in the same week.) June is normally dry, hot, clear, and breezeless. Sudden, frequently violent thunderstorms are not uncommon during July/August. Generally, though, for the June–September summer season, temperatures are comfortable: mid-40s to mid-80s. Autumn is short, and like spring can be fickle: warm and sunny one day, cool and cloudy with a breeze blowing the next. The first flakes usually start falling about the end of October, but the snow doesn't normally get serious until Thanksgiving. Winter days are clear and crisp during stable weather, and cold and stormy during unsettled conditions.

Inner Canyon. For all practical purposes the inner Canyon is a desert. During the summer, temperatures often exceed 100° during the day with equally hot, strong upstream winds blowing mid-afternoon. The 4 to 15 inches of precipitation annually recorded at Phantom Ranch generally fall in the form of rain during July/August and January. However, storms on the rims can unexpectedly slop over into the inner Canyon at any time of the year.

North Rim. This area receives up to 30 inches of precipitation annually, with most of it falling in the form of snow during the winter months (100+ inches). Consequently, the North Rim's paved access roads are closed from late October to early May. The North Rim is approximately 1,500 feet higher than the South, and its weather is generally cooler and wetter. Summer days at the North Rim are usually clear and crisp, with periodic thunderstorms during July and August. Even in direct sunlight the days can be cool and the nights biting. There's nothing like the warm days of an Indian summer on the North Rim during the more stable weather of September. Whatever happens on the South Rim during late fall, winter, and early spring happens about twice as hard on the North Rim.

For up-to-date weather information call the National Weather Service: (602) 774-0301 or the Backcountry Reservations Office: (602) 638-2474.

The most comprehensive and up-to-date weather information for the Colorado Plateau and Grand Canyon area is broadcast over KCLS 610 AM Radio/Flagstaff after the 8:00 a.m., 12 noon, and 5:00 p.m. news.

For winter road conditions and high-profile-vehicle wind warnings in the summertime, call the Arizona Department of Public Safety: (602) 779-2711.

TRAINING

The price of admission into the incomparable land below the rim does not come cheap; nor is it without its own hazards. But if you prepare yourself physically, spiritually, and intellectually, you'll come out of the Canyon under your own power with unforgettable experiences.

Whether you're a veteran backpacker with thousands of miles under your Vibrams, a dedicated long-distance runner, or a rank beginner, you'll find hiking in the Grand Canyon unique. It is the reverse of mountain climbing.

First you breeze into the Canyon (probably carrying a Volkswagen-sized backpack), get tired, camp, then try to crawl out—your legs screaming with each step, the air growing thinner with each switchback. Don't overestimate your own abilities; and don't underestimate the arduous nature of inner-Canyon foot travel, or canyoneering. In fact, if 1984's search-and-rescue statistics are any indication, *way* too many hikers still make these mistakes. Grand Canyon park rangers spent a total of 1,818 hours—and $84,955—conducting search-and-rescue operations during 1984. Of the 219 hiker-related incidents, 18 involved lost hikers, 96 were due to illness, 3 were drownings, 2 involved climbing, and 100 were characterized as miscellaneous. And of the 1,099 evacuations, 931 people were "dragged out" by mules, 99 by air, 9 by stretcher, and 5 in body bags. Fifty-five made it out before the rangers could find them.

The moral: get in shape before you come to the Grand Canyon.

Physical Training

During the turn of the century, the Havasupai Sinyella was quoted on his training methods. "When I was about six years old my father said, 'Do not sleep after sunrise; wake as soon as daylight appears. Run toward dawn. You should do this every day. Run out as far as you can. Do not walk; run. Do this always when you are a young man too. Then you will be able to run fast, and when you race with someone you will win. If you do not, you will be beaten.'"

That kind of tight-lipped advice may have worked for several generations of Havasupai, Walapai, Hopi, Navajo, and Paiute who lived in and around the Grand Canyon because, for most, running, travel, trade, hunting, religion, and spiritual quest were intertwined throughout their lives. But the vast majority of us—even those holed up in the remote nooks and crannies of the U.S.—are inexplicably linked to city life. And while there is no question a regular program of running and cycling will improve our general condition for canyoneering, increase our red blood cell mass for aerobic activity (such as hiking uphill) and strengthen our legs for the demands of inner-Canyon foot travel, there's probably no better general training advice to follow than that of the preeminent Everesteer, Sir Edmund Hillary: "The only way to get in shape to climb mountains is to climb mountains." And the same holds true for canyoneering.

However, most of us don't live near enough to the Grand Canyon, or a scaled-down substitute, to use canyoneering as a viable form of training for our first big Grand Canyon hike. So whether you train by riding a mountain bike, wilderness running, or backpacking, you should try to simulate the following in your training:

- The total distance you plan on hiking in the Grand Canyon over the same—or shorter—period of time, carrying the same amount of weight.
- The total elevation gain and loss of your proposed hike. (For most rim-to-river trails and routes, figure a vertical mile down and up; double that for the popular Bright Angel/North

Kaibab and return trek. In other words, you'll have to hike up a mountan that has a similar elevation gain and loss; if it has only a 2,500-foot vertical elevation gain, hike it twice.)

- The environmental conditions of your proposed hike. You wouldn't want to train for a hike down the Hermit Trail in May by limiting all of your training to cycling or jogging through the local city park near sea level in the cool of spring. By the same token, you wouldn't want to train for a multi-day trek on the Tonto Trail (a desert) in the still-warm month of October by limiting all of your training to the boggy Sasquatch forests of the Northwest or the hickory-stippled slopes of Wisconsin's Kickapoo Valley. So plan your first Grand Canyon hike or two in an environment and season your body is already physiologically adapted to, and one your mind is psychologically comfortable with.

"Expect nothing, be prepared for everything," a sage Japanese brickbreaker once said. And if you apply that concept to the rest of your physical training for canyoneering, you should cover all the bases. In addition to simulating distance, total elevation loss and gain, environmental conditions, and hiking pace in your training, it should be well-rounded enough to comfortably deal with those unexpected situations that always rear their enchanting little heads while hiking a Grand Canyon miner trail. You may plan a comfortable hike down one of the nonmaintained miner trails, but Mother Nature usually has a way of rearranging the topography. So you want to be physically trained to climb under and over fallen trees with a pack on, or to hop over and dance around boulders with a pack on. And you can supplement your aerobic base of cycling, running, or hiking with those kinds of activities that will condition your stomach (where the movement of uphill hiking begins) and upper body. You may prefer swimming and Nautilus as many triathletes do; ballet, modern dance, or aerobics as does Bjorg Austrheim-Smith (four-time woman's champion of the Western States 100-miler); or yoga and martial arts as still others do. Add a thrice-weekly routine of bent-knee situps, plus pushups and/or pullups, and you still won't be too well trained for the physical demands of Grand Canyon hiking.

Psychological Training

Many backpackers are independent, strong-willed, right-brained performers who have their own ideas about breaking through the barriers of physical discomfort—while maintaining firm footing in the cerebral wildland of endurance activity. But there are a few psychic techniques we can take from the spoonbenders and firewalkers if we learn how to apply them to both our training and canyoneering. Perhaps the best-known of these is the power of positive thinking—the notion that you can set your mind to the goal of hiking in and out of the Grand Canyon, and enjoy it. Another technique is *disassociation*, which many long-distance runners use to remove themselves from the physical elements of running in order to enjoy the esthetic qualities of their journey. Try looking at the scenery and daydreaming the same way you do on a long automobile drive. *Concentration* is the flipside of disassociating. Use it when you're hiking a trail so narrow and precipitous—like the Boucher Trail along the Hermit Formation in winter, or the Beamer Trail after a good rain—that taking your mind even momentarily off the physical act of hiking, could cause you to fall. Practicing concentration on lifting, moving, and simply placing your foot will definitely help prepare you for the precipitous and exposed nature of canyoneering. *Pre-visualization* of your proposed hike before you go will also help stretch your psychic muscles, so once you're in the Grand Canyon you'll be psychologically equipped to deal with whatever emotions arise.

Perhaps the most important psychic technique to use for canyoneering is what I call *segmenting*. When American rock climber Bev Johnson became the first woman to climb solo El Capitan's imposing 3,000-foot high Salathe Wall, she said, "The only way to eat an elephant is one bite at a time." And I've found that holds true for hiking out of the bottom of the Grand Canyon. If you look up at the South Rim from Phantom Ranch and say, "I've got to make it all the way up *that* today!" the big picture may overwhelm you. But if you look at hiking little pieces of it, the climb out will become far more manageable. For instance, just concentrate on making it to the Tonto Formation. Then, after you've taken a reasonable break, focus on the next leg or series of switchbacks, and so on and so forth until you've finally topped out on the rim.

GEAR FOR THE PACK

Most hikers have their own system or way of doing things when it comes to food and gear. Still, there are several specific items that will make your Grand Canyon hike safer and more enjoyable. An internal-frame or soft pack is generally preferred for hiking nonmaintained trails and trans-Canyon routes, primarily because it fits your body better and thus makes negotiating precipitous ledges and rugged sections of trail easier and safer. External-frame packs have a tendency to catch wind, or act as a kite, and frequently bang against rock overhangs. And the last thing a hiker needs on an exposed Canyon trail or route is to be thrown off-balance.

Know your fluid requirements. If you prehydrate by drinking several quarts of water, you can probably make it to Phantom Ranch in the wintertime on two quarts of water. During the summertime, if you prehydrate with three or four quarts of water the evening before (so your urine is clear the morning of your hike), it'll still take you three to four quarts of water (more if you're not acclimated) to reach the South Rim from Phantom. And you either have to carry that water, or cache some of it on the hike down. Many hikers and runners add ERG, or powdered Gatorade, to their water to replace precious electrolytes lost through sweating. You'll probably also find this helpful for canyoneering, particularly in the warmer months. But bring more water than you think you'll need.

The following equipment list was compiled by GCNP backcountry rangers. (For further information, get a copy of John Hart's *Walking Softly in the Wilderness: The Sierra Club Guide to Backpacking*.)

Suggested Equipment for Grand Canyon Overnight Hiking

The essentials: water; purification tablets: iodine, chlorine or water purification pump; extra food; hat; sunscreen; sunglasses; topographic map; compass; flashlight; signal mirror and whistle; pocket knife; first aid kit: bandages, tape and surgical adhesive, moleskin, antiseptic, Ace bandage, nylon cord, safety pins.

Clothing: appropriate for season. Remember—guard against wind, wetness, and cold. Dress in layers! Bring only what you actually need, but keep the weight down! Shirts: heavy and light; pants: heavy and light; socks: 2 pairs heavy, 2 pairs light; boots or hiking shoes—broken in; underwear.

Food: meal items: well balanced, high in carbohydrates; snack items; vegetables and fruits (can be dried); drink mixes (e.g., ERG, Gatorade).

Kitchen/cooking: stove; fuel; cooking pot(s); plate, bowl, cup, knife, fork, spoon; can opener; matches (strike anywhere); salt, pepper, and other spices; plastic food containers; plastic bags.

Shelter: poncho or rainsuit; lightweight tent; sleeping bag or bedroll and foam pad; ground cloth.

Sanitation items: toilet paper and trowel; biodegradable soap; trash bags; pinch of lime or powdered bleach.

Personal items: toothbrush and paste; comb; washcloth; lip balm; foot powder; insect repellant; needle and thread; camera and film.

Suggested Season Substitutions for Winter

Clothing: wool cap; wool sweater; wool pants; wool socks; wool or polypropylene underwear; wool gloves or mittens; shirt and wind/rain parka; rainsuit; waterproofed boots, gaiters and instep crampons; light, waterproof tent; winter sleeping bag; space blanket.

In addition to the topographical maps listed at the end of each trail or route description, you would do well to get a copy of the *Geological Map of the Grand Canyon National Park, Arizona*, and section it into the eight quadrangles that comprise the heart of Grand Canyon National Park, Arizona: Nankoweap, Vishnu Temple, De Motte Park, Bright Angel, Powell Plateau, Havasupai Point, Kanab Point, and Supai (all 15-minute). When used with these individual quadrangles, and cross-referenced with each trail or route description and Michael Young's "Geology" (see Chapter 4), the colorful *Geological Map of the Grand Canyon National Park, Arizona*, will prove to be an invaluable reference for the less traveled and more remote Canyon trails and routes. It's published by the Grand Canyon Natural History Association (P.O. Box 399, Grand Canyon, AZ 86023) in conjunction with the Museum of Northern Arizona (Rt. 4, Box 720, Flagstaff, AZ 86001) and can be purchased for a nominal price by writing to either of their offices.

The USGS quadrangles listed at the end of each trail and route description can be purchased by writing: Branch Distribution, U.S. Geological Survey, Federal Center, Denver, CO 80225.

One other map worth acquiring, if it's not already in your collection, is *The Heart of the Grand Canyon*, compiled by eminent cartographer Bradford Washburn and published by the National Geographic Society, Washington, DC 20036. This masterpiece literally zooms in on the Bright Angel Quadrangle area and colorfully highlights it in great topographical detail.

HIKING BELOW THE RIM

Caches. Let's say you're going to hike down the Tanner Trail, or any other rim-to-river trail, spend a day at the river, then hike out the same trail. Unless you enjoy carrying the additional weight as a workout, there's really no practical reason to carry everything you're going to need for the hike out all the way down to the river. So pick one or two spots along your descent route, say one-third and two-thirds of the way down, where you can cache food and water for the return hike. Make sure your food is animal-proofed and keep your water in the shade.

Method of Travel. During the summertime, which is absolutely the worst time of the year to hike *into* the

Grand Canyon, you should plan on leaving the river or Phantom Ranch no later than 5:00 a.m. if you want to beat the heat to the Tonto Formation. That means, eat breakfast and pack everything except your sleeping gear the night before. If you sleep in, and get caught on the Tonto in the heat of the day, wait till high noon passes before you start walking again. In wintertime you might want to sleep in a bit longer, but you want to be on the trail by daybreak so you're hiking during the warmest part of the day. Also, the last mile or two out, most of the South Rim trails tend to be icy and treacherous if you reach them too late in the afternoon during winter months, due to their shaded northern exposures.

Hiking Techniques. Most Grand Canyon pilgrims have a tendency to walk very guardedly when descending into the Canyon, mainly because the awesome breadth and exposure can be so unnerving. This tendency leads to locking the knee each and every step. And the knee and hip joints just can't take that kind of stress—especially when you've got a pack on. So before you go to the Canyon, on one of your training hikes, try the *shuffle* when going downhill. All you do is relax your body and legs, waddling from side to side, so the downhill torque and stress are absorbed in your calves and quadriceps instead of your ankle, knee, and hip joints. Should you fall while you're hiking downhill, which happens to the best of us, fall uphill on your buttocks. There are numerous places in the Grand Canyon where you simply cannot afford to do a cartwheel, with or without a pack.

Almost the opposite holds true for hiking uphill out of the Canyon. Going up, use the *rest step*. It consists of taking a short- or moderate-length step, then locking your knee so your body is resting on the skeletal structure of that leg while the opposite leg is taking the next step. Lock, rest, step, and so on until you're all the way out. Otherwise, if you have a tendency to just march on out without locking your knees, the constant churning of the leg muscles can be utterly exhausting.

WATER

> We have run out of food and water. God help us. We're trying to get to water.
>
> —*Incident Report*
> Grand Canyon National Park

They never made it, and the note those two hikers left before they fell to their deaths is a cry that's been echoed around the world for as long as man has tried to cross the Earth's great deserts on foot. But the Grand Canyon isn't merely a desert; it's an inverted desert mountain range whose few reliable water sources can be far more difficult, precipitous, and dangerous to reach for the uninitiated than those cool deep wells and fly-infested seeps that pockmark the relatively flat deserts of the Gobi, Outback, Sahara, and more forgiving arid reaches of the Southwest.

Historically, Native American runners and traders like the Mojave, Walapai, Havasupai, and Hopi traveled long distances across northern Arizona, frequently under miserable conditions, to trade bighorn sheepskins or caulky red ochre paint for seashells, turquoise, pottery, and other precious, easily transportable goods. They were able to undertake and endure these arduous trading forays to one another's distant villages not only because they were well conditioned and had a photographic knowledge of the terrain, but because they planned their treks to link one perennial or seasonal water source to the next. And you would do well to follow this historic precedent by planning your own inner-Canyon trek so it links one known water source with the next.

Water Treatment. A study completed in 1980 by the U. of Arizona's School of Renewable Resources concluded that all side streams in the Grand Canyon, as well as the main stem of the Colorado River, need to be treated before drinking, because of the high fecal-coli counts. Of the numerous methods backpackers use to treat drinking water, perhaps the most widely practiced is the use of chlorine; although, one authority warns: "Simple chlorination is unpredictable, and may be useless against bacteria when water is contaminated with organic material." If you suspect your watersource may be home to the devastating intestinal amoeba *giardia*—a safe bet in the Canyon—you may opt to pack an Iodine Crystal Kit. That's assuming you're not sensitive to iodine or have been treated for hyperthyroidism; if you have any doubts, it'd be safer to boil your water or pack a small water purification pump. Investigate the best method of water purification for yourself *before* your hike.

Water Sources

Colorado River. For those canyoneers hiking down rim-to-river trails and routes where there are no reliable springs or seeps, it's recommended you use the Colorado River as your principal water source to replenish depleted reserves. Use the water treatment methods described above. If the Paria or Little Colorado is flooding, the Colorado River will usually become heavily laden with sediment. If you find it necessary to use this water because it's your only, or best, water source, and you're not dying of thirst, let the water stand overnight (so the particulates have time to settle) before pouring it into another container(s) for treatment.

Perennial Water Sources

According to the Cooperative National Park Services Resources Studies Unit, "Sources are classified as perennial on the basis of detailed historic records indicating the source has not gone dry within historic times or on the presence of maidenhair fern." The following list has been compiled from their study, "An Inventory and Classification of Surface Water Resources in G.C.N.P., AZ," as well as from the Western Speleological Institute's Technical Note #36, the Backcountry Reservations Office's "Water Sources in Grand Canyon National Park," and the author's field notes.

Perennial Water Sources

Warning: Conditions in the backcountry continue to change. Check with the BRO on the latest status of these water sources and others before betting your life on them.

Below the South Rim

From the Little Colorado River on the east end of the Grand Canyon at River Mile 61½, proceeding west to Havasu Canyon at River Mile 157.

Name	*Location*	*Source*
1. Little Colorado River	River Mile 61½, east end of Beamer Trail.	Blue Springs
(*WARNING:* High radioactive spill in Rio Puerco tributary. *DON'T DRINK!*)		
2. J.T. Spring	Hance Canyon, east arm of Grandview Trail.	Muav Limestone
3. Grandview Spring	Hance Canyon, east arm of Grandview Trail.	Muav Limestone
4. Grapevine	East fork of Grapevine Canyon, off Tonto Trail.	
5. Burro Spring	Pipe Creek, on Tonto Trail west of S. Kaibab.	Bright Angel Shale
6. Pipe Spring	Pipe Creek, Tonto Trail west of S. Kaibab.	Bright Angel Shale

Perennial Water Sources (continued)

Warning: Conditions in the backcountry continue to change. Check with the BRO on the latest status of these water sources and others before betting your life on them.

7. Garden Creek	Bright Angel Trail.	Muav Limestone
(*DON'T DRINK!* Due to high fecal coli. Use developed water sources.)		
8. Monument Creek	Tonto Trail, 10½ miles west of Indian Gardens.	
9. Hermit Creek	Tonto Trail, 2½ miles west of Monument Creek.	
(*DON'T DRINK!* Due to high fecal coli. Use Colorado River.)		
10. Santa Maria Springs	Hermit Trail, below junction of Dripping Springs Trail.	Esplanade Sandstone
11. Dripping Springs	Boucher Trail, mile west of Hermit Trail junction.	Coconino Sandstone
12. Boucher Creek	Boucher Trail, upstream of Boucher Creek camp.	
13. Slate Creek	Tonto Trail, 5 miles west of Boucher Creek camp.	Muav Limestone
14. Turquoise Canyon	Tonto Trail, 11½ miles west of Slate Creek.	Bright Angel Shale

15. Copper Canyon	Tonto Trail, 4½ miles west of Bass Canyon.	
16. Royal Arch Creek	Below Apache Trail.	Elves Chasm
(*DON'T DRINK!* Due to high fecal coli. from lower and middle Elves.)		
17. Forster Canyon	River Mile 123	Bright Angel Shale
18. Hundred and Forty-Mile	River Mile 140	Bright Angel Shale
19. Olo Canyon	River Mile 145½	
20. Matkatamiba Canyon	River Mile 148	
21. Havasu Creek	Havasupai Indian Reservation	Havasu Springs
(*DON'T DRINK!* Semi-treated sewage pumped into creek below Supai.)		
22. Havasu Springs	Havasupai Indian Reservation	Supai Group

Below the North Rim

From Little Nankoweap Creek on the east end of the Canyon at River Mile 52, proceeding west to Kanab Creek at River Mile 143½.

Name	*Location*	*Source*
1. Nankoweap Creek	Nankoweap Trail along Nankoweap Creek.	Muav Limestone

Perennial Water Sources (continued)

Warning: Conditions in the backcountry continue to change. Check with the BRO on the latest status of these water sources and others before betting your life on them.

2. Cliff Spring	Cliff Spring Trail below Cape Royal.	Toroweap Formation
3. Clear Creek	Clear Creek Trail, east end.	
4. Bright Angel Creek	Bright Angel Campground.	North Rim
(*DON'T DRINK!* Due to high fecal coli. Use developed water sources.)		
5. Phantom Creek	N. Kaibab Trail, 2 miles north of Phantom Ranch.	Muav Limestone
6. Ribbon Springs	N. Kaibab Trail, 5½ miles north of Phantom Ranch.	Muav Limestone
7. Transept Spring	Transept Canyon, north of Cottonwood Campground.	Muav Limestone
8. Roaring Springs	N. Kaibab Trail, 10 miles north of Phantom Ranch.	Muav Limestone
9. Crystal Creek	North Rim trans-Canyon route, Crystal Creek.	Tapeats Sandstone
10. South Big Springs	West of Big Spring Canyon at head of Shinumo Creek.	

11. Shinumo Creek	River Mile 108¼	Muav Limestone
12. White Creek	Below east side of Muav Saddle.	
13. Hundred and Twenty-Mile Creek	River Mile 120, Blacktail Canyon.	
14. Bedrock Canyon Creek	River Mile 130½	
15. Galloway Canyon Creek	River Mile 131½	
16. Stone Creek	River Mile 132	
17. Tapeats Creek	River Mile 134	
18. Tapeats Spring	Tapeats Cave above Thunder River confluence.	Muav Limestone
19. Thunder River	Thunder River Trail at Tapeats Creek confluence.	Muav Limestone
20. Thunder Spring	Thunder River Trail, below Redwall.	Muav Limestone
21. Deer Creek	River Mile 136	
22. Deer Spring	Surprise Valley Trail, below Redwall.	Muav Limestone
23. Unnamed seep	River Mile 138	Tapeats Sandstone
24. Kanab Creek	River Mile 143	

Seasonal Water Sources

If you are planning an inner-Canyon trek that does not link together a sufficient number of perennial water sources to ensure a safe and rewarding outing, it is strongly advised you plan your trek so it coincides with the late-winter/early-spring runoff, when a greater number of tributary drainages might be running with water; or if you're looking to do a high-country trek closer to either the North or South rims, the July/August rains can generally be counted on to supply some marginal water sources in the form of *tinajas*, or rain pockets, before they succumb to evaportion. However, lightning and flash floods present their own hazards during the summer.

The following tributary drainages have been recorded as having seasonal water, but this list is to be used only as a planning aid. *Never* trust these without first checking with the Backcountry Reservations Office. The BRO maintains up-to-date files on backcountry water sources, based on ranger patrols and hiker reports.

Emergency Water

If you find yourself running low on water, and you are hampered by either distance or some geological barrier from reaching the Colorado River, a perennial water source, a seasonal water source the BRO has confirmed in advance as being reliable, or a developed water source on either of the rims, you have several alternatives *during the wet seasons*. Rain frequently collects for short

Seasonal Water Sources

The following tributary drainages have been recorded as having seasonal water, and this list is to be used only as a planning aid. Never trust these without first checking with the Backcountry Reservations Office. The BRO maintains up-to-date files on backcountry water sources, based on ranger patrols and hiker reports.

Below the South Rim (East to West)

Name	*Location*	*Comments*
1. Tanner Canyon	Fork below Desert View	Marginal, off trail
2. Seventy-Five Mile Canyon	West fork	Difficult to reach
3. Red Canyon	Below point trail descends Redwall	
4. Cottonwood Creek	Middle fork	In reeds. (Not O'Neil Springs)
5. Boulder Creek	Marked by spring	Marginal
6. Lonetree Canyon	Marked by spring	Marginal
7. Cremation Canyon	East wall	Marginal
8. Horn Creek		More reliable
9. Salt Creek		Marginal
10. Ruby Canyon	Above Tonto Trail	*Tinajas*

Seasonal Water Sources (continued)

The following tributary drainages have been recorded as having seasonal water, and this list is to be used only as a planning aid. Never trust these without first checking with the Backcountry Reservations Office. The BRO maintains up-to-date files on backcountry water sources, based on ranger patrols and hiker reports.

Below the South Rim (East to West)

Name	*Location*	*Comments*
11. Serpentine Canyon	Above Tonto Trail	*Tinajas*
12. Bass Canyon	Bedrock tanks	
12. Garnet Canyon		*Tinajas*
13. Chemehuevi Point	Seep west of point above Apache Trail	
14. Fossil Bay, main arm	Seeps below Coconino	
15. Keyhole Natural Bridge	Spring to west	

periods of time in wide, but shallow, rain pockets on broader sections of Tapeats Sandstone, Esplanade Sandstone, and Hermit Shale. Zip-locking baggies are best for removing water from these shallow *tinajas*. If you're not in the vicinity of any of these formations, you can pretty well surmise from the list of perennial water sources that your best bet is to look for indicator plants (like maidenhair fern) in the Muav Limestone, Bright Angel Shale,

Below the North Rim (East to West)

Name	Location	Comments
1. Kwagunt Creek		More reliable
2. Sixty-Mile Creek	Near Butte Fault	Marginal
3. East fork of Carbon Creek	Avoid seep	May be poisonous
4. Lava Canyon	Runoff	
5. Basalt Creek	North of where map says "Basalt"	
6. Unkar Creek	Runoff	
7. Asbestos Canyon	Below Tonto Formation in main arm	
8. Vishnu Creek	Near Tonto Formation	Runoff and *tinajas*
9. Trinity Creek	Near Tonto Formation	Terrible tasting
10. Dragon and Crystal creeks	Runoff	
11. Tuna Creek	Runoff	
12. Powell Spring		Marginal
13. Saddle Canyon		Runoff and *tinajas*

Redwall Limestone, or whichever formation is in the closest proximity to your predicament.

Again, don't plan extended hikes away from perennial water sources during the hot and dry months unless you

Water Requirement Charts

A. Number of Days of Expected Survival in the Desert, No Walking at All:

Max. daily shade temp. F.	*Available water per man, U.S. quarts* 0	*1*	*2*	*4*	*10*	*20*
120 degrees	2	2	2	2.5	3	4.5
110	3	3	3.5	4	5	7
100	5	5.5	6	7	9.5	13.5
90	7	8	9	10.5	15	23
80	9	10	11	13	19	29
70	10	11	12	14	20.5	32
60	10	11	12	14	21	32
50	10	11	12	14.5	21	32

The importance of temperature reduction to the survivor is highighted by the following in Chart A: Temperature 120°, water available 2 quarts, days of expected survival 2; reduce the temperature to 100°, and 2 quarts of water will extend your life expectancy THREE TIMES. This importance to a potential "survivor" cannot be overemphasized. Night travel, or better, NO TRAVEL, is stressed.

At equal temperatures, the body requires two to three times as much water to maintain water balance in the desert as it requires in the jungle with its high humidity.

Dehydration: An increase in body temperature of 6 to 8 degrees above normal (98.6) for any extended period causes death. (from "The Physiology of Man in the Desert" by Adolph & Associates)

know *exactly* what you're getting yourself into. Assuming you can find any, you probably won't be able to stomach eating all the barrel cactus it takes to replenish massive fluid deprivation.

B. Number of Days of Expected Survival in the Desert, Walking at Night Until Exhausted and Resting Thereafter:

Max. daily shade temp. F.	*Available water per man, U.S. quarts* 0	*1*	*2*	*4*	*10*	*20*
120 degrees	1	2	2	2.5	3	
110	2	2	2.5	3	3.5	
100	3	3.5	3.5	4.5	5.5	
90	5	5.5	5.5	6.5	8	
80	7	7.5	8	9.5	11.5	
70	7.5	8	9	10.5	13.5	
60	8	8.5	9	11	14	
50	8	8.5	9	11	14	

Effects of Loss of Body Fluid

% of Loss	*Effect*
2½%	Dehydration commences
5%	Nausea
6–10%	Giddiness, headaches, limbs itch
15%	Death imminent in 90 degree weather
25%	Death even in cool climates

Water Requirements

If you were to look at the big picture of hiking in the Grand Canyon, you'd see that the greatest percentage of potential hazards that can befall both the unwary and experienced backpacker are water-related: either too much of it, or not enough of it.

By far the highest number of unfortunate hiker-related incidents have to do with *not enough water*, primarily because too many hikers choose to do their inner-Canyon hiking during the warmest and driest months of the year. But even those hikers who plan their outings for the relatively cool months of April and May are still faced with the prospect of heat cramps, heat exhaustion, and frequently deadly heat stroke. Why? Because their bodies simply aren't prepared for the sudden heat that claims those environmentally adapted to hiking during the cold winter and cool spring months.

That leaves the hiker coming to the Grand Canyon during April and May two alternatives: overdress during your training, to simulate warm desert environment, and/or prehydrate before your most strenuous hiking days—in the process continually replenish your lost fluids by overdrinking. Thirst is a poor indicator of your fluid requirements. It's far better to use the color of your urine as a clue to your fluid needs. If it's clear, you're doing great. But once it starts turning yellow, you're getting into fluid deprivation and need to fill up the tank. Once it turns dark yellow, well, you're getting into serious problems.

The preceding water requirement charts should be used as a guideline for your fluid requirements, with the qualifier that section B was based on walking at night over relatively flat desert. (Don't walk at night in the Grand Canyon, unless you know what you're doing and where you're going.)

If you're walking during daylight hours with a pack

on, figure on doubling or trebling these fluid requirements—depending on your fitness, acclimatization, air temperature and humidity, terrain, elevation gain and the weight you're carrying.

Again, the best treatment is prevention, and the best practical indicator is your urine; so you might consider leaving your vitamins in the car until you return, because they have a tendency to turn your urine yellow. Remember, you lose water three ways: perspiration, urination, and breathing. And—if you're sitting on the hot ground (midsummer in the Inner Gorge, it's 140–160 degrees)—heat conduction.

For a detailed discussion of the treatment of heat cramps, heat exhaustion, and heat stroke, get a copy of *Medicine for Mountaineers* (The Mountaineers/Books, 715 Pike Street, Seattle, WA 98101).

HAZARDS

Sunburn. Prevent by wearing long-sleeve, white cotton shirts, and a white cotton hat.

Sunglare. Only polarized sunglasses and certain brands of glacier goggles will block out harmful ultraviolet rays.

Flash Floods. These occur suddenly, usually during summer rains when several inches of precipitation can pelt the higher elevations in a relatively short period of time. This peak runoff normally has only one way to go, *downhill*, and if you happen to be hiking along the bottom of one of the named tributary canyons which frequently act as funnels for this tremendous runoff, chances are you won't have time to climb to higher ground. In which case, you may suddenly find yourself bodysurfing to the Colorado River—and your death. If you doubt the power and danger of a Grand Canyon flash flood, ask any boatman who's rafted Crystal Rapid before and after the awesome flash flood of 1966 created one of the most treacherous rapids in North America; or ask any of the boatmen and passengers who were taking out at Diamond Creek during the summer of 1984 and scrambled for their lives when a flash flood came thundering down Diamond Creek and swept all of their boats, gear, and a stakeside truck (!) into the Colorado River. So stay out of the main canyons, creeks, and drainages during the July/August rains.

Lightning. Lightning will present problems during the rains if you're in an open area or shallow cave, standing on a ridgetop, or hunkered down under a lone tree. Stay out of these areas during lightning storms, and head for the boulder fields and protected areas such as forests, or any other site you feel will offer you some protection.

Rockfall. In the Grand Canyon, a rockfall is generally caused in one of three ways: by a sonic boom, a storm, or hikers. The sonic booms you can do nothing about except write your representatives in Congress. When hiking cross-country or along any of the trails, make sure you're out of the fall line of rocks that can be knocked down by other parties or members of your own party. And exercise care as to where you place your hands and feet. As far as storms are concerned, the most predictable areas for rockfall are those polished streaks that adorn so many canyon walls; they turn to waterfalls during the rains and carry debris and rubble with them. Stay away from their fall line.

Sprains. Storms, erosion, and hikers are constantly changing conditions of Grand Canyon trails and routes. So make sure your footwear will meet the demands of the terrain you're hiking and provide you with adequate ankle support.

River Crossings. There have been numerous drownings of experienced canyoneers who've been ill-prepared for crossing the Colorado River. Unless you've practiced river crossings elsewhere, with a pack on, it's definitely not advised to attempt your first on the Colorado. While historic pre-dam records indicated the Colorado River at Diamond Creek sometimes reached a surface temperature near 80 degrees during the hottest part of summer, the post-dam river temperature is closer to 40 degrees on the east end of the Grand Canyon, where many river crossings are attempted. Even if you're wearing a full-length wetsuit, a human being normally can't handle that kind of cold-water immersion for more than a few *active* minutes without succumbing to hypothermia—and death. That's in the calm stretches of river, where your crossing should be made.

If your cross-river trek is planned for April through September, you can usually get a commercial river outfitter to take you across the river. But remember, they've got their own passengers and a schedule to maintain, so you may have to wait for a while at an opportune pickup point before you get a ride.

If your cross-river trek does not fall within the commercial boating season—and you *must* cross the river—consider these two types of inflatable rafts:

An inflatable raft or canoe, minimum size 3½′ × 6′ × 12″ tubes (approximate weight, 10–15 lbs.), commonly referred to as a two-man raft, is a reasonably stable craft. Seams should be sealed so that there is a rounded surface, not a 'trim' on the outside perimeter of the tube. No more than two persons with packs should use such a craft at any one time (shuttle if necessary). Life preservers, either Type II or Type III, must be worn while crossing.

An air mattress is lighter to carry, but more dangerous to use. It's easy to upset even in seemingly flat water, which has its own tricky currents in the form of eddies, whirlpools, and boils. And the Colorado is just too cold to swim across most times of the year, even if you don't have a pack on. Contact the Backcountry Reservations Office for further recommendations on techniques, gear, and best crossing sites.

Creek Crossings. Several hikes described in this guide require creek crossings. But there are certain times of the year, such as during heavy spring runoff, when you just *can't* ford creeks like Shinumo, Tapeats, Saddle Canyon and others without endangering your life. So plan your hikes into these areas before or after heavy spring runoff and summer rains. (Check with the BRO on the latest conditions.) During the years of particularly heavy precipitation and runoff, these seasons may be extended on either end.

If for some reason your route or situation requires you to ford a creek before or after spring runoff, and you feel the crossing will be a marginal one for you, select the area you feel is safest, e.g., not at the top of Deer Creek Falls, Thunder River, Lower Tapeats Narrows, etc. Heave your pack across to the other side. Then put on your inflatable, U.S. Divers' life vest, and make your crossing as carefully as possible. If you get knocked off your feet, lie on your back, arms paddling at your sides, knees bent, and legs pointed downstream, and hope like hell you can grab a limb or tree root before you're swept over Never Never Falls. Unless you're an experienced climber who's set up Tyrolean traverse river crossings elsewhere, *don't use a rope*. It'll drag you to the bottom like an anchor, and the more your pard heave-hos on the other end, the more fishlike you'll become.

Hypothermia. "Killer of the unprepared." Commonly referred to as "exposure" in your local newspaper headlines, hypothermia is simply the rapid cooling of your body's inner core. While the inner Canyon should be considered desert, the Tonto Formation on up to both rims can be considered a mountain environment. There are certain times of the year, however, when your body can lose heat in either of these environments.

To prevent hypothermia you must, in all circumstances, be able to keep yourself warm. This can be no easy task

Wind Speed Cooling Power of Wind

mph	*Temperature (F)*										
Calm	40	30	20	10	5	0	−10	−20	−30	−40	−50
	Equivalent Chill Temperature										
5	35	25	15	5	0	−5	−15	−25	−35	−45	−55
10	30	15	5	−10	−15	−20	−35	−45	−60	−70	−80
15	25	10	5	−20	−25	−30	−45	−60	−70	−85	−100 –
20	20	5	−10	−25	−30	−35	−50	−65	−80	−95	−110 –
25	15	0	−15	−30	−35	−45	−60	−75	−90	−105	−120 –
30	10	0	−20	−30	−40	−50	−65	−80	−95	−110	−125 –
35	10	−5	−20	−35	−40	−50	−65	−80	−100	−115	−130 –
40	10	−5	−20	−35	−45	−55	−70	−85	−100	−115	−130 –
	Danger			Increasing Danger (Flesh may freeze within 1 minute)				Great Danger (Flesh may freeze within 30 seconds)			

Example: At 10°F, a 25 mph wind speed produces a −30°F chill temperat

if you are wet and/or if the wind is blowing. Think about this carefully when you select clothing and gear for your pack.

For a detailed discussion of cause, treatment, and prevention of hypothermia, read *Medicine for Mountaineering*. This same excellent source also addresses *Frostbite*, which several experienced canyoneers fell victim to not long ago.

Poisonous Bites and Stings. Of the three species of rattlesnake that inhabit the Grand Canyon, the most common is the timid Grand Canyon "pink." Don't put your hands or feet where you can't see, and you've nothing to worry about. However, if you *do* get bit, there are no less than five methods of treatment; all are controversial. Ask any three doctors, and you'll see what I mean. Current methods include: (1) cut and suck, *terrible*; (2) ligature/cryotherapy, may cause cold damage to affected limb; (3) antivenom, causes anaphylactic shock if you're allergic to horse serum—and you don't know that until you're injected; (4) hydra-cortisone injections—a doctor in Texas has been very successful with this; (5) do nothing, sit still, don't panic, send your pard for help, and statistics prove you'll survive. If you get up and start walking, and you have been envenomated (which happens only 50–75% of the time, and you'll *know* if you have been), complications arise in minutes.

Scorpions like to cling to dark, damp places, such as the bottom of your groundcloth, so shake out your boots and sleeping bag every morning. If you get bit, you'll get pretty nauseous, maybe even cramp up, but you'll probably survive to make the climb out.

One far more common type of bite you might encounter is that of a red ant. Treat with ammonia and watch your food scraps and crumbs or the buggers will beat a path straight to your hands and ankles.

For further information on treatment of poisonous bites and stings, as well as practical applications of desert survival, send for an excellent free booklet, *Desert Sur-*

vival, published by the Maricopa County Department of Civil Defense and Emergency Services (2035 N. 52nd Street, Phoenix, AZ 85008).

EMERGENCY EVACUATION

All right, you did all your homework—your training, your reading; you bought all the right gear, achieved the proper mental attitude, the whole ball of wax. But somehow you still managed to get in trouble. What are you going to do now that you (or your pard) have broken a leg, or met one of the other Grand Canyon dragons face-to-face? After you've administered first aid, you have to decide whether one of you is going to go for help, or whether you're both going to sit where you are and wait for help to come. And only *you* can properly decide that. If you've got adequate water, food, shelter, and clothing—which you should—and you're too far from either the rim or the river, your best bet might be to sit tight, flash signs to one of the airtour operators or commercial airliners with your signal mirror. If they've seen your flash, they'll notify GCNP authorities; so don't quit flashing until you hear the sound of their voices or the *whup-whup-whup* of Mother Ship. If they bring in a helicopter, remember to stay clear. Let them come to you.

If you're too far away from the developed sites or pavement on either of the rims, or just plain closer to the river, that'll be your best bet during the commercial river season if you know a sure way down to the river. Again, they have their own passengers to take care of and schedules to follow, so it had better be an *emergency*; if it is, they'll take care of you. They carry major first-aid kits, should hold an Advanced First Aid or EMT card, and carry air-net radios; those radios can send messages out at 122.9 mc and/or 123.05 mc. Stay out of their way, and let them do what they know how to do. The message they'll broadcast will probably be: "Emergency, emergency, require helicopter, require helicopter, Mile-____, Colorado River, Mile-____, Colorado River. Notify NPS, Grand Canyon."

Before you leave your injured partner and head for the creek, write down time of trauma, condition, medication administered (if any), location of victim, and any other pertinent information you think a successful treatment and evacuation might require. Keep a cool head, and take something down to the river a boatman will be able to see or hear when you try flagging him or her down: red or yellow shirt or jacket, a mirror, a whistle, etc. And don't try flagging them down in the middle of a rapid or immediately below it. Pick a calm stretch of water where they have enough time to pull over, or a spot where they've pulled over for lunch, camp, or to scout a rapid.

Note that there is no scheduled air traffic over some parts of the river. Among these are Marble Canyon between Rider Canyon (Mile 17) and 60 Mile Canyon; Stephen and Conquistador isles (Miles 117–122); and Deer Creek to Vulcan's Anvil (Miles 138–178). It may be advisable to move to an area where more air traffic occurs, if possible. Or try flashing any of the rim overlooks or the Desert View Watch Tower.

WILDERNESS ETHICS

> The richest values of wilderness lie not in the days of Daniel Boone, nor even in the present, but rather in the future.
>
> —*Aldo Leopold*

As hikers and canyoneers we have the desire and, in many cases, the ability to reach remote areas of the Grand Canyon that most of its 2½ million annual visitors will see only in a scenic photograph. And that's the primary reason we have the potential to inflict the most—sometimes irreversible—physical damage upon its fragile ecosystems. More damage than the mule-riding concessions, which use only the maintained South Kaibab, Bright Angel, North Kaibab, and Uncle Jim trails; and more than the heavily regulated, closely monitored commercial river concessionaires whose boatmen guide most of the riverside day hikes. So that leaves us with the responsibility to clean up our own act, and that of others, so that future generations of canyoneers can enjoy the pristine qualities of Grand Canyon National Park. Failing this, national park rangers will have no recourse but to enforce backcountry regulations more severely.

Note these rules:

1. Don't use firearms. 36 CFR 2.4(a). This includes bows and arrows.

The Grand Canyon is not an armed camp. So if you want to engage the enemy, see your local recruiter; they could use a few good men. Their toll-free number is 1-800-241-3903. Nor is the Grand Canyon a hunting preserve. Unless you'd enjoy taking lunch with the U.S. magistrate, complete with an armed escort, "go ahead, make *everybody's* day" and leave your weapons at home.

2. Don't use motorized vehicles or wheeled vehicles on trails. 36 CFR. The trails were not constructed for motorcycles, baby buggies, bicycles, and similar vehicles. They can create a hazard for you as well as other hikers.

Probably the classic incident involving this regulation was the citation of a Colorado River boatman for rolling 10 cases of beer down the Bright Angel Trail on a hand dolly in order to resupply a thirsty river party. He was not only cited under this law, but had to push his still-loaded hand dolly back up the steep South Kaibab.

3. Don't take dogs or other pets below the rim. 36 CFR 2.15(a)1. As much as little Bozer may look like White Fang sitting next to the fireplace, he is an exotic species when it comes to the inner Canyon. And most exotic species, including modern man, have a difficult enough time trying to adapt to the peculiarities and hazards of canyoneering—not to mention disturbing wildlife and other hikers. You can arrange for his personal lodging at the South Rim kennels. (Call Grand Canyon National Park Lodges at (602) 638-2631 for further information.)

4. Do not cut switchbacks or take shortcuts. 36 CFR 2.1(b). If you're hiking either a maintained or nonmaintained trail, stay *on* the trail. Cutting switchbacks isn't going to get you there any faster, but it does cause erosion, contributes to the damaging and confusing braiding of trails, and definitely poses a danger to people hiking in the fall line of rocks below. If you're doing a cross-country or trans-Canyon route, use some common sense with regard to disturbing and trampling fragile plants and delicate surface areas covered with cryptogamic soil; one footprint in this erosion-controlling soil will remain for a hundred years.

5. Do not throw or roll rocks into the Canyon. 36 CFR 2.1(a)3. Everybody's had the urge to throw a rock or push a boulder off a cliff to watch and listen to it explode far below, including no less than early alpine mountaineer Sir Martin Conway, who wrote in *The Alps from End to End*: "We amused ourselves by throwing stones down the slope we had come up and watching them vanish in the fog." But serious injuries and at least one fatality have occurred in the Grand Canyon from boulder trundling. Resist the temptation.

6. Set up camp away from your water source. Arizona state law prohibits camping within a quarter mile of a water source. With the particular scarcity of water sources in the Grand Canyon, that general rule becomes especially critical. So set your camp up at least 300 feet away from the nearest stream, spring, or pothole. When camping in developed zones and recognizable areas of undeveloped, threshold, and primitive management zones with preexisting campsites, use them whenever possible. When camping in areas without preexisting campsites, try to pick an area that doesn't require gardening (clearing away vegetation, leveling a tent site, delimbing trees, etc.) and that's far from archaeological and historical sites.

7. *Don't set wood or charcoal fires*. 36 CFR 2.13(a)1. For many wilderness enthusiasts, the opportunity to sit around a warm campfire at night howling at the moon is often the high point of many backpacking trips. Unfortunately, due to the shortage of wood and the dangers of wildfire, open fires are not permitted in Grand Canyon National Park unless it's a life-threatening emergency.

8. *Dig privies away from the nearest water source*. Before commercial river outfitters were required to carry human waste out of the Grand Canyon, over 20 tons of feces were being deposited on the dissipating beaches of the Colorado River. The backcountry is undergoing a similar, if more widely dispersed, threat from slowly decomposing human waste. And that problem has the potential to be a greater threat to both this fragile ecosystem and the health of other hikers. So select an area at least 300 feet from the nearest water source and your neighbor's camp when privies are not available, and dig a cathole 6 to 8 inches deep with your plastic trowel. After use, fill the hole up completely, then tromp the soil. Burning toilet paper has caused numerous wildfires in the Grand Canyon; pack it out in zip-locking baggies, adding a pinch or two of lime or powdered Clorox for sanitary reasons.

The Canyon's soft sandstones make excellent toilet paper substitutes.

9. Don't fish without a license. 36 CFR 2.3(a). Many of the tributary drainages along the Colorado River, such as South Canyon, Bright Angel, and Tapeats Creek, to name a few, have excellent trout fishing. However, fishing by anyone 14 years or older requires a valid Arizona fishing license or a nonresident permit. These can be purchased at Babbitt's General Store on the South Rim, or at nearby Arizona sporting-goods stores. Several river outfitters, such as Grand Canyon Expeditions, Inc., offer special river trips keyed specifically to the needs of fishermen. (For further information contact: Grand Canyon Expeditions, Inc., P.O. Box O, Dept. NPS, Kanab, UT 84741; 801-644-2691.)

10. Do not dig up, collect, or otherwise remove plants, rocks, animals, or other natural or cultural features. 36 CFR 2.1(a)1. After 20 years of research and an estimated 1,000 hours of helicopter flight time, Dr. Robert C. Euler and his staff of researchers at GCNP discovered over a thousand historic and prehistoric sites in the Grand Canyon. Not all of them were Anasazi sites, which comprise the majority of the Canyon's 2,000 recorded archaeological sites. Some were those of the "ancient hunters known as the Pinto Basin Culture," who may have been responsible for constructing delicate split-twig figurines of deer and bighorn sheep, archaeologists believe, as effigies to ensure a successful hunt. Other sites were those of the Southern Paiute Indians, "ancestors of the Walapai and Havasupai. They settled along the South

Rim and utilized portions of the inner Canyon south of the Colorado River." Still others were those of prosectors who came to the Canyon during the late 1800s looking to strike paydirt.

So if you come upon any of these historic or prehistoric sites while camping or hiking, leave them alone. Don't camp in them or climb around them; they're a nonrenewable resource. That includes potsherds, arrowheads and the like; leave them for the next visitor to enjoy. Besides, they're protected by federal laws such as the Archaeological Resources Act of 1979 and the Antiquities Act of 1906, which carry stiff federal sentences for first offenses.

11. Don't write on, scratch, or otherwise deface natural features, signs, buildings, or other objects. 36 CFR 2.31(a) and 36 CFR 2.1(a)1.

12. Do not feed wild animals. 36 CFR 2.2(a)2. "But the squirrels will eat it." Wrong. Little squirrels don't eat Pop Tarts, orange peels, or Ding Dongs, any more than you and I get down on all fours and start munching on the nearest bush.

13. Carry out your own trash. 36 CFR 2.14(b). And your neighbors' too.

Name it, and it probably will take years to decompose, if it decomposes at all in the arid soils and desert environment of the inner Canyon: aluminum packages, cigarette butts, pull-tabs, grease, food scraps, etc. So bring along a double-strength garbage bag, and seal all of your trash in it before packing it out.

14. If you see someone in trouble, give him a helping hand.

15. *If you make a positive identification of a rare sighting*, such as a mountain lion in the inner Canyon, a desert bighorn on either of the rims, a feral burro anywhere, or stumble across what looks like undiscovered historic or prehistoric artifacts, *fill out the Natural History Observation Cards, which are available at the Backcountry Ranger Office.*

PART TWO

TRAILS OF THE GRAND CANYON

CHAPTER 8

South Rim

RIM TRAILS

If you're short on time, just getting in shape, or have arrived at the Grand Canyon in midsummer—as most visitors do—the Canyon's rim trails make an excellent alternative to *inner*-Canyon hiking. For all practical purposes there are only two rim trails located on the South Rim: the South Rim Nature Trail and the Comanche Point Trail.

South Rim Nature Trail

See Chapter 5 for access points and route description.

Comanche Point Trail

The first leg of the Comanche Point Trail is a nonmaintained jeep road used primarily by Navajo families who live and graze sheep on the reservation lands adjoining the eastern boundary of Grand Canyon National Park. According to John C. Van Dyke, who wrote of his extended visit to the Grand Canyon in 1919 in *The Grand*

Canyon of the Colorado, the trail out to Comanche Point is "an old Mormon wagon-road." And being a former wagon road, it is not advisable to take even a four-wheel-drive vehicle down it during the summer rains or winter months; there are several steep pitches north of Cedar Canyon which are prett' near impossible to drive up after a moderate rain or snowfall.

As far as backcountry foot travel is concerned, this trail is of primary interest to those skilled rock climbers interested in climbing Comanche Point Pinnacle, the Lost Arrow Spire of the Grand Canyon, located several confusing rappells below 7,073′ Comanche Point; for canyoneers interested in scrambling up 6,000′+ Espejo Butte, located several trailless miles north of Comanche Point along the rim of the Palisades of the Desert; and for those hikers who'd like to explore the cooler pinyon-juniper country of the South Rim during the summer, while taking in a breathstopping view of the Painted Desert and eastern Grand Canyon.

To reach Comanche Point, park your vehicle at the East Entrance Ranger Station a half mile east of Desert View. Follow this rock-strewn dirt track approximately 2½ miles downhill around the east arm of Tanner Canyon to BM 6641. Turn left, descend into and climb out of Straight Canyon, covering another 2½ to 3 miles before reaching a T junction designated on your Vishnu Quadrangle map by BM 6634′ and/or two black squares that represent dwellings. Turn left again, this time striking out cross-country through the pinyon and juniper in a N/NE direction for half to three quarters of a mile until you're overlooking the drainage immediately below (east of) the word "Palisades" on your quadrangle. Pick your way into this drainage and follow it north for approximately one mile to the base, or southeast slope, of Comanche Point. (Seasonal water is sometimes found in this drainage.) The first summit you see is a false one, tallying up to an 800′ vertical climb in about three quarters of a mile to reach the apex of Comanche Point. The afternoon winds sweeping up out of the inner Canyon are normally pretty strong, so you may want to place your camp on the leeside of Comanche Point on one of several suitable flat areas between its summit and the drainage.

Once on top you'll no doubt see, as George Wharton James noted in 1910, that "the walls are precipitous to three thousand five hundred feet below, and the outlook afforded is about seventy miles in either direction, up and down the Canyon." (Assuming, that is, the Page and Four Corners power plants aren't belching out gray plumes of sulfer dioxide.) Several very experienced canyoneers have descended into Comanche Creek via the saddle between Comanche Point and BM 6831, but this airy and precarious route is a semitechnical one and is best reconned and/or approached from below before considering a descent.

ELEVATION:	7,400 feet to 6,300 feet to 7,073 feet.
MILEAGE:	Approximately 7 miles one way.
VEGETATION:	Pinyon/juniper.

WATER:	Seasonal *only*. (See description.)
CACHE POINTS:	BM 6641′ at the Cedar Mountain turnoff, and/or BM 6634 at T junction.
SEASONS:	Spring through fall. Wintertime may require a good mountain tent, cross-country skis, and other winter camping gear.
MAPS:	Vishnu Quadrangle (15 minute), and South Kaibab National Forest Map. Write: Forest Supervisor, Kaibab National Forest, Route 1, Box 142, Williams, AZ 86046.
NEAREST SUPPLY POINTS:	G.C. Village, Cameron, Flagstaff, and Williams.

RIM-TO-RIVER TRAILS—MAINTAINED

At present two rim-to-river trails located on the South Rim are maintained by National Park Service trail crews. These two, the South Kaibab and the Bright Angel trails, are without a doubt the most heavily used trails in Grand Canyon National Park. They are perhaps the easiest rim-to-river trails, offering inexperienced canyoneers a challenging introduction to inner-Canyon hiking while providing them with a base of experience to draw upon for more difficult Canyon treks later on. (Harvey Butchart took his first hike down one of these two trails, the South Kaibab in 1945.) If you haven't hiked into the Canyon before, you should consider hiking one or both of these trails—either one way, or tying both of them together in a loop hike—before striking out for the Great Unknown.

The South Kaibab and Bright Angel trails are also used by the Fred Harvey mule concession to ferry dudes and supplies to and from Phantom Ranch, as well as to "drag out" hikers. And chances are, if you're hiking either of these trails, you'll come face-to-face with one of these mule trains; if you do, the wrangler will most likely ask you to step to the high side of the trail until he moves his pack string past. If you should hear a pack string coming your way, you can make the wrangler's job a little easier if you take the high ground at a wide spot on the trail before they reach you.

Please Note: The maintained rim-to-river trails, such as the South Kaibab and Bright Angel, as well as the seven nonmaintained rim-to-river trails, will provide the major avenues of ingress and egress for those canyoneers hiking any, or all of, the South Rim's trans-Canyon trails and routes. Because trans-Canyon trails and routes are described east-to-west, descriptions of both the maintained and nonmaintained trails will also be listed in a geographical order of east-to-west, rather than according to difficulty. (The approximate difficulty of each of the rim-to-river trails will be listed at the end of the South Kaibab Trail description.)

South Kaibab Trail

Unlike many of the other rim-to-river trails, which were Indian routes improved upon by prospectors during the late 1800s, the South Kaibab was constructed by the National Park Service in 1924 primarily as an alternate to the Bright Angel Trail because hosteler Ralph Cameron had a franchise to charge a $1 toll to anyone riding or hiking down it. It was down the South Kaibab's steep, thigh-pummeling 6.3 miles that 42 Havasupai Indians carried eight steel cables, one at a time, in order to help construct the new Kaibab Suspension Bridge across the Colorado River. According to former ranger-naturalist J. Donald Hughes's *The Story of Man at Grand Canyon*, each of those cables was "550 feet long, 1½ inches in diameter and weighed 2,320 pounds." The procession looked like "some giant squirming centipede."

To reach the South Kaibab trailhead, take the shuttle bus (summer only) or your own vehicle out the East Rim Drive to Yaqui Point. The trail is well marked all the way to the Colorado River, with aluminum placards identifying each of the major geological formations you'll descend through en route to the river. In the 2.2 miles to Cedar Ridge you'll hike through first the Kaibab Limestone, then the Toroweap Formation, and finally the Coconino Sandstone before reaching the Hermit Shale that comprises Cedar Ridge; the hike to Cedar Ridge and back is a fine introductory day hike. There are privies there, and a birds-eye view of 6,072′ O'Neil Butte, named

The view from Yaqui Point. *Photo by George H. H. Huey.*

after Rough Rider William Owen "Buckey" O'Neil, who fought in Cuba during the Spanish-American War.

The trail angles off the east side of Cedar Ridge through the Supai Formation, then corkscrews through the Redwall Formation—covering 3 miles from Cedar Ridge to the Tonto Trail junction. A full day or two east is the Grandview Trail, and 4.2 miles west is Indian Gardens and the Bright Angel Trail. (For trail descriptions of the Tonto east and west of the South Kaibab, see "Trans-Canyon Trails and Routes," p.193.)

Going in, the Tonto Formation makes an excellent rest or lunch stop, and you can usually find some shade in the Tapeats Sandstone immediately below the Tipoff, a quarter mile further. From the Tipoff, it's a little under 2 miles to the Kaibab Suspension Bridge, and another quarter mile to the Bright Angel Campground and ranger station.

Additional Considerations: Many first-time canyoneers use the South Kaibab Trail as their major ingress point for completing the popular South Kaibab/Bright Angel loop hike, or for hiking to Phantom Ranch and spending the night before hiking back out the Bright Angel Trail or continuing up the North Kaibab Trail. (See Chapter 9 for the North Kaibab Trail description.)

WARNING: Don't attempt hiking out the South Kaibab during the hot summer months or warm, dry months of spring and fall.

ELEVATION:	7,260 feet to 2,480 feet.
TOTAL ELEVATION LOSS & GAIN:	9,560 feet (4,780 vertical feet each way).
MILEAGE:	6.7 one way to Bright Angel Campground.
VEGETATION:	Mountain Transition Zone to Lower Sonoran Desert.
WATER:	Colorado River and B.A. Campground only!
CACHE POINTS:	Cedar Ridge and the Tipoff.
SEASONS:	Fall through spring. Summer can be deadly.
MAP:	Bright Angel Quadrangle (15 minute).
NEAREST SUPPLY POINTS:	G.C. Village, Flagstaff, Williams, Cameron.
DIFFICULTY:	The following list has been compiled in sequential order—from easiest to most difficult—and has been included as a planning aid for those who want to increase their backcountry experience in increments, rather than in leaps and bounds: 1. Bright Angel 2. South Kaibab

3. Hermit
4. Grandview (Horseshoe Mesa loop)
5. South Bass
6. Tanner
7. Boucher
8. New Hance

Bright Angel Trail

In addition to going from top to bottom, the reverse of mountain climbing, most rim-to-river trails fall into one of two major categories: ridge trail or drainage trail. The South Kaibab is a ridge trail because it crests or parallels Cedar Ridge most of the way into the Canyon. It offers exposed hiking and spectacular views en route. The Bright Angel Trail, on the other hand, is a drainage trail because it follows and criss-crosses Garden Creek most of the way to its confluence with Pipe Creek near the river in the Vishnu Schist. Because the B.A. is a drainage trail, the hiking isn't as airy nor are the views as spectacular as those of the ridge trails.

The Bright Angel was originally a footpath used by Havasupai Indians to reach their gardens at present-day Indian Gardens. The route—unlike many of the miner trails that had to be blasted through different formations—utilized a natural break through that upper geological barrier known as the Bright Angel Fault. Prospectors improved the Havasupai trail in the 1890s and pegged it the Cameron Trail. The name stuck until Coconino County finally wrested control of the trail from Ralph Cameron in 1928. It was officially pegged the Bright Angel Trail by the U.S. Board of Geographic Names in 1937.

To reach the Bright Angel trailhead, stroll a few minutes west of the Bright Angel Lodge and you're there. Like the South Kaibab, the Bright Angel Trail is well marked for all of its 9½ miles to Bright Angel Campground on the north side of the Colorado River. One and a half and 3 miles down the trail there are resthouses built in the 1930s by the CCC. At a switchback some folks call Two Mile Corner, there are pictographs dating back to A.D. 1300. Any of these three points will make an invigorating morning saunter.

Indian Gardens is 4.7 miles down the trail, and if you're used to remote backcountry travel you might not be prepared for the developments that have taken place since the prospectors first arrived in the 1890s. There is a fully staffed ranger station, a developed campground, a corral, toilets, water, and shade in the form of massive cottonwood trees. Indian Gardens is a good turnaround point for a day hike, as is the well-marked 1½-mile-long trail out to Plateau Point; that's pretty near where the first airplane landed in the Grand Canyon and where you'll get your best views of the Inner Gorge on this trail.

To reach the river, continue beyond the Tonto Trail junction and descend into Tapeats Narrows before tackling the Devil's Corkscrew; the latter switchbacks through the Vishnu Schist and will take you to the Pipe Creek resthouse near the river. This is where you pick up the

River Trail and follow it east for 1.7 miles to that glistening silver suspension bridge. If you make a left and cross this bridge, Bright Angel Campground (and water) is not more than a half mile beyond; if you keep going straight, you'll reach the foot of the South Kaibab Trail and the old suspension bridge a mile farther.

Additional Considerations: If you're planning a rim-to-rim hike from the North Rim to the South Rim, consider coming out the Bright Angel Trail; it's a few miles longer than the South Kaibab but not as steep, so your legs will have some respite on the long haul out. There's water besides.

ELEVATION:	6,860 feet to 2,400 feet.
TOTAL ELEVATION LOSS & GAIN:	8,920 feet (4,460 vertical feet each way).
MILEAGE:	9.5 one way to Bright Angel Campground.
WATER:	Indian Gardens, Colorado River, and Bright Angel Campground.
CACHE POINTS:	Immediately below the Tonto Formation in the shade and seclusion of Tapeats Narrows.
SEASONS:	Fall through spring. Summer's hot.
MAP:	Bright Angel Quadrangle (15 minute).

NEAREST SUPPLY POINTS: G.C. Village, Flagstaff, Williams, Cameron.

Phantom Ranch

When Major John Wesley Powell and his pards first came down Big Red in 1869, they stopped near a little creek they fondly dubbed Bright Angel; they were looking for timbers to replace the oars they'd trashed upstream. Perhaps the most startling discovery Powell made during that layover was the small group of Indian ruins he described in his river log, adding (perhaps as an afterthought): "It is ever a source of wonder to us why these ancient people sought such inaccessible places for their homes."

Not far from where Powell first discovered those ruins, David Rust established a tent camp in 1903 for hunters and tourists. The Fred Harvey Company thought it was an equally enchanting area, bought it in 1921, and hired Mary Jane Colter as the architect to design what today is a must overnight for the majority of Canyon hikers and mule riders. One can't help but wonder what Powell would think about that today.

RIM-TO-RIVER TRAILS—NONMAINTAINED

During the Grand Canyon's gold rush of the late 1800s, some 84 trails supposedly cut their way into the heart of the Canyon. Whether or not 84 trails actually existed still remains to be seen. Whatever the total number of miner

Footbridge over Bright Angel Creek at Phantom Ranch. *Photo by George H. H. Huey.*

trails was, only a handful of those hand-forged routes are still used today—and they exist primarily in the form of nonmaintained rim-to-river trails. Because these trails are not presently maintained by NPS trail crews, the conditions you'll find them in depends on a number of factors, the most significant of which is how much use they see by backcountry visitors. Trail conditions vary from the well-groomed Yellow Brick Road nature of the Hermit to that gnarly avalanche of a route called the Old Hance. But whether you call these historic pathways trails or routes is not important, because each will offer you its own peculiar characteristics, challenges, and rewards.

Tanner Trail

Somewhere to the west of Tanner Canyon—no one's pinpointed the exact spot—a soldier of fortune by the name of García López de Cárdenas first discovered the Grand Canyon in 1535. At the time, most visiting Spaniards came to the Southwest in quest of gold or souls or both. Cárdenas was no different. Under direct orders from the Grand Wazoo of Southwest exploration, Francisco Vásquez de Coronado, Cárdenas was sent on a wild-goose hunt to look for the legendary Seven Cities of Gold. What the tough mercenary and his men found instead were insurmountable odds in their unsuccessful three-day attempt to reach the Colorado River on foot somewhere near Tanner Canyon. "What appeared to be easy from above was not so, but instead very hard and difficult."

Indeed, this has been the case with most subsequent Grand Canyon explorers, adventurers, and hikers.

If in fact it was Tanner Canyon that Cárdenas' men tried to descend, they no doubt missed—or lost—the old Hopi route that once descended the east arm of Tanner Canyon. Mormon pioneer and prospector Seth B. Tanner rebuilt the upper third of this trail circa 1884, beginning near Lipan Point, to reach his copper diggings near the Colorado River. This same trail, a.k.a. Horsethief Trail, was used during Prohibition by moonshiners who transported their ''furniture polish'' from stills near the river to the thirsty revelers at the South Rim village.

To reach this historic spoiler's route, take the East Rim Drive out to Lipan Point. The trailhead is just east of the parking lot.

As late as 1970, the Tanner, Boucher, Thunder River, and several other miner trails required some real route-finding ability—not necessarily to keep from getting lost, but to stay on the trail. Today the Tanner Trail is so popular, you can follow it with one eye closed all the way to the river. At a moderate pace, it takes about an hour to descend the first series of switchbacks to what is called Seventy-five Mile Saddle; that's the first major saddle you'll come to, and the trail stays just to the east (right, going down) of its Supai Sandstone crest. From here the trail contours around the base of Escalante and Cardenas buttes across a broad section of Supai Sandstone; if you're not deadheading to meet a river trip or some other schedule, the area below the Escalante/Cardenas saddle is a great place to camp. If you use care, the summits of these buttes are enjoyable half-hour scrambles from their saddle, offering the best panoramic views on the Tanner.

Back to the trail. Once you've contoured the base of Cardenas Butte, this ridge trail begins its enchanting little descent of the Redwall, and going in or coming out these steep, rocky switchbacks comprise what is probably the toughest stretch of the Tanner.

Once the trail finally breaks out of the Bright Angel Shale, it heads almost due north along a ridgetop of Tapeats Sandstone before sliding off its east side through a standing wave of Dox Sandstone all the way to the *rio*. Going down, this section of the Tanner is the most enjoyable, because you feel like you're flying.

If you reach the river during boating season, you may find a camp of river runners camped near the mouth of the Tanner Trail, but the area is such a large one, there's no reason to feel crowded. Just head west along the sand dunes a ways, and you'll have the solitude you came to enjoy.

Additional Considerations: Going east, the Tanner provides access to the Beamer Trail (see below) and the Little Colorado River. Going west, there is a challenging route along the south side of the river that'll take you all the way to Hance Rapids and the start of the Tonto Trail (see below).

ELEVATION:	7,360 feet to 2,700 feet.
TOTAL ELEVATION LOSS & GAIN:	9,320 feet (4,660 vertical feet each way).

MILEAGE:	10.4 miles.
WATER:	Colorado River only.
CACHE POINTS:	Seventy-five Mile Saddle, and top of the Redwall.
SEASONS:	Fall through spring. Summers are hot and can be deadly. No water, and virtually no shade.
MAP:	Vishnu Temple Quadrangle (15 minute).
NEAREST SUPPLY POINTS:	G.C. Village, Flagstaff, Williams, Cameron.

New Hance Trail

One of the most famous quotes concerning a Grand Canyon trail was written by Rough Rider Bucky O'Neil in the guest book Captain John Hance kept at his ranch on the South Rim. It read: "God made the cañon, John Hance the trails. Without the other, neither would be complete." According to geologist Edwin McKee, who described a number of the Canyon's historic trails in the classic *Inverted Mountains*, the "Old Trail" that Hance built down Hance Canyon in 1883 to reach his asbestos mines on the north side of the river was a refurbished Indian trail used for hundreds of years by the Havasupai. But if any permanent traces of this famous trailblazer's original rim-to-river route still exist, to this day they continue to elude the footsteps of most experienced canyoneers. Even in its prime during the 1880s, the Old Trail was such a steep and precipitous bugger that Hance had to use ropes to lower tourists and guests down one particularly nasty section of cliff. Those guests included Mrs. Edward Ayres who in 1882 reputedly became the first woman to reach the bottom of the Grand Canyon. By 1900 the trail was washed out and practically inaccessible, so Hance built the Red Canyon (or New Hance) Trail to reach the inner Canyon and to meet the growing numbers of tourists who'd responded to earlier newspaper ads like: "Being thoroughly conversant with all the trails leading to the Grand Canyon of the Colorado, I am prepared to conduct parties thereto at any time. I have a fine spring of water near my house on the rim of the Canyon, and can furnish accommodations for tourists and their animals" (*Arizona Champion*, 1886).

To reach the head of the New Hance Trail requires more effort than most other rim-to-river trails on the South Rim. It's approximately one mile west from Moran Point in the northwest quarter/section of Section 14. If for some reason you should miss the trailhead, which should be marked by a fair-sized cairn (or WC on your Grandview Point Quadrangle), just remember you want to descend the head of the Red Canyon drainage immediately east of Coronado Butte and you shouldn't have any problem picking up the start of the trail in either the Kaibab Limestone or Toroweap Formation. The descent of these top two formations, as well as the Coconino Sandstone, is short, steep, and rocky; so make sure you're on the trail before you go plunging off into the abyss and

The view from Moran Point overlooking the New Hance Trail. *Photo by George H. H. Huey.*

get rimrocked. Except during heavy snows—which have a tendency to bury this first stretch of trail all the way down to the Hermit Shale saddle between the rim and Coronado Butte—and immediately after heavy spring runoff, the route is clearly defined if you scout the way.

Once you've reached the Coronado Butte saddle, the trail veers generally northeast as it snakes its way through the Hermit Shale, Esplanade Sandstone, and lower Supai. You may encounter a rockslide or two, depending on what's eroded, and the footing can be loose. So take your time and exercise care in negotiating this section and locating the beginning of the Redwall descent; that *should* be marked by a totem-sized cairn. The Redwall descent won't be any easier than what you've just done, but your legs will be more tired and the rock more crumbly; so use your best judgment as to pace and foot placement.

Below the Redwall the trail tracks across the Tonto, which until recently was criss-crossed by a confusing series of feral burro trails. Since this exotic species has been removed from the Canyon, this section across the Tonto is now much easier to follow. Just about where you want to tip off the Tonto, there should be a drainage on your left and one on your right. Make sure you descend into the eastern drainage (right-hand side, going down); this is the one that will get you down to the creekbed below and to Hance Rapids at the mouth of Red Canyon a few boulder-strewn miles further.

Additional Considerations: If you're planning on doing the New Hance/Tonto/Grandview loop hike, you'll find it easier going down the New Hance and up the Grandview, rather than the other way around.

ELEVATION:	6,982 feet to 2,600 feet.
TOTAL ELEVATION LOSS & GAIN:	8,764 feet (4,382 vertical feet each way).
MILEAGE:	8 miles.
WATER:	Colorado River only.
CACHE POINTS:	Coronado Butte saddle, and top of the Redwall.
SEASONS:	Fall and spring. Upper sections can be treacherous in winter snow. Summertime can be unforgiving.
MAPS:	Grandview Point and Vishnu Temple quadrangles (both 15 minute).
NEAREST SUPPLY POINTS:	G.C. Village, Flagstaff, Williams, Cameron.

Grandview Trail

Of all the Grand Canyon prospectors who sought to fulfill their wanderlust and dreams of gold dust in the unexplored reaches of the inner Canyon, Peter D. Berry was perhaps the most successful. But the Mother Lode he struck was in the form of high-grade copper ore he discovered 3 miles below Grandview Point on Horseshoe Mesa. He called it the "Last Chance Mine," and according to J. Donald Hughes, "8 or 10 mules, each carrying 200 pounds" were used to carry out the prizewinning ore to a stamp mill located on the rim above. Berry was prescient, because he took some of that money and built the Grandview Hotel in 1895, which proved to be the leading tourist hostel at the Canyon until the Santa Fe Railroad ran a track from Williams up to the South Rim a dozen miles west of Berry's place. That pretty well took care of his dude ranching profits, and when the bottom dropped out of the copper market in 1907, Berry sold his mining operation to newspaper magnate William Randolph Hearst.

Of all the rim-to-river trails, the Grandview is probably the least practical for reaching the Colorado River. Most people who hike the Grandview Trail use it primarily to hike down to and around Horseshoe Mesa.

To reach the Grandview Trail, drive out to Grandview Point and pick up the trailhead there. While the trail is obvious and straightforward enough all the way down to Horseshoe Mesa, several of the upper switchbacks are still rip-rapped with iron rods and logs from the heyday of the Last Chance Mine. There are also several exposed sections in the Toroweap Formation that can be slippery and dangerous during icy winter conditions, and spectacular most other times of the year. Once you reach the Hermit Formation, the trail skirts the west side of a Coconino Sandstone fin before continuing through the Esplanade Sandstone and lower Supai Group to the neck of Horseshoe Mesa.

Once atop Horseshoe Mesa, you have numerous options. You can camp there and explore the mining relics that still litter the area. You can take the eastern spur trail into Hance Canyon and take the Tonto Trail east down to the river; or, from Hance Canyon, you can take the Tonto Trail west around the base of Horseshoe Mesa and come up either the spur trail that ascends the northwest arm of Horseshoe Mesa past the Cave of the Domes, or the spur trail that continues around the base of that arm and ascends Cottonwood Creek. Or any variation thereof. Without a pack, you can day hike all the way around the base of Horseshoe Mesa and have enough time to reach camp before nightfall.

Additional Considerations: If you're interested in doing your first multiday inner-Canyon trek, the Grandview/Tonto/Bright Angel loop is a challenging, if fairly straightforward, three to four day introduction to the rigors and rewards of trans-canyoneering.

ELEVATION:	A—7,406 feet to 4,932 feet on Horseshoe Mesa. B—4,932 feet to 4,000 feet on Tonto Trail.
TOTAL ELEVATION LOSS & GAIN:	A—4,948 feet (2,474 vertical feet each way).

	B—1,864 feet (932 vertical feet each way).
MILEAGE:	3 miles to Horseshoe Mesa. 4–5 miles around base of Horseshoe Mesa.
WATER:	Grandview and J.T. springs, east arm of Grandview Trail below Redwall Formation.
CACHE POINTS:	Coconino saddle approximately 1 mile below Grandview Point and Horseshoe Mesa—depending on hike planned.
SEASONS:	Spring and fall. Early morning summertime, the hike to Horseshoe Mesa and back is a good day hike. In wintertime you might need instep crampons for the top switchbacks.
MAPS:	Grandview Point and Vishnu Temple quadrangles (both 15 minute).
NEAREST SUPPLY POINTS:	G.C. Village, Flagstaff, Williams, Cameron.

Hermit Trail

The first leg of the original Hermit Trail was constructed in 1896 by a New York prospector named Daniel Hogan.

The trail was improved with inlaid cobblestones and extended by the Santa Fe Railroad around 1913 as the first of two Canyon trails that sought to bypass the tolls charged by Ralph Cameron to descend his Bright Angel Trail. The Santa Fe Railroad folks ran a way station at the end of the trail, called Hermits Camp, which provided an overnight stop for saddle-weary dudes until the 1930s.

The area this now-abandoned trail descends is called the Hermit Basin Natural Area; it comprises 1,280 acres and "was established to exemplify the geological strata and phenomena of the Grand Canyon" (Hermit Basin Natural Area Abstract). Two trails descend into this remarkable basin; the Hermit Trail descends the east wall below Hermits Rest, and the Dripping Springs/Boucher Trail descends the west wall. Of these two trails, the Hermit is the easiest and no doubt the safest because of its seemingly maintained nature. It's also a popular introductory hike for those hikers who've already done the Bright Angel and South Kaibab and are looking to extend their horizons without getting in over their heads on one of the more difficult rim-to-river trails.

To reach the beginning of the Hermit Trail, take the West Rim Drive 8 miles to Hermits Rest. (A "Hiker's Special" shuttle bus makes regularly scheduled runs to Hermits Rest during the summer.) From Hermits Rest, you walk a dirt road a few minutes west to the trailhead. The trail drops an abrupt 1,400 vertical feet in the 1.3 miles it takes to reach the Waldron Trail junction and is clearly marked. The Waldron Trail, which comes in from the left (south), was the original section of the Hermit constructed by Hogan from Horsethief Tank into Hermit Basin. (The Waldron trailhead can be reached by taking the Rowes Well Road from Grand Canyon Village to Horsethief Tank.) From the Waldron Trail junction, turn right (north) and proceed another .3 mile to the Dripping Springs/Hermit Trail junction.

To continue down the Hermit Trail, turn right (north) and follow this cobblestone stairway through the Supai Sandstone Formation past Santa Maria Spring. The hike down to this spring makes an excellent morning walk and provides some of the best views of this awesome drainage. Just beyond Santa Maria Spring, the trail descends completely through the Supai Formation and stays atop the Redwall past Four Mile Spring to Cathedral Stairs; the hikes to Four Mile Spring (dry) and the top of Cathedral Stairs are both good day hikes. The latter provides a raptor's view of 4,540′ Cope Butte, used by the Santa Fe Railroad when it ran its aerial tramway from Pima Point all the way down to Hermits Camp.

To reach Hermits Camp, continue down the Cathedral Stairs to its junction with the Tonto Trail; the camp is another mile to the south atop the Tonto Plateau. Hermit Rapids can be reached by following the bed of Hermit Creek another 1½ miles. During the river-running season, you can enjoy the vicarious thrill of whitewater rafting by watching boatmen run one of the most fun stretches of river in the Canyon—the wavetrain of Hermit Rapids.

Additional Considerations: The Hermit Trail is frequently used for the Bright Angel/Tonto/Hermit loop, one of the most popular multiday loop hikes in the park.

ELEVATION:	6,640 feet to 2,400 feet.
TOTAL ELEVATION LOSS & GAIN:	8,480 feet (4,240 vertical feet each way).
MILEAGE:	8.5 miles one way to the river.
WATER:	Santa Maria Spring and Colorado River. High fecal coli. count in Hermit Creek.
CACHE POINTS:	In seclusion of Dripping Springs Trail junction, top of Cathedral Stairs, and Hermits Camp—depending on hike planned.
SEASONS:	Fall through spring. Summer's hot.
MAPS:	Bright Angel Quadrangle (15 minute) and S. Kaibab N.F. Map for Waldron Trail.
NEAREST SUPPLY POINTS:	G.C. Village, Flagstaff, Williams, Cameron.

Boucher Trail

If there is one trail in Grand Canyon National Park the author is reluctant to describe, it's the Boucher Trail. It's one of the most spectacular trails and one of the more difficult. If you continue to tread lightly, it will remain one of the most pristine.

The Boucher Trail was constructed by French-Canadian prospector Louis D. Boucher before 1893. He called it the Silver Bell Trail and started the first leg a few miles west of the Waldron trailhead near Eremita Mesa to reach his camp and oasis at Dripping Springs. He continued the Silver Bell Trail down to Boucher Creek, where he prospected for graphite, planted a fine little orchard, and delighted tourists until about 1910. It's been said of Boucher that "he rode a white mule and told only white lies," a claim the tall-speaking John Hance couldn't make—not with his tales of riding his horse Darby across the Grand Canyon on a cloud-hopping journey to the North Rim.

The most commonly used access to the Boucher Trail is reached by taking the Hermit Trail down from Hermits Rest 1.6 miles to the Hermit Trail junction. The road out to the Eremita Mesa trailhead can be more difficult to follow than the trail itself and is frequently impassable during summer rains, winter snows, and spring thaws.

From the Dripping Springs/Hermit Trail junction, turn left (west) and follow the Dripping Springs Trail 1.1 miles along the very rim of the Supai Formation to its junction with the Boucher Trail, which can be picked up by crossing the Dripping Springs drainage. If you walk up the bed of this little drainage, you'll reach Dripping Springs. The 2.7-mile walk from Hermits Rest down to this spring is a good day hike, even during the relatively hot summer months if done early in the morning. The Boucher

Trail continues north from the Dripping Springs drainage and follows the very rim of the Supai Formation for approximately 2½ miles to Yuma Point. This leg, from the Hermit Trail junction to Yuma Point, is probably the most exposed and exciting hiking in the Grand Canyon. But it can be quite dangerous if you attempt to hike it during icy winter conditions, because there are sections where you're literally walking on the *very* edge of the Hermit Formation. The abyss yawns below your footsteps.

The trail contours around the base of Yuma Point for another half mile before it begins its descent through the Supai Formation; there are several sections along this descent that require the use of hands and feet, as well as an open eye for the actual line of descent the trail takes to the bed of Travertine Canyon. Once you're in the bed of this canyon, the trail follows the west side of this drainage to the saddle immediately below Whites Butte. The trail through the Redwall is picked up just west of the Whites Butte saddle and runs basically due north the 1.3 miles it takes to reach its junction with the Tonto Trail. This is probably the most grungy and difficult section of the Boucher Trail, primarily because the trail descends through the Redwall and Muav limestones rather abruptly.

It's a clearly marked half mile from the Tonto Trail to Boucher Trail. From Boucher Creek, you have the option of camping in the vicinity or boulder-hopping another 1½ miles down Boucher Creek to the river.

Additional Considerations: The Boucher Trail is frequently used as the first leg of the increasingly popular

Boucher/Tonto/Hermit loop hike, or to start the long trek across the Tonto to the head of the South Bass Trail.

ELEVATION:	6,640 feet (Hermits Rest) to 2,325 feet at the river.
TOTAL ELEVATION LOSS & GAIN:	8,630 feet (4,315 vertical feet each way).
MILEAGE:	10.8 miles one way to the river.
WATER:	Dripping Springs, Boucher Creek, Colorado River.
CACHE POINTS:	Dripping Springs drainage, Yuma Point, and Whites Butte saddle.
SEASONS:	Spring and fall. Winter can be treacherous along the exposed sections of Supai, and summers can be unkind.
MAPS:	Bright Angel Quadrangle (15 minute) and S. Kaibab N.F. Map for Eremita Mesa trail-head.
NEAREST SUPPLY POINTS:	G.C. Village, Flagstaff, Williams, Cameron.

South Bass Trail

Of all the prospectors who came to the Grand Canyon,

perhaps none had a greater effect on the development of the area than William Wallace Bass. He came to the Canyon for his health in 1884, married Ada Diefendorf eleven years later, raised four children—the first family on the South Rim—and didn't succumb to ill health until he was 84. During his forty-odd years at the Canyon, the tireless Bass built a seventy-mile road for tourists from Ashfork to Bass's Camp on the South Rim, delivered mail from the Grand Canyon Village to Havasupai, went to Washington to drum up support for the first school in Havasupai, led the first cross-Canyon treks for tourists from the South to North rims, built trails, and prospected.

The first leg of the Bass Trail was originally the Mystic Springs Trail, which the Havasupais used for years before the spring vanished, following an earthquake. Bass improved this trail and extended it down to the river in order to take tourists up to the North Rim, as well as to haul out asbestos and tend to his garden along Shinumo Creek.

To reach the South Bass Trail requires more effort than any other rim-to-river trail on the South Rim. The trailhead is located approximately 4 miles north of the Pasture Wash Ranger Station at the end of the Pasture Wash Road. (See S. Kaibab National Forest Map for directions to Pasture Wash Ranger Station.) The entire road, from the Rowes Well Road turnoff to the trailhead, is frequently impassable during summer rains, winter snows, and spring thaws. But if you've done the navigation necessary to reach this remote trailhead, you shouldn't have any problem following the South Bass Trail 7 miles down to the river.

The trail drops 1,400 vertical feet in the 1½ miles it takes to reach the broad sweep of the Esplanade Sandstone that comprises Darwin Plateau, Spencer Terrace, and Huxley Terrace. You can pick up the Apache Trail on the Esplanade, but you'll have to start looking for the junction not long after you break away from the Hermit Shale, especially if you're the first one on it in the spring; this junction has been wheeled at 1.45 miles from the trailhead. It's just under a mile across the Esplanade to where you begin your descent through that formation. Mystic Springs (dry) makes a good day hike from the rim, and you can reach it by following the edge of the Esplanade west and then north along the rim of the Darwin Plateau until you reach the neck of Spencer Terrace on the northwest side of Mt. Huethawli.

To continue down the South Bass, it's another mile from the top of the Esplanade due east of Mt. Huethawli to the top of the Redwall. From here it's 2 miles along this sometimes brush-covered trail to the Tonto Trail junction, and another mile down Bass Canyon to Bass Rapids. You'll have to look for the cairn before beginning this last pitch, because the creekbed drops off abruptly just short of the river. If you're headed to the North Rim, the area below Bass Rapids and above Shinumo Creek is the most likely spot to catch a ride across the river.

Additional Considerations: The South Bass Trail is frequently used for the Boucher/Tonto/South Bass trek, and if you haven't been up or down either the Boucher or the

South Bass, you'll probably find it easier to descend the Boucher and exit the South Bass. It is, however, safer to be dropped off at the South Bass and come out the Hermit if you haven't been up the Boucher. If the Pasture Wash Road gets buried in snow or becomes otherwise impassable, the trek from the Pasture Wash Ranger Station to Grand Canyon Village is not the most delightful stroll to undertake after marching 35 or 40 miles across the Tonto. Plan this shuttle carefully.

ELEVATION:	6,648 feet to 2,200 feet.
TOTAL ELEVATION LOSS & GAIN:	8,896 feet (4,448 vertical feet each way).
MILEAGE:	6.9 miles.
WATER:	Colorado River.
CACHE POINTS:	Esplanade Formation, and Tonto Plateau.
SEASONS:	Spring and fall. Access road impassable most of winter without cross-country skis. Summer's hot.
MAPS:	Havasupai Point Quadrangle (15 minute) and S. Kaibab N.F. Map.
NEAREST SUPPLY POINTS:	G.C. Village, Flagstaff, Williams, Cameron.

TRANS-CANYON TRAILS AND ROUTES—NONMAINTAINED

You've hiked most or all of the South Rim's rim-to-river trails, and now you're looking to do something other than hike to the Colorado River and back. What are your options? You can link several of the rim-to-river trails on the South Rim with those on the North Rim and do rim-to-rim treks. (See Chapter 9 for North Rim trail descriptions.) Or you can tackle either multiday or multiweek trans-Canyon trails and routes that traverse the heart of the Grand Canyon east to west, or vice versa. If you're interested in starting off your canyoneering career with one of the more popular multiday treks, it's possible to descend any of the previously described rim-to-river trails, follow one of the major geological benches or other natural lines of weakness east- or westward, then exit any of the other rim-to-river trails. The loops you decide to embark on will depend on your own canyoneering experience and how many days you want to be in the field. However, if you're interested in undertaking a multiweek trek, it's possible to hike all the way from Cameron on the Navajo Indian Reservation, down the Little Colorado River Gorge, through the heart of the Grand Canyon (resupplying at Phantom Ranch or G.C. Village) to Supai on the Havasupai Indian Reservation—and beyond.

The following section will describe the major routes from the confluence of the Little Colorado and Colorado rivers leading westward to Apache Point near the eastern border of the Havasupai Indians' Traditional Use Area. (The Little Colorado River Gorge from Cameron to its confluence with the Colorado River, and the Havasupai lands west of Apache Point, as well as their major access points, are described in Chapter 11.) Taken individually, it will be possible to combine certain sections of the trans-Canyon trails and routes with specific rim-to-river trails for multiday loop hikes. Or combined all together, it'll be possible to take that multiweek trek from one end of the Grand Canyon to the other.

Note that each of the trans-Canyon trails and routes will be described east-to-west and each links one individual section with the next.

Beamer Trail

Ben Beamer was yet another prospector who came to the Grand Canyon in the late 1800s to find the Mother Lode. He built a section of trail from Palisades Creek to the mouth of the Little Colorado River that no doubt was used earlier by the Hopi to reach their sacred salt mines in the eastern Grand Canyon. This section of trail gave Beamer the access he needed to link together the old Tanner Canyon Trail with his stone house at the mouth of the Little C. This stone house was actually a Pueblo Indian ruin—built into the convoluted walls of the Tapeats Sandstone—that Beamer refurbished and lived in for the two years he prospected and farmed in the area.

The Beamer Trail begins—or ends, depending on which

direction you're coming from—near the mouth of the Little Colorado River by the last sand spit deposited on the left (south) bank. It climbs no more than several hundred feet through the Tapeats Sandstone, and is marked by both cairns and hiker use. Once you've topped out on this Tapeats Sandstone bench, the trail stays atop it all the way to Palisades Creek. Like the Tonto Trail, the Beamer is neither flat nor straight. It curves in and out of drainages cut by headward erosion, frequently descending 50 to 100 vertical feet into each drainage before climbing out the opposite side. Just make sure you see the trail or cairns on the opposite sides of each of these minor drainages before descending into them, and you'll save yourself some time and unnecessary scrambling.

About the time you reach the last major drainage opposite (or across the river from) the mouth of Carbon Creek, the Beamer Trail suddenly braids off on three different and distinct levels. Like the Boucher Trail, there are certain sections of the Beamer that aren't all that much fun to be on if you're wearing an external-frame pack and encounter strong upstream winds. In this section, taking the highest trail, which is marked by cairns, might be safer for you than traversing the outer rim 200 feet above the river. The Beamer Trail continues contouring the Tapeats Sandstone until you're overlooking Palisades Creek. This is where the Beamer makes an abrupt and well-marked descent through the Dox Sandstone to the mouth of Palisades Creek.

From Palisades Creek, the trail is straightforward

enough through the sand, boulders, and tammies—passing the McCormick Mine en route—until you encounter the first of two sections of Dox Sandstone that have to be negotiated before you reach the mouth of Tanner Canyon. This first section of Dox begins just opposite of the north end of the exposed sandbar on the left side (facing downstream) of the river, at River Mile 66½. If high water has covered up this sandbar, you can tell you're at your first section of Dox Sandstone, because there's no longer any beach to walk on. Two faint trails traverse their way through the Dox to the next beach, less than a half mile downstream. The lower route can be followed at low water, though there are a couple of boulder moves you might find awkward with a pack on; or you can take the upper route, which is marked by cairns.

Once you're through this section of Dox, the trail links up with the next section of beach and remains on it until you've crossed the mouth of Comanche Creek and reached the next major drainage to the west of it. Here you'll encounter the second section of Dox Sandstone. As in the first section, two routes traverse their way through this formation. The upper route may require a little more walking because it climbs to the top of the Dox, but it's more clearly marked and safer than the lower route. There are several exposed boulder moves near the west end of the low route where a fall would necessitate a potentially dangerous cold-water swim—assuming one can swim with a heavy pack on.

Once you're through this section of Dox, it's a few

minutes' stroll to the expanse of the Tanner Canyon delta and the bottom of the Tanner Trail.

Additional Considerations: The Beamer Trail is most frequently done as an out-and-back hike from the top of the Tanner Trail simply because it's far easier to drive to the Tanner trailhead than it is either to drive the maze of unmarked roads leading out to the head of Salt Trail Canyon (the main access route into the Little Colorado River Gorge) or to hike the entire Little Colorado River Gorge from Cameron to the north end of the Beamer.

PRIMARY ACCESS TRAILS & ROUTES:	Tanner Trail, Salt Trail Canyon, Little Colorado River.
ELEVATION:	2,725 feet to 2,650 feet, at river level.
TOTAL ELEVATION LOSS & GAIN:	1,000 feet plus or minus (approximately 500 vertical feet each way).
MILEAGE:	Approximately 8 to 9 miles one way.
WATER:	Colorado River.
CACHE POINTS: (If hiked out-and-back from Tanner trailhead.)	Mouth of Tanner Canyon, and Palisades Creek.

SEASONS:	Fall through spring. Summer's hot, and upstream winds can be unusually strong.
MAP:	Vishnu Temple Quadrangle (15 min.)
NEAREST SUPPLY POINTS:	G.C. Village, Flagstaff, Williams, Cameron.

Tanner Canyon to Red Canyon

At one time the 2½-mile section betweeen the mouth of Tanner Canyon and Cardenas Creek used to be a faint path. But so many river runners have hiked it over the years that there is now a distinct trail.

From Tanner Canyon the trail heads west along the contact point of Dox Sandstone and the south end of Tanner Beach. So if you're unsure as to which of several braided trails to take, head south across the beach until it merges with the Dox and you'll pick up the trail to Cardenas Creek, which for the most part follows this contact line all the way.

Once at Cardenas Creek you'll take another river-runner trail, which climbs abruptly to the top of the Unkar Overlook. By lying on your stomach you'll get an incredible view of Unkar Rapids several hundred feet below. When Welshman Colin Fletcher first backpacked this route in 1966, the river was a veritable trickle at 1,260 cubic feet per second; that was low enough for him to walk along the south side of Unkar Rapids at river level. But chances are the river won't be that low when you do this section; so from the Unkar Overlook you'll have to follow this increasingly faint trail up a ridge of Dox Sandstone until you find the next cairn, or until you can eyeball a route down into the head of the first major drainage west of the Unkar Overlook. If you use care, you shouldn't have much problem picking your way back down to the river.

Assuming the river isn't cranking along at 30,000 cfs or more, you can follow the left-hand (south) side of the river through the tammies, along upward-sloping steps of Hakatai Shale all the way to Escalante Creek. (If high water has covered this section along the river, you'll have to take the high route by contouring the talus from Unkar Overlook to Escalante Creek. The author has not hiked the high route, so a description of it is not included here. It's marked infrequently by cairns, but if you've got the canyoneering experience to be hiking the Tanner/Red Canyon route, you shouldn't have any major problems finding the safest path.)

The bed of Escalante Creek drops off near the river. Cairns mark the way through the series of three pour-offs standing between you and the beach below. If for some reason you can't find the cairns, eyeball the safest route—and don't burn your bridges by down-climbing something you can't climb back up. Each of these three obstacles can be negotiated by locating and following their weakest lines, which have a tendency to diagonal off to the west.

You can follow the beach at Escalante all the way to Papago Canyon (again, assuming it's not buried by high water). Call the BRO for river-flow information. If you'll look closely, there is a route that climbs and then traverses the sandstone ledges above. It has a tendency to diagonal up and west to the top of the rockslide, which is your descent route back down to river level. From the bottom of this rockslide, it's another 30–40-minute hike along the beach to Hance Rapids and the terminus of both the New Hance and Tonto trails.

Additional Considerations: If you're planning on doing this loop, you might consider following the Tanner Trail downstream to Hance Rapids, then exiting either the New Hance or Grandview trails. If you run into any problems negotiating either of the two cliff sections, you might be able to catch a ride around these obstacles with river runners. Or, if you're planning your trek for the warm weather, you'll have the option of making use of the two springs on the east arm of the Grandview Trail rather than having to face the long, hot, and waterless hike up the Tanner at the end of your trek.

PRIMARY ACCESS TRAILS & ROUTES: Tanner Trail, New Hance Trail, and Tonto/Grandview Trail.

ELEVATION:	2,650 feet to 2,550 feet, at river level
TOTAL ELEVATION LOSS & GAIN:	2,000 feet plus or minus (approximately 1,000 vertical feet each way for the route described).
MILEAGE:	Approximately 10 miles one way.
WATER:	Colorado River, Grandview and J.T. springs on the east arm of the Grandview Trail below Redwall Formation.
CACHE POINTS:	None.
SEASONS:	Fall through spring. Summer's hot.
MAPS:	Vishnu Temple and Grandview Point quadrangles (both 15 minute).
NEAREST SUPPLY POINTS:	G.C. Village, Flagstaff, Williams, Cameron.

Tonto Trail—Red Canyon to Bass Canyon

The mouth of Red Canyon at Hance Rapids marks the beginning of the Tonto Platform and the 70-odd-mile-long Tonto Trail. The platform itself is the broadest of all the major terraces and talus slopes coursing their way east- and westward through the Grand Canyon, except for certain sections of the Esplanade Sandstone near the west end where the Tonto tends to peter out. This desert plateau may look flat when viewed from either rim, but don't be fooled. And the nonmaintained trail that snakes its way across it is more of a roller-coaster ride than the hoped-for flat hiking one imagines a trail crossing a plateau should be. In its broadest sections, usually between major and minor drainages, the Tonto Trail has a tendency to contour the outer rim of the platform, sometimes skirting the very edge of the Tapeats Sandstone; if there is flat hiking on the Tonto, this is where it'll be. The steepest sections, however, appear when the trail contours each of the major drainages cut by headward erosion. Going into these drainages the trail generally makes an abrupt descent, while coming out of them it has a tendency to climb abruptly—hence the roller-coaster aspect.

If there's a debilitating nature to the Tonto Trail, it's in trekking in and out of these drainages. What looks close is far, primarily because there are very few shortcuts across these drainages; when you think there is one, it'll generally cliff-out in the Tapeats. Consequently, each and every minor drainage usually has to be contoured before you reach the head of the major drainages. And what before may have looked close—when you were standing on the Tonto Platform looking across the mouth of one of these major drainages—will suddenly hit you as being very far. That may have something to do with the manner in which the Tonto Trail was constructed.

Of it James Wharton James wrote in 1910 in *The Grand Canyon of Arizona*: " . . . the trail made centuries ago by mountain sheep, small bands of which are still to be found in the remoter corners of the Canyon—then followed by the Indians, whose moccasin feet made less impression upon it than did the hoofs of the sheep. And in the two or three decades just passed, a few white men trod it. Perhaps Powell, or some of his men, or Stanton, walked where we now walk, or ride, and surely some of those early mining prospectors of the Canyon—Ashurst, McClure, Marshal, Hance, Boucher, Berry, Brashear—once went this way."

Whatever your own impressions of hiking the Tonto Platform are, the Tonto Trail is the major east-west thoroughfare through the Grand Canyon.

Red Canyon to Hance Creek

This first section is perhaps the steepest and rockiest stretch of the Tonto Trail. Standing at the mouth of Red Canyon, look up and to your west and you can see the trail climbing out of the west side of Red Canyon. Pick it up at the top of a large sand dune before it tackles a steep section of Hakatai Shale. Between the Hakatai Shale and Mineral Canyon, you'll have to pick your way from one cairn to the next as the trail probes its way through the slumps, landslides, and rockfalls. Once through this craggy section, you'll skirt the Bass Formation near the mouth of Mineral Canyon for a few minutes before tying together once again with the Hakatai, which will take you about halfway up the east side of Mineral. You'll cross Mineral Canyon here. (Hiking down this section from Hance Creek to Red Canyon, you may mistake some of the old burro trails while crossing this section. They go down Mineral Canyon to the river, not over to Red Canyon.) Once across Mineral Canyon, the trail climbs back through the Hakatai Shale to a place called Shady Overhang, which is located at the head of the small canyon between Mineral Canyon and Hance Creek; it's a good lunch or rest spot.

From Shady Overhang, the trail climbs up through the Tapeats Sandstone and finally tops out on the Tonto Platform below Ayer Point. You'll stay on the platform, skirting the Tapeats along the east side of Hance Creek until you're just about opposite the saddle, or neck, of Horseshoe Mesa. This is where the trail leaves the Tonto Platform and descends back through the Tapeats and links up the eastern spur of the Grandview Trail coming down from Horseshoe Mesa, J.T. Spring, and Grandview Spring.

Additional Considerations: If you're planning on making a loop hike using the New Hance, Tonto, and Grandview trails, and you haven't hiked the New Hance before, you might find it more satisfactory to descend the New Hance and exit the Grandview. There is no permanent water on the New Hance for the climb out, whereas you can get water at J.T. Spring and Grandview Spring about halfway on your climb out of the Canyon.

PRIMARY ACCESS TRAILS & ROUTES:	New Hance Trail and eastern spur of Grandview Trail.
ELEVATION:	2,550 feet at Hance Rapids to approximately 3,900 feet at junction of eastern spur of Grandview.
TOTAL ELEVATION LOSS & GAIN:	1,350 feet plus or minus vertical elevation gain.
MILEAGE:	Approximately 4½ miles one way.
WATER:	Colorado River and J.T. and Grandview springs.
CACHE POINTS: (If hiked out-and-back from Grandview trailhead.)	Hance Creek and Shady Overhang.
SEASONS:	Fall through spring. Summer's hot.

MAPS: Vishnu Temple and Grandview Point quadrangles (15 minute).

NEAREST SUPPLY POINTS: G.C. Village, Flagstaff, Williams, Cameron.

Hance Creek to Cottonwood Canyon

When the prospectors of the late 1800s abandoned their mines, they turned loose their exotic African burros. The burros prospered in the warm inner Canyon, and several decades later their population numbered in the hundreds. But their very presence threatened the native, and more timid, desert bighorn sheep by destroying its habitat. And until National Park Service biologists destroyed over 2,000 of them, and Cleveland Amory saved several hundred more, they also played havoc with some of the inner-Canyon trails—most notably the Tonto. That's kind of ironic because *Equus asinus* did as much to develop and maintain large sections of the Tonto Trail as the prospectors who led them. But once they were turned loose to roam at will, they had a knack for braiding many sections of the Tonto into a confusing array of dead ends, cul-de-sacs, and seemingly aimless wanderings. That presented the hiker with the dilemma of choosing which of these nonmaintained trails to follow.

Today, all but a handful of these clever animals are

gone from the park; though there remain several sections of the Tonto Trail that still bear the marks of their feral wanderings. One of these sections is the stretch of Tonto between Hance Creek and Cottonwood Canyon, which contours the base of Horseshoe Mesa. While there is never any doubt where you are geo- or topographically, there are several short sections on the north side of Horseshoe Mesa that require more care in following the cairns that mark the best of several trail alternatives.

Cave of the Domes Trail leading up the north side of Horseshoe Mesa is picked up shortly after contouring around the east arm of Horseshoe Mesa, while the west arm of the Grandview Trail is picked up as soon as you reach the drainage of Cottonwood Creek. Like the east arm of the Grandview Trail, both of these trails will take you back up to Horseshoe Mesa, where you can link up with the Grandview proper.

Additional Considerations: This section of Tonto is most frequently done as a loop hike, using the Grandview Trail as the main trail to enter and exit the Canyon. However, if you're doing a loop around Horseshoe Mesa, you might consider going down either the west arm of the Grandview or Cave of the Domes trails and coming up the east arm at Hance Creek, so you can replenish your water at J.T. or Grandview springs.

PRIMARY ACCESS TRAILS & ROUTES: Grandview Trail and New Hance Trail.

ELEVATION:	3,900 plus or minus feet at Hance Creek to 4,000 plus or minus feet to 3,700 plus or minus feet at Cottonwood Creek.
TOTAL ELEVATION LOSS & GAIN:	300 plus or minus vertical feet each way.
MILEAGE:	Approximately 3½ miles from east arm to west arm trail junctions.
WATER:	J.T. and Grandview springs, and Colorado River.
CACHE POINTS: (If hiked from Grandview Trail.)	Horseshoe Mesa.
SEASONS:	Fall through spring. Summer's hot.
MAPS:	Vishnu Temple and Grandview Point quadrangles (both 15 minute).
NEAREST SUPPLY POINTS:	G.C. Village, Flagstaff, Williams, Cameron.

Cottonwood Canyon to South Kaibab Trail

Assuming one of the old feral burro trails doesn't lead you off on a half-day tangent, it's 18 miles along the main arm of the Tonto Trail from Cottonwood Creek to the Tonto's junction with the South Kaibab Trail. Compared to the 40-odd-mile stretch of Tonto between the Boucher and South Bass trails, this popular stretch is relatively easy to follow, though care is required on several sections.

From Cottonwood Creek, it's 3.43 miles to the head of Grapevine Creek. This creek is significant from a couple of standpoints: it's the only perennial water source on this stretch of the Tonto; and it's the longest tributary drainage cutting through the Tonto Platform below the South Rim—longer than Hance Creek to the east, and Slate Creek and Serpentine Canyon far to the west. From that standpoint alone, it can be particularly debilitating to walk from one side of Grapevine Creek to the other at the end of a weary day. So don't expect to flash it in an hour, because it *is* farther than it looks. You should also pay particular care in following the cairns when hiking into and out of the east and west sides of Grapevine, because the trail is not as clearly defined in the narrower sections of Tapeats Sandstone as it is on the broader stretches of the Tonto Platform.

It's 5.82 miles from Grapevine Creek around the base of 5,368′ Lyell Butte to Burro Creek, and if you haven't been tempted to try a shortcut on the meandering Tonto Trail, the notion just might strike you while you're hiking out the west side of the Grapevine. There you'll be faced with the classic question that's faced every canyoneer who's spent any time hiking the Tonto Platform: "Is it shorter and faster to go up and over, or better to go all the way around?" It's a question many have answered the hard way. In this particular instance, the carrot being dangled in front of you is the Muav Limestone saddle between the east arm of Lyell Butte and another smaller and unnamed butte, designated on your map as 4396. Unless you're prepared for adventure, go around. Boulder Creek is one of three seasonal water sources you might be able to make use of on this stretch of Tonto if you plan your hike for mid-spring. (Check with the BRO on conditions of this seasonal water source and others.)

From Boulder Creek to Lonetree Canyon, it's 2.88 miles. And there aren't any real mysteries in following this section of trail going into Lonetree, the second seasonal water source.

It's 3.09 miles from Lonetree Canyon to the east arm of Cremation Canyon, the last seasonal water source, and the only real puzzle on this stretch is after you climb out through the Tapeats on the west side of Lonetree and regain the Tonto Platform; there you'll regain several feral variations of the true Tonto Trail. Let cairns, footprints, and common sense be your guide.

From the east arm of Cremation to the west arm, it's a well-marked .82 mile. Don't let the sudden appearance of Hakatai Shale in the middle and west arms throw you off. From the east arm, the trail climbs out of the Tapeats Sandstone, over a pinched-out section of Tonto Platform, then descends back into the Hakatai in the middle arm; from the middle arm, it climbs over another pinch of Tonto Platform before descending back into the Hakatai

Shale in the west arm. If you encounter any problems with this section, most likely it'll have to do with the heat which seems to collect in this tributary canyon. This part of the canyon was once a vast urn for the prehistoric Indians who cremated their dead on the rim and hurled the ashes into the abyss.

Once you've started out the west arm of Cremation Canyon, it's only 1.63 miles to the junction of the Tonto Trail; the way should be obvious.

Additional Considerations: Assuming you've planned your trek along the South Kaibab/Tonto/Grandview loop to coincide with reliable seasonable water sources, it's really up to you whether you do this loop east-to-west or vice versa. However, if you've checked with the BRO, and their records indicate the only water source you can rely on along this stretch is the perennial one in Grapevine Canyon, you would do well to consider hiking down the South Kaibab across the Tonto, then out the Grandview; that way, you could make better use of Grapevine as your primary water source—and perhaps layover day—before climbing out the west arm of the Grandview Trail.

PRIMARY ACCESS TRAILS & ROUTES:	Grandview Trail and South Kaibab Trail.
ELEVATION:	3,700 feet plus or minus at Cottonwood Creek to 3,900 feet plus or minus at South Kaibab Trail.

TOTAL ELEVATION LOSS & GAIN:	Approximately 1,000 feet plus or minus one way.
MILEAGE:	18 miles one way.
WATER:	Grapevine Creek.
CACHE POINTS:	None.
SEASONS:	Fall through spring. Summer can be deadly.
MAPS:	Vishnu Temple, Grandview Point, and Bright Angel quadrangles (15 minute).
NEAREST SUPPLY POINTS:	G.C. Village, Flagstaff, Williams, Cameron.

South Kaibab Trail to Bright Angel Trail

While the 4.1-mile stretch of the Tonto Trail between the South Kaibab and Bright Angel trails is not maintained, it is perhaps the most well-worn and easily identifiable stretch of Tonto Trail along its entire 70-odd-mile course. Pipe Springs and Burro Springs, both perennial water sources, are located midway between the South Kaibab and Bright Angel trails.

Additional Considerations: If you're in good shape, but only have time for a day hike, the 13-mile-long South Kaibab/Tonto/Bright Angel loop is a good outing. Waterwise, it's best to descend the South Kaibab and exit the Bright Angel.

PRIMARY ACCESS TRAILS & ROUTES:	South Kaibab Trail and Bright Angel Trail.
ELEVATION:	3,900 feet plus or minus at South Kaibab Trail to 3,900 feet plus or minus at Bright Angel Trail.
TOTAL ELEVATION LOSS & GAIN:	200 plus or minus vertical feet one way.
MILEAGE:	4.1 miles one way.
WATER:	Pipe Springs, Burro Springs, and Indian Gardens.
CACHE POINTS:	None.
SEASONS:	Fall through spring. Summer's hot.
MAP:	Bright Angel Quadrangle (15 minute).
NEAREST SUPPLY POINTS:	G.C. Village, Flagstaff, Williams, Cameron.

Bright Angel Trail to Hermit Trail

For all practical purposes, the 12-mile-long stretch of Tonto Trail between the Bright Angel and Hermit trails is as easy to follow as the 4.1-mile section of Tonto Trail between the Bright Angel and South Kaibab. Mileages for this section (from Indian Gardens) are as follows: 2.52

miles to Horn Creek campsite (seasonal water); 7.29 miles to Salt Creek campsite (seasonal water); 9.38 miles to Cedar Springs campsite; 10.70 to Monument Creek campsite (perennial water); and 12.32 miles to the Granite Rapids campsite or 12.05 miles to the Hermit–Tonto trail junction.

Additional Considerations: This is the most popular multiday loop hike in Grand Canyon National Park; if you plan your hike when the seasonal water sources on this loop are reliable (normally the spring), you're going to have to book Backcountry Reservations far in advance. However, if your schedule coincides with the drier hiking seasons, and records at the BRO indicate that Monument Creek is the only reliable water source, consider hiking down the Bright Angel and out the Hermit; that way you can make better use of Monument Creek as your primary water source—a good spot for a layover day, too—before climbing out the Hermit Trail.

PRIMARY ACCESS TRAILS & ROUTES:	Bright Angel Trail and Hermit Trail.
ELEVATION:	3,900 feet plus or minus at Bright Angel Trail to 3,400 feet plus or minus at Hermit Trail junction.
TOTAL ELEVATION LOSS & GAIN:	Approximately 1,000 feet plus or minus one way.

MILEAGE:	12 miles one way.
WATER:	Indian Gardens, Monument Creek, Colorado River.
CACHE POINTS:	None.
SEASONS:	Fall through spring. Summer's hot.
MAPS:	Bright Angel Quadrangle (15 minute).
NEAREST SUPPLY POINTS:	G.C. Village, Flagstaff, Williams, Cameron.

Hermit Trail to Boucher Trail

This section of the Tonto is becoming increasingly popular with hikers because it's relatively short, 6.3 miles, and because a challenging loop hike can be done by using only one trailhead: In the case of the Hermit/Tonto/Boucher loop, that's Hermits Rest, which is easily accessible. However, because this section of the Tonto Platform is one of the narrowest below the South Rim, the trail itself is difficult to follow and contours generally steep talus slopes. Consequently, a bit more care is required in scouting the way for cairns and footprints than on several of the more heavily used sections of Tonto.

From the Hermit Trail junction to Travertine Canyon, it's a shade under 4 miles; the 2.75-mile section from Hermit Creek to Monument has a tendency to play tag with the Tapeats Sandstone most of the way, except where the trail hooks back over the Tonto Platform before descending into the mouth of Travertine Canyon.

It's 2.34 miles from Travertine Canyon to the Boucher Trail junction, and the first piece of this section has a tendency to hang near the Tapeats until you reach the north side of Whites Butte, where it regains the Tonto Platform for a mile or so before descending to Boucher Creek (perennial water).

Additional Considerations: This loop is most frequently done by descending the Boucher Trail and exiting the Hermit Trail—primarily because most people find it easier to climb out the more obvious Hermit than the less frequently used Boucher Trail. Knowledgeable canyoneers do it both ways, and strong day hikers have trekked it in 8 to 9 hours.

PRIMARY ACCESS TRAILS & ROUTES:	Hermit Trail and Boucher Trail.
ELEVATION:	3,400 feet plus or minus at Hermit Trail junction to 3,100 feet plus or minus at Boucher Trail junction.
TOTAL ELEVATION LOSS & GAIN:	Approximately 300 plus or minus vertical feet one way.
MILEAGE:	6.3 miles.
WATER:	Hermit Creek, Boucher Creek, and Colorado River.

CACHE POINTS:	None.
SEASONS:	Fall through spring. Summer can be unforgiving.
MAP:	Bright Angel Quadrangle (15 minute).
NEAREST SUPPLY POINTS:	G.C. Village, Flagstaff, Williams, Cameron.

Boucher Trail to South Bass Trail

If there is a No Man's Land aspect to any section of the Tonto Trail, it's the 30-mile stretch between Boucher Creek and the South Bass Trail. The reason is simple: If you get into trouble anywhere on this stretch, and you can't walk out under your own power, you either have to signal with your mirror for help or—failing that, due to poor visibility or stormy conditions—send your partner for help, either out the Boucher Trail to Hermits Rest or the South Bass Trail to the seasonally staffed Pasture Wash Ranger Station. One other emergency alternative can be considered during the river-running season, and that's to hike to the Colorado River for help, using either Boucher Creek, Ruby Canyon, Serpentine Canyon, or the South Bass Trail.

Be all that as it may, this is not to say this section of the Tonto doesn't offer its own unique rewards to experienced hikers; it does, primarily in the form of solitude and the opportunity to experience the Canyon's natural rhythms for more than a few hours at a time. It's just that a trek along this route should be well planned and not taken any lighter than one along the Tanner to Red Canyon route, or any of the other more remote treks in the Canyon.

From the Tonto/Boucher Trail junction, it's less than half a mile to the Boucher Creek camp. The Boucher Rapids trail junction is .36 mile down Boucher Creek at its confluence with Topaz Canyon. To reach Boucher Rapids, turn right at this junction and boulder-hop a little more than a mile to the river. To continue west along the Tonto Trail, however, you have to hike up the west side of Topaz Canyon for about a quarter of a mile until it starts climbing back up through the Vishnu Schist and Tapeats Sandstone and regains the Tonto Platform southeast of Marsh Butte.

It's 5 miles from Boucher Creek to Slate Canyon, the first perennial water source on this route. While this section of the Tonto Trail isn't indelible, you shouldn't have any problems following it all the way to the South Bass Trail as long as you exercise good judgment in trail and route finding. This section of the Tonto Trail stays atop the Tonto Platform, except where it shortcuts the heads of tributary drainages like Slate, Sapphire, the two unnamed drainages between Shaler Point and Le Conte Plateau, and Ruby and Serpentine canyons. These shortcuts have a tendency to make abrupt descents and ascents through the Tapeats Sandstone before linking up with the next section of Tonto Platform. All of the shortcuts should be marked with cairns and/or footprints.

From Slate Canyon it's 4½ miles to the head of Agate

Canyon; the only thing to remember is that the trail in Agate Canyon follows the contact point between the Tapeats and Tonto before climbing back atop the Tonto Platform and descending into Sapphire. From Agate Canyon to Sapphire it's 2.05 miles; the trail shortcuts the head of Sapphire, then climbs back atop the Tonto and stays there all the way to the head of Turquoise Canyon 2.72 miles farther. Turquoise Canyon is the second perennial water source on this route and a good objective for your first day's hike west of Boucher Creek. From Turquoise to Jasper Canyon it's 2.4 miles, and from Jasper to Jade Canyon it's another .73 mile; these are the two unnamed drainages between Shaler Point and Le Conte Plateau that were no doubt given names by river runners who refer to the 6-mile stretch of river between Agate Canyon and Serpentine Canyon as "the gems"; the trail shortcuts both Jasper and Jade canyons.

From Jade Canyon to Ruby Canyon it's 2.69 miles; the trail shortcuts the head of Ruby Canyon, which is also the first seasonal water source west of Boucher Creek. It's 1.54 miles between Ruby and Quartz canyons, and 1.93 miles between Quartz and Emerald canyons; these are the two unnamed drainages between Ruby and Serpentine. The trail does not shortcut either of these canyons, but generally rims the top of the Tapeats Sandstone.

From Emerald Canyon to Serpentine Canyon, the next seasonal water source, it's 1.37 miles; the trail only cuts off a small piece of Serpentine before beginning the 3.81-mile haul to Bass Canyon.

Additional Considerations: If you're not trekking all

the way from one end of the Canyon to the other, and just want to do this remote loop using the Boucher and South Bass trails, consider going in on the South Bass and out the Boucher or Hermit trails.

PRIMARY ACCESS TRAILS & ROUTES:	Boucher Trail and South Bass Trail.
ELEVATION:	3,100 feet plus or minus at Boucher Trail junction to 3,200 feet plus or minus at South Bass Trail junction.
TOTAL ELEVATION LOSS & GAIN:	Approximately 2,000 plus or minus vertical feet one way.
WATER:	Boucher Creek, Slate Canyon, Turquoise Canyon, and Colorado River.
CACHE POINTS:	None.
SEASONS:	Fall and spring. Summer can be deadly, and winter snows usually prevent access to South Bass trailhead.
MAPS:	Bright Angel and Havasupai Point quadrangles (both 15 minute) and S. Kaibab National Forest Map.
NEAREST SUPPLY POINTS:	G.C. Village, Flagstaff, Williams, Cameron.

The Apache Trail

If you look at either the map at the end of this guide, or the Havasupai Point Quadrangle, you'll notice a trail immediately west of the upper end of the South Bass Trail that heads over to Apache Point. According to Frank J. Taylor and Miner Raymond Tillotson (the latter a former superintendent of Grand Canyon National Park) who co-wrote the 1930s classic *Grand Canyon Country*, " . . . in the earlier days, came the Apaches on their expeditions to raid the stores of corn and other foodstuffs harvested by the Havasupai Indians." Their raids no doubt had something to do with how the Apache Trail got its name; this was the same trail that Harvey Butchart (in *Grand Canyon Treks*) said, " . . . Captain Burro started to build . . . which would go from the Bass Trail to his home in Supai." At one time that trail traversed, for the most part, the Esplanade Sandstone situated approximately 1,500 vertical feet below the South Rim; thus it provided both the Havasupais and William Wallace Bass with an easier means of traversing that cinnamon-red terrace from east to west.

However, what once existed on the ground, and what still exists on most topographical maps, no longer exists *in situ* today. The Apache Trail is, for the most part, a route that requires as much care and route-finding ability as the Tanner to Red Canyon route. To compound matters, access to Apache Point at the western end of the present Apache Trail has to be approved in advance by the Havasupai Indian Tribe, whose Traditional Use Area includes the access roads that lead to both Topocoba Hilltop and Apache Point. (For further information on obtaining permission for crossing, and hiking in, the Havasupais' Traditional Use Area see "Havasupai Indian Reservation" below.) Consequently, if you're an experienced-enough canyoneer to be trekking the Apache Trail,* but for some reason cannot obtain permission to cross Havasupai land, the only other way to hike this route is to do it out-and-back from the South Bass Trail. And unless you plan your trek to coincide with the wettest spring months, when seasonal water is plentiful (along with emergency water in the form of *tinajas*), there really isn't a practical way to carry all the water you'll need to do this arduous multiday route.

From the South Bass Trail, the route has a tendency to cling to the steep talus of the Hermit Shale all the way around both Chemehuevi and Toltec points; if you never knew what a Sidehill Gianther was before you tackled this route, you would after you completed it. The main reason is that your left foot is usually two feet higher than your right, which makes for some interesting locomotion—and for some cramps to be worked out later on. The only water source on this first stretch is a seasonal one located in the first drainage west of Chemehuevi Point, but you'll have to use as much care finding it as you will following the Apache Trail.

Just about the time you reach the northernmost arm of the three separate points that comprise Montezuma Point, the trail drops back down to the Esplanade for about half a mile, then climbs back up to the Hermit Shale in the first drainage south of that northernmost arm. It stays on the Hermit Shale until you reach Point Huitzil, where it begins its descent back down to the Esplanade in the first major drainage south of this point. For the most part, the South-Bass-to-Point-Huitzil leg is physically the most difficult stretch of the Apache Trail. But the route-finding challenge isn't over until Apache Point.

West of Point Huitzil, the Apache Trail stays on the Esplanade Sandstone around Point Centeotl and Point Quetzal; since the Esplanade is virtually devoid of continuous stretches of soil, the only way to know if you're on the historic course of this trail is to look for the occasional rock cairn; they provide the only real clues that this actually was a trail at one time. Failing that remember to stay on the Esplanade Sandstone until you reach the second major drainage south of Apache Point; the route goes up the north side of this drainage and regains the Hermit Shale, where it remains until you reach the head of the first major drainage south of Apache Point. It uses this steep drainage to climb through the Coconino Sandstone, and contours the Toroweap Formation around to the west until you find the breaks in the Kaibab Limestone, which will provide access to the top of Apache Point.

Additional Considerations: This remote route requires careful planning, good physical conditioning, and a thorough background in canyoneering and route-finding techniques.

Assuming you've obtained permission to cross and hike

in the Havasupais' Traditional Use Area, take the Apache Trail west from the South Bass to Apache Point, then a compass bearing west through the pinyon-juniper to Topocoba Hilltop, then down the Topocoba Trail to Supai is an excellent way to conclude a multiweek trans-Canyon trek from the Little Colorado.

One of the most appealing aspects of this route is that it traverses one of the highest terraces in the Grand Canyon, and in doing so you don't get that swallowed-up-whole feeling you frequently get hiking remote sections of the Tonto.

PRIMARY ACCESS TRAILS & ROUTES:	South Bass Trail and Apache Point. (To reach Apache Point you have to shoot a compass bearing from BM 6165, which is located approximately 2 miles north on the road from Mexican Jack Tank.)
ELEVATION:	5,200 feet plus or minus at South Bass Trail to 6,400 feet plus or minus at Apache Point.
TOTAL ELEVATION LOSS & GAIN:	Approximately 2,500 plus or minus vertical feet one way.
MILEAGE:	Approximately 18 miles one way.
WATER:	None.

CACHE POINTS: None.

SEASONS: Spring and fall. Summer can be deadly; winter access can be impossible.

MAPS: Havasupai Point Quadrangle (15 minute) and South Kaibab National Forest Map.

NEAREST SUPPLY POINTS: G.C. Village, Flagstaff, Williams, Cameron.

HAVASUPAI INDIAN RESERVATION

One of the most popular hikes in the Grand Canyon is the delightful 8-mile trek to the modern Havasupai village called Supai; it's situated in a virtual canyon paradise, which has been described with almost as many colorful adjectives as the Grand Canyon itself. At one time a dozen trails led down to the aquamarine waters of Havasu Canyon, but today there are only two trails hikers are allowed to use: the popular Hualapai Trail, the main means of access for hikers and mule riders from Hualapai Hilltop to Supai; and the seldom-used Topocoba Trail, which at one time was followed by early postmen carrying mail from Grand Canyon Village to Supai.

The reason for this seeming shortage of trails is simple enough: Many of the old trails and routes to Supai cross the Havasupai's ancestral lands, and there are many areas within these ancestral lands officially referred to as the

Havasupais' Traditional Use Lands that the Havasupai revere as sacred. Justifiably, the Havasupai don't want non-Indian visitors in these sacred areas, which they refuse to identify to outsiders for fear the areas will be treated as less than sacred and, perhaps, vandalized or pillaged in the process. If their historic encounters with and broken promises from the white man are any indication, their fears are very real. And until the *Memorandum of Understanding Between the Havasupai Tribe and the National Park Service Regarding the Havasupai Traditional Use Lands* is signed by both the chairman of the Havasupai Tribal Council and the superintendent of Grand Canyon National Park, hiker use is limited to the Hualapai Trail and the Topocoba Trail. Permission must be obtained from the Havasupai Tribe to hike either of these trails. (According to tribal Vice-Chairman Rex Tilousi, permission to use the Topocoba Trail must also be obtained from the BRO at Grand Canyon National Park.) Direct your inquiries concerning these trails, and other areas you might wish to hike, to: Wayne Sinyella, Chairman, Havasupai Tribal Council, P.O. Box 10, Supai, AZ 86435; (602) 448-2961. Just remember in your requests that it's the Havasupais' land you wish to visit, and you'll receive a courteous and friendly reply.

Hualapai Trail

To reach the trailhead for the Hualapai Trail at Hualapai Hilltop, drive 34 miles west of Seligman or 7 miles east of Peach Springs on U.S. 66 to the Supai turnoff. A 62-

mile-long paved road heads across the Blue Mountains, Aubrey Cliffs, and Coconino Plateau to Hualapai Hilltop. There are no services on this road!

The 8-mile-long Hualapai Trail is well worn and easy to follow. From Hualapai Hilltop it switchbacks through the Coconino Sandstone and drops approximately 1,100 vertical feet to the floor of Hualapai Canyon in just over a mile of hiking. It stays in the bed of this canyon all the way to its confluence with Havasu Canyon 5½ miles farther, in the process descending narrow clefts of Esplanade and Supai sandstone. There is no perennial water along this stretch, and the first you'll encounter is that trickling out of Havasu Springs near this confluence.

From this point on, the character of the trail changes from that of dry, sometimes sparsely shaded desert canyon hiking to a lush riparian habitat sprouting up out of the middle of an awesome drainage that begins in Williams, AZ, 80 miles due south—finally emptying into the Colorado River. Cataract Canyon and its tributary canyons drain some 3,000 square miles of the Coconino Plateau; in the process, this runoff continues to provide the lifeblood of existence for the Havasupai people, as well as an occasional threat to hikers and river runners if they happen to be playing near the mouth of Havasu Canyon during one of its seasonal flash floods.

It's 1½ miles from Havasu Canyon to the village of Supai, which is located in a verdant, U-shaped canyon surrounded by impressive cliffs of Supai Sandstone. Directly east from the village are two towering spires of rock, which the traditional Havasupai know and revere as *wigleeva*; one is male, the other is female, and together they watch over the Havasupai people and their crops.

Once in Supai, all hikers must check in with the Havasupai Tourist Enterprise to secure their permits. (It's strongly recommended that you book reservations at least 6 months in advance by contacting Havasupai Tourist Enterprise, Supai, AZ 86435; (602) 448-2121. If you haven't, and you've hiked all the way to Supai anyway and find both the campgrounds and the two tribal lodges full, you'll have to hike all the way back out.) A $10 entrance fee is charged for each hiker entering Supai, along with a $9-a-head daily camping fee; this money is used by the Havasupai to support the tribal government and to maintain campgrounds and trails.

Accommodations in Supai: There are two lodges, the Supai Lodge and Schoolhouse Canyon Lodge, which are available for $8 per person a night. A village cafe also operated by the Havasupai offers a menu of Indian fry bread, burritos, and other hot meals. Mail can be sent out of Supai via packtrain every Monday, Wednesday, and Friday. And horses can be rented to ride into and out of Supai from Hualapai Hilltop, or to carry the packs of weary party members. For further information on accommodations and services offered, contact the Havasupai Tourist Enterprise.

Campgrounds: The Navajo Campground is located 1½ miles below—or north of—Supai, near Navajo Falls; it's a total of 9½ miles from Hualapai Hilltop, while the

Havasu Creek. *Photo by George H. H. Huey.*

Havasu Campground is yet another half mile beyond. A freshwater spring is located on the west side of Havasu Creek, midway between Havasu and Mooney falls, and is well marked.

There are three waterfalls in the vicinity of the campgrounds; south to north, they're Navajo, Havasu, and Mooney. Of the three, Mooney is without a doubt the most spectacular. It's located just below Havasu Campground, and is reached by descending a steep stairway etched into the travertine and protected by a chainlink guardrail.

No overnight hiking is allowed below Mooney Falls. However, the hike to Beaver Falls (another 3 miles downstream from Mooney) and the hike to the Colorado River confluence (7 miles downstream from Mooney) both make excellent daylong outings if you have the time and energy. Both of these roundtrip hikes are straightforward enough, though some attention must be paid each of the numerous times the trail crosses Havasu Creek. Some route-finding ability is also necessary when the trail winds around the travertine cliffs on the east side of Havasu Creek above Beaver Falls. If you keep your eyes open for footprints on these craggy sections, and for the cairns that mark all of the creek crossings, you shouldn't have any problems staying oriented.

Warning: Don't drink the water out of Havasu Creek.

If you decide to hike to the Colorado River, be careful scrambling around the slick Muav Limestone near the river's edge; a hiker recently disappeared in the cold, swift-moving current long before a valiant Colorado River boatman was able to reach her.

Additional Considerations: Spring is definitely the most crowded time to be hiking to, or camping below, Supai. So unless you enjoy crowds, you might plan your visit for another time. Also, the Havasupai flying squirrels are something else to reckon with; no, they don't actually fly, but the author has watched them make four- and five-foot leaps into unwary hikers' packs, which were carefully suspended with cordage textbook-fashion from tree limbs. So if you're camping in one of the crowded campgrounds during peak hiking season, and someone in your party isn't watching your packs, these amazing (and fat) little buggers will probably compromise your security system.

PRIMARY ACCESS TRAILS & ROUTES:	Hualapai Trail, Topocoba Trail, and Colorado River.
ELEVATION:	5,100 feet plus or minus at Hualapai Hilltop, 3,195 feet at Supai, 1,780 feet plus or minus at Colorado River.
TOTAL ELEVATION LOSS & GAIN:	3,810 vertical feet (1,905 each way) Hualapai Hilltop to Supai.

	2,830 vertical feet (1,415 feet each way) Supai to Colorado River.
MILEAGE:	8 miles to Supai, 11 miles to Havasu Campground, 14 miles to Beaver Falls, 18 miles to Colorado River.
WATER:	Havasu Springs, Supai, campgrounds, and Colorado River. (*Don't* plan on using river water, as access is extremely dangerous.)
CACHE POINTS:	Secluded areas of Hualapai Canyon.
SEASONS:	All year. Summer is *hot* hiking, but the swimming's great.
MAPS:	Supai, Kanab Point, and Tuckup Canyon quadrangles (all 15 minute).
NEAREST SUPPLY POINTS:	Seligman, Peach Springs, Supai.

CHAPTER 9

North Rim

One of the most overlooked—and rewarding—hiking opportunities in Grand Canyon National Park are the trails and nonmaintained jeep roads that probe the sub-Alpine forests of the North Rim. When summertime temperatures turn the inner Canyon into a virtual oven—and hikers who've survived it into ashen-faced apparitions returning from the Land of the Dead—there is no better place to hike than the cool forests of the North Rim. The Anasazi had enough sense to make seasonal migrations back up to the lofty heights of the North Rim long before inner-Canyon rocks became too hot to touch. So if your vacation time is limited to summer months, you'd probably find it far more enjoyable to limit your Grand Canyon hiking to the supernal reaches of the North Rim. Unlike the heavily visited South Rim, which basically has only a handful of hiking opportunities atop the rim, the North Rim offers a wide selection of rim trails that can keep even the most avid backpacker busy for a month; they include everything from the half-mile-long hikes out

Quaking aspen, North Rim. *Photo by George H. H. Huey.*

to Cape Royal and Bright Angel Point to multiday treks that will take you all the way from Saddle Mountain on the east to Muav Saddle on the west—and beyond.

RIM TRAILS—EAST

Bright Angel Point Trail

See Chapter 5, "Above the Rim."

Uncle Jim Trail

The trailhead for the Uncle Jim Trail is located on the North Rim entrance road 2 miles north of Grand Canyon Lodge and begins on the east end of the North Kaibab Trail parking lot. The first mile of this well-marked 5-mile loop is also the first mile of the Ken Patrick Trail, and it skirts the very rim of Roaring Springs Canyon offering splendid views en route to the junction of these two trails. There should be a sign at this junction that reads "Old Kaibab Trail 2.5, Uncle Jim Point 1.2." Turn right at this junction (south), and about a quarter mile beyond you'll come to another junction where you'll have the option of taking the left fork (which makes a beeline through the woods to 8,336′ Uncle Jim Point) or the right fork (which continues to skirt the rim of Roaring Springs Canyon). Either way, the short, challenging hike out to Uncle Jim Point leads you to a fine picnic-style scenic vista.

Ken Patrick Trail

The 12-mile point-to-point hike along the Ken Patrick Trail from the North Kaibab Trail parking lot to Point Imperial is more of an intense introduction to orienteering and route finding than a well-marked afternoon hike. From the junction of the Ken Patrick and Uncle Jim trails, the trail contours the west slope of the Roaring Springs drainage. Though the trail remains easy enough to follow for the next couple of miles, it's rocky and makes sudden descents and ascents where it follows the bed of Roaring Springs drainage.

Three and one half miles out from the parking lot, you'll reach the old Bright Angel trailhead. From here the trail disintegrates, or goes underground, and what remains of it is anybody's guess all the way to the Cape Royal Road—though, if you're attentive, you'll occasionally discover pieces of the trail that verify you're on the right course through the New Mexico locust. Care must be taken where the trail is intersected by old fire roads; where the real fun begins, though, is where the Ken Patrick is covered with "blow-down," or fallen timber, and there your hiking consists of crawling under or climbing over these giant pick-up stix.

Pat yourself on your back once you've reached the Cape Royal Road, cross it, then descend the trail back into the trees. From this paved, serpentine crossing, the trail skirts the very rim of the Canyon all the way to Point Imperial, and once again offers exposed views en route.

Even though this trail doesn't go to the bottom of the Canyon, it offers the same adventurous elements of those inner-Canyon routes.

Cape Royal Trail and Cliff Springs Trail

See Chapter 5,"Above the Rim."

Saddle Mountain to Point Imperial Trail

This is actually an old fire road, and it's located in the same cul-de-sac as the Nankoweap trailhead at the end of USFS Road 610. The turnoff for Road 610 is located a mile south of the Kaibab Lodge on the North Rim entrance road 4 miles north of the NPS Entrance Station. It's about 15 miles on USFS 610 to road's end at the eastern edge of the old Grand Canyon National Park boundaries. From this cul-de-sac, head south until you pick up the old fire road that generally contours the rim for approximately 3 miles to Point Imperial.

This short trail can be used a number of ways: as an addition to the Ken Patrick Trail; an out-and-back hike from Point Imperial; or as the beginning of the Saddle Mountain to Muav Saddle hike. Though off-season, it provides an excellent means of winter access to the North Rim when the National Park Service locks up the North Rim Entrance Station and road; the reason is that USFS Road 610 from De Motte Park lies outside park boundaries and remains open until it's buried by the first snow.

RIM TRAILS—WEST

Transept Trail

This 1½-mile-long trail is one of the real bonuses for staying in what otherwise might be a crowded campground. It leaves the North Rim campground just west of the general store and contours the edge of the Transept a well-marked 1½ miles to Grand Canyon Lodge. Next to Phantom Creek, the Transept is the largest tributary drainage of Bright Angel Canyon, and a hike along its rim offers views as spectacular as any secluded vista in Grand Canyon National Park.

Widforss Trail

If you enjoyed an out-and-back hike along the Transept Trail, and want to get an even more secluded view of this magnificent drainage, the 10-mile out-and-back hike along the enchanting Widforss Trail is the ticket. It's well marked, has gentle gradients, and makes one of the best day hikes on the North Rim. To reach the Widforss trailhead, drive a mile north of the North Rim campground and turn left on the dirt road adjacent to the North Kaibab parking lot; it's a mile to the trailhead, which is located on the north side of this road.

From the parking area, the trail should be obvious all the way to Widforss Point; it climbs gently, skirts the north and northeastern arms of the Transept, then heads south through the woods, terminating several miles later at the head of Haunted Canyon; it's as inspiring a lunch stop as any on the North Rim, with excellent views of Manu Temple and Buddha Temple.

Powell Plateau

One of the most appealing aspects of the North Rim is that it drains—and thus erodes—into the Grand Canyon, unlike the South Rim, which has a tendency to drain away from the Canyon. In addition to the uplifting and faulting of the area north of the Grand Canyon, this erosion has created some significant plateaus in Arizona. From west to east they are Shivwits, Uinkaret, Kanab, and the Kaibab Plateau, which comprises most of the North Rim. Extending beyond the Kaibab are three subsidiary plateaus: Fishtail, Powell, and Wahlala. Of the three, Powell Plateau is perhaps the most appealing to explore on foot. While Fishtail is smaller and more remote than Powell, it's topographically lower in elevation, more arid, and for the most part is covered with pinyon/juniper. Wahlala, on the other hand, is a bit larger, but the paved access out to Cape Royal inhibits, to some extent, what would be the natural charm of the area had it otherwise remained a bit more remote. Powell Plateau has the best of both Fishtail and Wahlala; it's remote, but it's situated at over 7,000 feet in elevation. Consequently, its entire northern third is covered with some of the most impressive untouched stands of ponderosa pine on the heavily logged North Rim; these stands of ponderosa, intermixed with oak, start merging with pinyon/juniper about midway across the plateau until you reach its southern end, where pinyon/juniper becomes the dominant vegetation.

One of the most unique aspects of this isolated plateau, however, is not its vegetative mix, but its significance as a temporary habitation site for the Anasazi between A.D. 1050 and A.D. 1150. According to the data collected and compiled by Richard W. Effland, Jr., A. Trinkle Jones, and Robert C. Euler, 85 sites were recorded on Powell Plateau, with a density of sites averaging out to 33 per square mile and a density of rooms of 71 per square mile. These scientists suggest "that there were 650 to 700 rooms used by prehistoric people living on the plateau." (Do not disturb any of these sites if you happen across one.)

Powell Saddle Trail

To reach Swamp Point and the trailhead for both the Powell Saddle and the North Bass trails, take USFS Road 422 west from Arizona 67; the turnoff is located a mile south of the Kaibab Lodge. Take USFS Road 422 to USFS Road 270 and turn left (south). Follow USFS Road 270 to USFS Road 223, turn right (west), and take 223 to USFS Road 268B. Road 268B will eventually take you out to Swamp Point and the trailheads. (Please note: There are two North Kaibab National Forest maps in circulation with conflicting information on this stretch of road. Get the Interim Edition 1983, or later if it's available, with the correct road numbers out to Swamp Point.)

From 7,517′ Swamp Point, the trail drops 800 vertical

feet in the mile of switchbacks it takes to reach 6,711′ Muav Saddle. This is the geological confluence of the Crazy Jug and Muav faults, which provides a natural passageway for the North Rim trans-Canyon route (see below). The trail up to Powell Plateau is marked by a large cairn in Muav Saddle: turning left (east) will get you started down the North Bass Trail, while turning right (west) and heading along the crest of Muav Saddle will get you started on the Powell Saddle Trail. Immediately below the west side of Muav Saddle is a rickety old cabin built by the CCC, which is sometimes used by cross-country skiers during late winter and early spring. The CCC also built the trail up to Powell Plateau, which switchbacks 1½ miles through the Toroweap Formation and New Mexico locust until it tops out in the ponderosa forests 900 vertical feet later. Once atop the plateau, the trail is marked by blaze marks that have been etched and painted into these beautiful trees. The blaze marks aren't at all frequent, however, and you'll have to look for each of these marks before proceeding if you're intent on staying on the historic course of this trail as it skirts the west rim of White Creek until it begins disappearing somewhere in the head of Dutton Canyon.

Additional Considerations: The hike out to Powell Plateau makes a fine day hike from Swamp Point. But since you've taken the effort to drive all the way out to Swamp Point, you might as well spend a day and a night atop this incredible plateau and experience an altogether different kind of Grand Canyon hiking.

PRIMARY ACCESS TRAILS & ROUTES:	Powell Saddle Trail, North Bass Trail (from the river), Saddle Canyon route (from Thunder River).
ELEVATION:	7,517 feet at Swamp Point to 6,711 feet at Muav Saddle to 7,685 feet atop Powell Plateau.
TOTAL ELEVATION LOSS & GAIN:	3,590 feet (1,795 vertical feet each way).
MILEAGE:	Approximately 5 miles one way to Dutton Canyon.
WATER:	Below east side of Muav Saddle near base of Coconino at head of White Creek. Secondary trail leads to it.
CACHE POINTS:	Muav Saddle.
SEASONS:	Spring through fall. Winter access difficult from either South or North rims due to snow.
MAPS:	Powell Plateau Quadrangle (15 minute) and North Kaibab National Forest Map.
NEAREST SUPPLY POINTS:	Fredonia, Page, Vermillion Cliffs, Jacob Lake, North Rim.

Saddle Mountain to Muav Saddle

Just as it's possible to traverse the inner Canyon eastward and westward below the North and South rims, it's also possible to traverse the Grand Canyon atop the North Rim. One practical and enjoyable route, of many possible variations you may plan on your own, is the 39-mile Saddle Mountain to Muav Saddle route; it makes use of both rim trails and old fire roads to traverse one of the prettiest forests in the Southwest, which also has some of the more incredible views to be seen in any life zone—be it desert, canyon, or mountain environment.

This route traverses a fair-sized piece of the 350-square-mile Kaibab Plateau, which is capped by a layer of Kaibab Limestone, a 250-milion-year-old fossilized seabed which acts as a veritable sponge for the 27 inches of precipitation the North Rim receives on average each year. In the process, this moisture—which falls mainly in the form of snow—fills a subterranean aquifer that feeds natural hydrants below the North Rim like Vasey's Paradise, Cheyava Falls, Roaring Springs, Tapeats Creek, and Thunder River. While this route will take you through a sub-Alpine forest and fern-decked meadows (or "parks," as they like to call them in these parts), you're still going to have to concern yourself with water whether you take this route or one of your own design simply because the Kaibab Limestone is so porous.

From east to west, the route is as follows:

a. Saddle Mountain to Point Imperial: 3 miles; at-large camping; no water.

b. Point Imperial to North Kaibab trailhead parking lot via Ken Patrick Trail: 12 miles; selected camping (check with North Rim BRO); seasonal water at Neal Springs and North Rim campground.

c. North Kaibab Trail parking lot to Widforss Trail parking lot: 1 mile; camping at North Rim campground; water at North Rim campgound.

d. Widforss Trail parking lot to Crystal Ridge/Milk Creek area via Marble Flats and Point Sublime Trail: approximately 9 miles; camping at large, with fine choices between Milk Creek and Crystal Creek; seasonal water en route, check map and North Rim BRO. Use Bright Angel and De Motte Park quadrangles (both 15 minute) and follow your nose if winter snows have knocked down road and trail signs.

e. Crystal Ridge/Milk Creek area to Muav Saddle via Kanabownits Spring, Crescent Ridge, Big Springs Canyon, BM 8356, and Swamp Ridge (USFS Road 268B): approximately 14 miles; camping at large, with fine choices at Crescent Ridge; seasonal water en route, check map and North Rim BRO. Use De Motte Park and Powell Plateau quadrangles (both 15 minute), and North Kaibab National Forest Map.

Additional Considerations: This is only one possible route of many that traverse the Kaibab Plateau; there are as many alternate routes as there are old fire and logging roads to be explored on foot, horseback, or even in a vehicle. For further information, maps, and road conditions for the North Kaibab write: Fredonia Ranger Station, Kaibab National Forest, Fredonia, AZ 86022.

RIM-TO-RIVER TRIALS—MAINTAINED

There is only one rim-to-river trail below the North Rim that's presently maintained by National Park Service trail crews: it's the 14-mile-long North Kaibab Trail, and without a doubt it's the most heavily used trail below the North Rim. Mule-riding concessions also use this trail, and according to the August 1983 Backcountry Management Plan they " . . . have the right-of-way on all trails . . . " So if you encounter a mule train, take the high side of the trail before it reaches you.

North Kaibab Trail

The first known modern man to pioneer a route down Bright Angel Creek from the North Rim was Francois Emile Matthes, a cartographer who was surveying the area in 1902 for the United States Geological Survey. The route Matthes and his men used descended the short, northern arm of Bright Angel Canyon and crossed Bright Angel Creek 94 times before reaching the Colorado River. An original section of this trail, called the Old Kaibab Trail, can be reached by taking the Ken Patrick Trail 3½ miles from the North Kaibab Trail parking lot; this now-abandoned stretch of trail links up with the modern North Kaibab Trail at the confluence of Roaring Springs and Bright Angel Canyon.

A year later the Grand Canyon Transportation Company was formed by E.D. Woolley, who had the brainstorm of bringing tourists across the Canyon to visit the remote North Rim; his line of ascent was the route Matthes descended the year before. Serious trail construction didn't begin until 1924, however, and when the entire cross-Canyon trail was completed in 1928, "the total cost," according to Tillotson and Taylor's *Grand Canyon Country*, "rim to rim, was approximately $147,500, exclusive of the Kaibab Suspension Bridge, which added $39,500."

To reach the head of the modern North Kaibab Trail, drive 2 miles north of Grand Canyon Lodge; the parking lot is on the right (east) side of the road. Like its counterpart below the South Rim, the South Kaibab, your course along the North Kaibab is an easy to follow one all the way to the Colorado River; the only difficulties you may encounter, aside from its length and steepness, are the rockslides that periodically cover upper sections of the trail during spring thaw or after a summer squall.

By far the steepest section of the North Kaibab Trail is the declivitous 4.7-mile stretch it takes from the trailhead down Roaring Springs Canyon to its confluence with Bright Angel Canyon—dropping some 3,400 vertical feet; en route to the confluence, you'll pass Roaring Springs Campground on the right. The buildings and house you'll pass on the left are occupied and maintained by Park Service personnel who operate the Roaring Springs pumphouse, which supplies Grand Canyon Village with water via a cross-Canyon pipeline.

From this confluence it's another 2 miles down Bright Angel Creek to Cottonwood Campground; there's a seasonally staffed ranger station there. A mile beyond, you'll

Ribbon Falls. *Photo by George H. H. Huey.*

come to Ribbon Falls Trail Junction and footbridge; the nonmaintained trail leading to Ribbon Falls is marked by cairns, as is the ford of Bright Angel Creek further to the south. (During heavy spring runoff it's extremely dangerous to attempt fording Bright Angel Creek; so stick to the footbridge.)

It's another 6 miles down Bright Angel Creek to the Phantom Ranch/Bright Angel Campground area; less than a mile north of Phantom Ranch, you'll pass the junction of the Clear Creek Trail (see below).

Additional Considerations: The hike down from the North Kaibab trailhead to Roaring Springs and back is an excellent day hike, as is the hike up from Bright Angel Campground to Ribbon Falls and back. The North Kaibab Trail is frequently used by hikers in combination with the South Kaibab or Bright Angel Trail to make a cross-Canyon hike. So if you're hiking north-to-south, you'll find it easier and safer to hike out the Bright Angel Trail; whereas, if you're hiking south-to-north, you might find it a shade easier to descend the South Kaibab.

PRIMARY ACCESS TRAILS & ROUTES:	North Kaibab trailhead, Old Kaibab Trail, Bright Angel Trail, and South Kaibab Trail.
ELEVATION:	8,241 feet at trailhead to 2,425 feet at Colorado River.
TOTAL ELEVATION LOSS & GAIN:	11,632 feet (5,816 vertical feet each way).

MILEAGE:	14 miles one way.
WATER:	Roaring Springs, Bright Angel Creek, Transept Spring, Ribbon Springs (heavy lime), Phantom Creek, Bright Angel Campground.
CACHE POINTS:	Secluded areas of Roaring Springs, and Ribbon Falls Trail junction.
SEASONS:	June through September from the North Rim; all year from the South Rim—though expect deep snows and harsh conditions above Roaring Springs during winter months.
MAP:	Bright Angel Quadrangle (15 minute).
NEAREST SUPPLY POINTS:	Fredonia, Page, Vermillion Cliffs, Jacob Lake, North Rim, and G.C. Village.

RIM-TO-RIVER TRAILS—NONMAINTAINED

On the North Rim, there are only three nonmaintained rim-to-river trails that see any regular use at all: the popular Thunder River Trail (Bill Hall variation); the increasingly popular Nankoweap Trail; and the seldom-used North Bass, or Shinumo, Trail. Unlike the majority of nonmaintained rim-to-river trails on the South Rim, however, which have relatively easy access and tend to be clustered in one general area, all of these North Rim trails require long drives over secondary roads to reach their remote trailheads. For the most part, the North Rim trails are both longer and have a greater elevation loss and gain than those on the South Rim; they also visit relatively seldom-explored areas of Grand Canyon National Park, where the consequences of poor planning, insufficient canyoneering experience, or an error in judgment might have disastrous consequences. So whatever preparation you did before hiking the South Rim miner trails, do it half again as much—before you tackle the Nankoweap, North Bass, or Thunder River trails.

Nankoweap Trail

Of the four rim-to-river trails that plummet off the North Rim, the colorful history award should go to the Nankoweap Trail. It was constructed by Major John Wesley Powell, geologist Charles Doolittle Walcott, and others during 1882 so Walcott could study "the Grand Canyon Series of rock layers." It was down the Nankoweap, which Walcott called "a perfectly frightful trail," that Utah horse thieves supposedly linked their Butte Fault route across the eastern Grand Canyon with the foot of the Tanner Trail on the other side of the Colorado River.

But perhaps the most outlandish tale concerning the Nankoweap involves government lion hunter Uncle Jim Owens, who was responsible for shooting some 532 mountain lions on the North Rim at the turn of the century. As a result of such drastic conservation measures, the Kaibab deer population mushroomed from around 4,000 to an estimated 30,000. So somebody said, "Why don't we hire us some Navajo trackers, beat the brush, and herd about 8,000 of them deer down the Nankoweap and up the Tanner Trail to the South Rim where they're hurtin' for deer anyway?" What these heavy thinkers didn't realize, however, is that even with the best Navajo trackers beating the brush and firing their "noisemakers," wild and half-starved mule deer would have none of it. This fact was headlined on page one of the Thursday morning, December 18, 1924, issue of the *Arizona Republican:*

KAIBAB DEER DRIVE IS CALLED OFF
Snowstorm Ends Plans of M'Cormick
Motion Picture Men Return to Flagstaff in
Blinding Snowstorm; Deer Scatter Widely

Even Tinseltown had gotten in on the act, which did nothing to alleviate the disaster of thousands of starving deer.

To reach the Nankoweap trailhead, take USFS Road 610 located a mile south of the Kaibab Lodge on the North Rim entrance road; follow USFS Road 610 east approximately 15 miles to road's end.

From the end of USFS Road 610, cairns should mark the trail's descent east off the rim to a saddle in the Toroweap Formation some 500 vertical feet below; from this saddle, you'll climb back up to a small hill to the east identified on your Nankoweap Quadrangle as 8839, contour the north side of it, then descend into an east/northeastern-running drainage. This drainage will provide you with a passage through the Coconino Sandstone immediately below. At the base of the Coconino, follow a ridge of Hermit Shale east for about a half mile before you drop down to the saddle in the Esplanade Sandstone at the base—immediately west—of Saddle Mountain.

For canyoneers wishing to explore the eastern Grand Canyon after winter snows have buried USFS Road 610, and for cross-country skiers who want to tour the North Rim without having to make the 40-mile trek in from Jacob Lake, winter access to the Saddle Mountain area is relatively easy. Take U.S. 89A approximately 21 miles west from Marble Canyon and turn left (south) onto USFS Road 445, which is also called the Buffalo Ranch Road. Drive USFS Road 445 approximately 25 miles to USFS Road 445G; turn right (west) onto 445G, and follow it another 4 or 5 miles to road's end. Be attentive for surveyors' flagging and widely spaced cairns, and you shouldn't have too much trouble following the southern arm of Saddle Canyon the 3 miles or so it takes to climb up to the Saddle Mountain saddle.

The Nankoweap Trail drops off the south side of the Saddle Mountain saddle through the Esplanade Sandstone, and contours the Supai Sandstone for approximately 3 miles before it begins its corkscrew descent through the

Redwall on the west side of Tilted Mesa; the stretch along the Supai Sandstone is dangerously exposed in two sections and takes inventive forks in one or two other stretches, so extra care and caution should be exercised along this stretch. Below the Redwall, pick your way down through the landslide, a pinch of limestone, and the Galeros Formation to the bed of Nankoweap Creek. Perennial water flows from the Muav Limestone into Nankoweap Creek, which normally surfaces along the 3-mile stretch of creekbed you'll follow from the foot of the Nankoweap Trail to the Nankoweap Delta adjacent to the Colorado River.

Additional Considerations: This difficult trail, which should not be attempted by inexperienced canyoneers, provides access to the Butte Fault Trail and is the first leg of the North Rim trans-Canyon route.

PRIMARY ACCESS TRAILS & ROUTES:	USFS Road 610 from the North Rim, USFS Road 445G from Houserock Valley, Colorado River, and Butte Fault Trail (route).
ELEVATION:	8,800 feet plus or minus at Nankoweap trailhead, 2,826 feet at Colorado River.
TOTAL ELEVATION LOSS & GAIN:	11,948 feet (5,974 vertical feet each way).

MILEAGE:	14 miles one way.
WATER:	Nankoweap Creek and Colorado River.
CACHE POINTS:	Saddle Mountain saddle, top of Redwall, and Nankoweap Creek.
SEASONS:	Early fall and late spring. Summers can be deadly, and winter access can be difficult and treacherous.
MAPS:	Nankoweap Quadrangle (15 minute) and North Kaibab National Forest Map.
NEAREST SUPPLY POINTS:	Fredonia, Page, Vermillion Cliffs, Jacob Lake, and North Rim.

North Bass Trail (aka Shinumo Trail and White Trail)

According to "Grand Canyon Nature Notes" dated September 8, 1933, a prospector by the name of White was the first to use the route up Shinumo and White creeks, which linked the Colorado River with the North Rim. Around 1887, William Wallace Bass developed White's route into a trail so that tourists who stayed at Bass Camp would also have a means of visiting the beautiful, yet remote, North Rim. George Wharton James describes a pack trip he took with Bass along the Canyon's first cross-Canyon trail system in *The Grand Canyon of Arizona*: "Another two or three weeks' delightful experience can be gained by arranging to go down Bass's Trail [the South Bass Trail], cross on his cable ferry, go up the Shinumo Trail to Powell Plateau, watch herds of protected and preserved deer and antelope, look lovingly upon the succulent and delicious pine-hens that live upon pinion nuts and roost in the branches of the pine trees of the Kaibab forest, and pleasantly saunter along out to Point Sublime."

A hike down the North Bass isn't much different today than it was in Bass's time over a century ago; it's remote and difficult, and wildly beautiful. Unlike most other rim-to-river trails, which periodically expose themselves to the expansive breadth of the Grand Canyon, the North Bass Trail has a distinctly narrower character. From Muav Saddle all the way to the Colorado River it follows the course of White Creek and Shinumo Creek—never once exposing itself to the Canyon itself. In short, a trek down the North Bass is more akin to hiking into a separate wilderness area within the Grand Canyon—a seldom-trod, undiscovered wildland that heeds its own primeval laws and offers its own sublime rewards.

To reach the North Bass trailhead at Swamp Point, see above under "Powell Saddle Trail" for access information and trail description to Muav Saddle. From Muav Saddle head east along the base of the Coconino Sandstone for about a half mile; the springs that feed White Creek are located along a secondary trail to the east of the steep descent you'll take almost straight down through very loose Hermit Shale. Once through the Hermit, you'll make several switchbacks in the Esplanade Sandstone before the Muav Fault provides a natural passage through the Esplanade to the Supai Sandstone below. You'll follow the bed of White Creek as it carves its way through the Supai Sandstone, bushwhacking half the time, boulder-hopping the other half, with your eyes focused on the route ahead for the next cairn or clue that'll take you to the top of the Redwall on the west side of White Creek. Stay on the west side of White Creek and pick your way through the pinyon and juniper as this wilderness route traverses a series of three saddles before beginning its descent through the Redwall. The Redwall descent should be marked by a totem-sized cairn, so don't attempt a descent of this formation without first locating it.

Below the Redwall switchbacks, the route continues following the west side of White Creek as it descends through the Muav Limestone. Once you reach BM 4000 on your Powell Plateau Quadrangle, the route crosses the east side of White Creek and stays there the next mile or so it descends through the Bright Angel Shale to BM 3486. Here the trail crosses back over to the west side, where it makes its circuitous descent through the Tapeats Sandstone and upper Vishnu—eventually coming out below the confluence of White and Shinumo creeks. The route criss-crosses Shinumo Creek several times, passing Bass's old camp on the left before gaining a well-marked trail used by river runners; it climbs out of the creek over BM 2917 before switchbacking down to the Colorado River below Bass Rapids. If you continued following Shinumo Creek, you'd be cliffed-out above the river.

Additional Considerations: If you're hiking the North Bass out-and-back from Swamp Point, take time to familiarize yourself with the climb back out by stopping every so often to look at the country you're leaving; it's definitely more difficult hiking up the North Bass than it is hiking down it. If you're interested in doing a cross-Canyon hike by going down the North Bass and out the South Bass, the best place to catch a ride with river runners across the Colorado River is at the beach camp at the foot of the North Bass below Bass Rapids.

Warning: This is the most difficult rim-to-river trail or route described in this guide.

PRIMARY ACCESS TRAILS & ROUTES:	Muav Saddle, Saddle Canyon, and South Bass via Colorado River.
ELEVATION:	7,517 feet at Swamp Point to 2,200 feet at the Colorado River.
TOTAL ELEVATION LOSS & GAIN:	10,634 feet (5,317 vertical feet each way).
MILEAGE:	14 miles one way.

WATER:	White Creek below Coconino on east side of Muav Saddle, Shinumo Creek, and Colorado River.
CACHE POINTS:	Muav Saddle, top of Redwall, and where trail first crosses Shinumo Creek.
SEASONS:	Late spring and early fall; summer can be unforgiving; winter access from South and North rims difficult; early spring runoff can make fording Shinumo Creek dangerous and/or impossible in several sections.
MAPS:	Powell Plateau Quadrangle (15 minute), North Kaibab National Forest Map.
NEAREST SUPPLY POINTS:	Fredonia, Page, Vermillion Cliffs, Jacob Lake, North Rim.

Thunder River Trail and Bill Hall Trail

Gold may have been discovered "in the sands at the mouth of Tapeats Creek," as the 1869 Powell Expedition reported, but no one has rediscovered it to this day. What the prospectors did discover after constructing this trail in 1876, however, and what hikers and river runners continue to discover, is another form of gold in three of the most beautiful, cataract-fed creeks anywhere: Deer Creek, Tapeats Creek, and Thunder River. Thunder River, which is said to be U.S. Senator Barry Goldwater's favorite place in Arizona, also has the unique distinction of being the shortest river in the world—tumbling, cascading, and roaring, as it does, out of the Muav Limestone to Tapeats Creek a half mile and 1,200 vertical feet below.

To reach the Thunder River trailhead at Indian Hollow requires more driving time than either the Nankoweap or North Bass trails, but if the number of hikers using the Thunder River Trail is any indication, the rewards are far greater. Turn west off Arizona 67 a mile south of the Kaibab Lodge onto USFS Road 422, and take this road approximately 18 miles to the turnoff for USFS Road 425. Turn left (south) on USFS 425 and drive approximately 10 miles to the junction of USFS Road 232. The Thunder River trailhead at Indian Hollow is at the end of USFS Road 232. (To reach the Bill Hall trailhead at Monument Point, however, stay on USFS Road 425, turn right on USFS 292, and make yet another right on USFS Road 292A and follow it to the end.)

From the Indian Hollow trailhead, the Thunder River Trail contours west along the rim for about a half mile to Little Saddle, where it makes its abrupt descent through the Toroweap Formation, Coconino Sandstone, and Hermit Shale to that broad, enchilada-red terrace called the Esplanade. It then contours its way eastward along the Esplanade for approximately 4 miles before linking up with the Bill Hall Trail coming down off Monument Point. (Whether you're descending the Thunder River Trail or the Bill Hall Trail, this junction is a good place to cache water for the hike out.)

The Bill Hall Trail from Monument Point to this junction leaves the west end of the Monument Point parking lot, and stays atop the rim by heading southwest over a little knoll called Millet 7206 for about a half mile to the southern tip of Monument Point; there it begins switchbacking through the Toroweap Formation and Coconino Sandstone to the Hermit Shale saddle between Bridger's Knoll and Monument Point. From the Bridger's Knoll saddle it heads almost straight down through the Hermit Shale to link up with the Thunder River Trail another three quarters of a mile below.

From the Thunder River/Bill Hall junction the trail is braided in sections, but continues its serpentine course along the Esplanade below the west slope of Bridger's Knoll.

From a geographical standpoint, you shouldn't go astray whichever slight trail variation you might take along this stretch of Esplanade; however, the area is covered with cryptogamic soil, and if you're not careful to follow the cairns marking the exact line of the Thunder River Trail, you can damage this fragile soil, which may bear the marks of your footprints for a hundred years or more.

Cairns mark the descent off the Esplanade, west then

south across the Supai, and through the Redwall to Surprise Valley. Near the head of Bonita Creek in Surprise Valley you'll come to another trail junction: the trail to the right (west) heads over to Upper Deer Creek Falls, Deer Creek Narrows, and Deer Creek Falls where it cascades into the Colorado River (see Tapeats Creek in Chapter 10). The trail to the left (east) is the Thunder River Trail, which is clearly marked as it switchbacks down to the headwaters of Thunder River. No camping is permitted in this area; however, it's a refreshing rest stop before continuing down to the campground below the confluence of Tapeats Creek and Thunder River. It's another 2 miles or so from this campground along Tapeats Creek to the Colorado River. But this well-marked trail, which is frequently used by river runners, crosses Tapeats Creek a number of times, and care must be exercised in fording it during spring runoff.

Additional Considerations: The Thunder River/Bill Hall Trail is the last leg of the North Rim trans-Canyon route. (See pps. 272–274.) Fishermen frequently use the Bill Hall Trail to fish the confluence of Tapeats Creek and the Colorado River, and canyoneers sometimes use it as the first, or last, leg of a Kanab Creek loop trek.

PRIMARY ACCESS
TRAILS & ROUTES: Indian Hollow, Monument Point, and Colorado River via Tapeats and Deer creeks.

ELEVATION:	6,400 feet at Indian Hollow, 7,206 feet at Monument Point, 1,955 feet at Colorado River.
TOTAL ELEVATION LOSS & GAIN:	*Maximum*—10,502 feet (5,251 vertical feet each way).
MILEAGE:	17 miles via Thunder River Trail to the Colorado River. 12 miles via Bill Hall Trail to the Colorado River.
WATER:	Thunder River, Tapeats Creek, Colorado River, and Deer Creek.
CACHE POINTS:	Surprise Valley and the Bill Hall/Thunder River trail junction on Esplanade.
SEASONS:	Thunder River Trail closed by USFS from June 15 to August 30 due to extreme heat. Spring and fall. Winter access difficult.
MAPS:	Powell Plateau and Kanab Point quadrangles (both 15 minute) and North Kaibab National Forest Map.
NEAREST SUPPLY POINTS:	Fredonia, Page, Vermillion Cliffs, Jacob Lake, North Rim.

TRANS-CANYON TRAILS AND ROUTES

If you have extensive canyoneering experience, feel comfortable trekking and scrambling for days on end over precipitous and uncompromising terrain with tenuous footing, can look at the lay of the land and pick the most natural route across it, *and* have both your wilderness and survival skills down pat in the event you get into trouble, then the virtually trailless trans-Canyon route below the North Rim may be the canyoneering challenge you've been looking for. In most sections it's no less difficult than the North Bass Trail; in fact, put about 12 to 15 North Bass treks back-to-back and that would be closer to the mark. However, whatever you've done on the relatively accessible South Rim is basically a romp in the city park compared to the objective hazards and rewards of trekking this remote, seldom-explored route. An accident in this inner-Canyon frontier would be like stepping off the face of the earth. Most likely, the grid searches by helicopters, professional trackers, and bloodhounds would fail to find you; if they did, the ravens would probably have gotten to you first. However, if you do undertake this trek—and exercise good judgment—you'll have the exceedingly rare opportunity to glimpse, if only for a few fleeting moments, the Grand Canyon the way it once was seen by the ancient masters of canyoneering, the Anasazi.

The following section will describe the major trans-

Canyon route from the Nankoweap Trail on the east end of the North Rim to the Thunder River Trail on the west end. Each of the individual sections of this route will be described east-to-west and will link one individual section with the next.

Nankoweap Trailhead to the Butte Fault Trail

The Butte Fault Trail is picked up approximately 100 yards above the foot of the Nankoweap Trail when it first joins Nankoweap Creek (see Nankoweap Trail above). Approximately 11 miles; camping at large, with many choices around Nankoweap Creek; water in Nankoweap Creek; use Nankoweap Quadrangle. *Escape routes* via Saddle Mountain to Pt. Imperial fire road and Nankoweap Creek to Colorado River.

Nankoweap Creek to Colorado River via Butte Fault Trail, East Fork of Carbon Creek, and Lava Canyon

The Butte Fault Trail isn't a trail any more than the North Bass Trail is one; however, it is a very distinct route that follows the geological fault line called the Butte Fault. This was the route horse thieves rode hell-for-leather with their stolen stock all the way across the eastern Grand Canyon; if they actually made that ride, they were outstanding horsemen. From Nankoweap Creek, you have two choices of routes that closely parallel one another to reach Kwagunt Creek: either follow the actual hogback of the Butte Fault on its east or west side up and over the saddle between Nankoweap Mesa and Nankoweap Butte down to Kwagunt Creek; or follow the north/south drainage system that contours the west side of Nankoweap Mesa.

Once you get to Kwagunt Creek, you'll no doubt have the feel for the Butte Fault and be able to see the lay of the land ahead. Continue following this fault line generally south below the Redwall Formation on the west slopes of Malgosa Crest, Kwagunt Butte, Awatubi Crest, and Chuar Butte to the east fork of Carbon Creek on the north side of Temple Butte. The inherent characteristic of this sometimes-debilitating section is that of a slow-motion roller-coaster ride as you struggle out of Kwagunt Creek, flank the west side of Malgosa Crest, then fly down into Malgosa Canyon and so on and so forth from Malgosa Canyon to Awatubi Creek; from Awatubi Creek to Sixty Mile Canyon; from Sixty Mile Canyon to the east fork of Carbon Creek.

From the head of the east fork of Carbon Creek, drop into this creekbed and follow it as it contours the west slope of Temple Butte to its confluence with the west fork of Carbon Creek. Once at this confluence, you can take the west fork all the way to the Colorado River; or you can follow it downstream for about a mile, where you can eyeball a route over the saddle between the west side of Chuar Lava Hill and BM 3741 into Lava Canyon, and thence to the river.

PRIMARY ACCESS TRAILS & ROUTES:	Nankoweap trailhead, Saddle Mountain, and Colorado River.
ELEVATION:	3,200 feet at Nankoweap Creek to 2,700 feet at Colorado River.
TOTAL ELEVATION LOSS & GAIN:	*Loss:* 6,700 vertical feet. *Gain:* 6,300 vertical feet.
MILEAGE:	Approximately 15 to 20 miles.
WATER:	Nankoweap Creek and River.
SEASONAL WATER:	Kwagunt Creek, Sixty Mile Creek, east fork Carbon Creek, and Lava Canyon.
SEASONS:	Fall through spring, though from a water standpoint spring would be best.
MAPS:	Nankoweap and Vishnu Temple quadrangles (both 15 minute) and North Kaibab National Forest Map.
ESCAPE ROUTES:	Via Nankoweap Trail to North Rim or Colorado River; Kwagunt Creek, east fork of Carbon Creek, and Lava Canyon to Colorado River.

Lava Canyon to Tanner Canyon via Beamer Trail

Cross Colorado River and follow Beamer Trail to Tanner Canyon (see Beamer Trail in Chapter 8). Approximately 4 miles; camping at large; water in Colorado River; use Vishnu Temple Quadrangle. *Escape routes* via Tanner Trail or river runners.

Tanner Canyon to Unkar Creek

Hitch a ride above Tanner Canyon Rapids, or cross river on west side of Tanner Canyon Delta above Basalt Canyon Creek. Follow right bank (north side) from Basalt Canyon Creek through heavy stands of tammies along Dox Sandstone to Unkar Creek; approximately 5 miles; no camping on Unkar Delta; water in Colorado River; use Vishnu Temple Quadrangle. *Escape routes* via Tanner Trail or river runners.

Unkar Creek to East End of North Tonto Plateau

This section gains the saddle between the Tabernacle and Rama Shrine. Immediately west of Unkar Creek is a prominent ridgeline of Dox Sandstone. Climb up this ridgeline (north) to a break in the Tapeats Sandstone, and take a narrow strip of Tonto Plateau to the saddle on the north side of the Tabernacle. Approximately 4 miles and 2,000 feet of elevation gain; camping at large; water in Colorado River, sometimes seasonal water in Unkar Creek; use Vishnu Temple Quadrangle. *Escape routes* via Tanner Trail or river runners.

The Tabernacle to Clear Creek via North Tonto Plateau

The Tabernacle saddle is the most practical starting point for using the north Tonto Plateau as the main thoroughfare for proceeding westward through the inner Canyon below the North Rim. But because the North Rim drains into the Canyon, the north Tonto is for the most part narrower, steeper, and rockier than the south Tonto. To make matters more interesting, the tributary drainages on the north Tonto are generally longer and steeper. And due to the fact that the north Tonto is devoid of trail until you reach the Clear Creek Trail, you'll have to decide if your best route is to follow the outer edge of the Tonto Plateau near the Tapeats rim, or whether you should stay high and hug the base of the Muav in order to shortcut what may seem like long and circuitous miles.

From the Tabernacle saddle, follow the Tonto around the south side of Sheba Temple to the head of Asbestos Canyon; there's a break in the Tapeats you'll have to eyeball in order to reach seasonal water on the floor of Asbestos Canyon or the Colorado River. To continue westward, take the Tonto from the head of Asbestos Canyon until you reach the base of the saddle on the north side of Newberry Butte; there's a break through the Muav in this saddle, which will cut a few miles off your Tonto route to the head of Vishnu Creek. If you do this route in the spring, you can generally find seasonal water in the head of Vishnu, which also makes a good camping spot.

It's a long but otherwise straightforward haul from the head of Vishnu Creek around the base of Hall, Hawkins and the Howlands buttes to the Clear Creek descent, with no shortcuts worth writing home about in between. The standard descent into Clear Creek is down the drainage running northeast from the Angel's Gate/Wotan's Throne saddle; however, if you're a fair climber, there's a steeper descent through the Tapeats into Clear Creek due north of the Howlands Butte off the point adjacent to number 4000 on your Bright Angel Quadrangle, and you'll be able to eyeball it to make sure it's the right chimney before commiting yourself. From the bed of Clear Creek at the foot of this descent line, head downstream (west) for a few hundred yards, before turning north up the main arm of Clear Creek where you'll pick up the Clear Creek Trail. There is perennial water in Clear Creek. Allow 1½ to 2 days minimum; selected camping; water in Clear Creek and Colorado River at mouth of Unkar Creek and Asbestos Canyon; seasonal water in floor of Asbestos Canyon at the head of Vishnu Creek; use Vishnu Temple and Bright Angel quadrangles. *Escape routes* to Colorado River via Unkar Creek and Asbestos Canyon, and to Phantom Ranch via Clear Creek Trail.

Clear Creek to Phantom Ranch via the Clear Creek Trail

This is unquestionably the best section of trail on this entire route, and it's straightforward and easy to follow all the way to the Phantom Ranch beer hall; 9 miles; selected camping; water in Clear Creek and Phantom Ranch; emergency water sometimes found in Sumner Wash in Tapeats; use Bright Angel Quadrangle.

Additional Considerations: The Clear Creek Trail is most frequently used by hikers coming down the South Kaibab and Bright Angel trails, normally a two-day trek from the South Rim. But once you've set up camp at Clear Creek, you can explore Cheyava Falls to the north, the Colorado River to the south, or just hang out and watch the cotton blow off the cottonwood trees.

Phantom Ranch to Crystal Rapids via Utah Flats and the North Tonto

From the north end of Bright Angel Campground (opposite the aluminum bridge spanning Bright Angel Creek), follow a track up through the schist to a notch through the Bass Formation, which is the passageway to the Hakatai Formation. The tendency is to want to climb high at this point, but stay in the Hakatai around the base of Cheops Pyramid until you reach the northwest arm of Ninetyone Mile Creek; climb up this arm to the Tonto.

From Ninetyone Mile Creek, stay on the Tonto around the base of Isis Temple to the northeast arm of Trinity Creek; this arm will take you to Trinity Creek, where seasonal water can sometimes be found, but it's pretty foul-tasting stuff. You can also use the upper-west arm of Trinity to regain the Tonto, but it's not much good as a shortcut if you don't need water.

Continue on the Tonto around the tentacles of Tower of Set, the head of Ninetyfour Mile, until you reach the westernmost arm coming down off Tower of Ra. This arm points to the general direction of the descent to Crystal Creek, but you'll have to eyeball the route down the correct drainage before committing yourself. This descent is longer, looser, and more difficult than the steep descent to Clear Creek. Allow 1½ to 2 days minimum; camping at large; water at Phantom Ranch and Crystal Creek; seasonal water sometimes available in Trinity Creek; use Bright Angel Quadrangle. *Escape routes* to Phantom Ranch and Crystal Creek at river via this route.

Crystal Creek to Tuna Creek via the North Side of the Colorado River

This little stretch through the schist and quartz is as short, difficult, and time-consuming as any mile-and-a-half on this route, and from Crystal Creek to Tuna Creek it's just a matter of picking and scrambling your way along the path of least resistance. Approximately 1½ to 2 miles; not the most ideal place to camp in the Canyon, but suitable spots can be found near Crystal Creek and mouth of Tuna; water in Crystal Creek and Colorado River; use Bright Angel and Havasupai Point quadrangles. *Escape routes* either back the way you came or with river runners who pull over to scout Crystal Rapids on the right bank several hundred yards above Crystal Creek.

Tuna Creek to the North Bass Trail via North Tonto

From the mouth of Tuna Creek, the first major fault to the west will take you back up through the schist and Tapeats to the Tonto Plateau. Once on the Tonto Plateau, stay on it around Scorpion Ridge and all the way through and around Monadnock Amphitheater, until you reach the western arm of Evans Butte. There are several faults leading into the Hotauta drainage, but you'll have to eyeball your line of descent to the foot of the North Bass Trail before you commit yourself; this descent is comparable to the Crystal Creek descent in steepness, length, and difficulty, so use extra care following one of several steep lines south of the south arm of Hotauta Canyon. Allow 1 to 1½ days minimum; camping at large; water at Colorado River; emergency water sometimes available in second major drainage north of the west pincher of Scorpion Ridge, and below Tapeats in both arms of Monadnock Amphitheater; use Havasupai Point Quadrangle. *Escape routes* either back the way you came or at Colorado River above and below Bass Rapids.

Bass Rapids to Muav Saddle via North Bass Trail

See North Bass Trail description, above; 14 miles and 5,317-vertical-foot elevation gain; camping at large; water in Colorado River, Shinumo Creek, and White Creek below east side of Muav Saddle; use Powell Plateau Quadrangle and North Kaibab National Forest Map. *Escape routes* out Swamp Point Road or at Colorado River.

Muav Saddle to Thunder River Trail via Saddle Canyon and Tapeats Creek

Head west off Muav Saddle straight down the drainage through the brush below the old CCC cabin, and follow it all the way to the Thunder River confluence. There is no trail along this stretch, but it's one of the prettiest stretches on the entire North Rim route. There aren't any real route-finding difficulties either, but several of the upper formations may require doubling back and scouting a descent line when cliffed-out; these pourovers can generally be gotten around on their right (or north) side—specifically the Esplanade and Supai sandstones. Surprisingly, the Redwall presents no difficulties other than an 8-foot jump into a small plunge pool, which can be downclimbed, and it's unquestionably the finest section of Saddle Canyon until you reach Tapeats Narrows. The narrows have to be crossed, as there's no practical way to skirt them above on the right all the way to Thunder River. Make sure your trip isn't planned during peak runoff. If it is, and you've succeeded in somehow fording—i.e., body-surfing—the narrows of Tapeats Creek, there's really no way to safely ford Tapeats Creek below the Thunder River confluence; you'll have to ford Tapeats Creek above this confluence, or find a stout-enough stalk from a century plant and pole-vault it, in order to reach the trunk of a cottonwood tree that spans the mouth of Thunder River and links you back up with the Thunder River Trail. Allow 1 to 1½ days; camping at large above Tapeats Narrows, in Tapeats Campground below; water in Muav Saddle springs, Tapeats Creek, and Thunder River; use Powell Plateau Quadrangle. *Escape routes* via Muav Saddle to Swamp Point, Tapeats Creek to Colorado River; and Thunder River to Monument Point.

Thunder River Trail Exit

See Thunder River Trail, above; 9 miles to Monument Point via Bill Hall Trail; camping at large above Redwall; water in Thunder River; use Powell Plateau Quadrangle and North Kaibab National Forest Map.

CHAPTER 10

The Colorado River

This guide would be incomplete if it ignored the numerous day hikes that can be taken from river level along the Colorado River.

Unlike the sections on the South Rim, North Rim, and Little Colorado River Gorge, which have a rim-to-river and trans-Canyon hiker's perspective and deal with those areas within—and immediately adjacent to—the old Grand Canyon National Park boundaries, the Colorado River section has more of a river-to-rim perspective and addresses the interests of both private and commercial river runners who raft from Mile 0 at Lees Ferry to Mile 225 at Diamond Creek—and beyond. As an aid to private river runners boating this stretch during the off-season, this section also includes practical river-to-rim escape routes in the event standard emergency-signal procedures prove unsuccessful. All hikes and escape routes are listed by River Mile and, when possible, topographical name in descending order from Lees Ferry to Lake Mead.

As an additional aid to this section, the author strongly recommends carrying two other guides in your ammo box. *The Colorado River in Grand Canyon: A Guide*, by Larry Stevens, is a comprehensive river guide illustrated with a map detailing, among other things, river-mile numbers, rapids, and some of the hikes described in this section (available at the Grand Canyon Natural History Association bookstore on the South Rim or by writing Red Lake Books, P.O. Box 1315, Flagstaff, AZ 86002). *A River Runner's Guide to the History of the Grand Canyon*, by Kim Crumbo, is just that, detailing the river's colorful history mile by mile and highlighted by a detailed series of river maps (available at GCNHA bookstore or by writing Johnson Publishing Company, 1880 South 57th Court, Boulder, CO 80301).

Lees Ferry Quadrangle (15 Minute)

Mile O, Lees Ferry

Lees Ferry is situated on the Colorado River near the mouth of the Paria Canyon—the first of four major tributary canyons that drain into the Colorado River in Arizona. While few river runners take the opportunity to explore this canyon before putting on the river, there are a number of destinations that make pleasant afternoon or early morning strolls. From the wooden bridge crossing the Paria River, you can head north and walk along a dirt road that will take you past "Lonely Dell" and the Lees Ferry cemetery to the southern boundary of the Paria Canyon Primitive Area. From here, a trail hugs the left (west) side of Paria River, which you can take past several other historic sites around the base of a bluff where the old grade parts with the Paria Canyon route. (For a detailed description of the 35-mile-long hike through the Paria Canyon Primitive Area, see *Hiking the Southwest*, a Sierra Club Totebook by Dave Ganci.) No spring water available for short day hikes.

Mile 3, Cathedral Wash

The mouth of this wash is sometimes used by river runners who put on the river too late in the afternoon to make more than a few miles. It's an enjoyable and straightforward 1½-mile hike up this wash to the Lees Ferry road; this route is sometimes used by boatmen to mail one last letter at the Marble Canyon, AZ, post office several miles further. You can hike to the rim from here in an emergency. No water en route.

Mile 8, Badger Canyon

You can take a mile hike up the boulder-strewn bed of Badger Canyon until it dead-ends, for all practical purposes, in an overhanging section of Kaibab Limestone. No water en route.

Mile 8, Jackass Canyon

This canyon is sometimes used by Navajo Indians to fish the Colorado River, and less successfully by pirate river runners netted in NPS stakeouts. Escape route to Highway 89A. Approximately 3 miles. No water.

Tanner Wash Quadrangle (15 Minute)

Mile 12, Salt Water Wash

It's a 4-mile hike up Salt Water Wash to Highway 89A. Cairns mark the way up the steep, boulder-clogged lower half of this route until the wash opens up and the walking becomes more enjoyable. Escape route: This is the last practical escape route to reach Highway 89A and the phone at Marble Canyon Lodge. No water.

Emmett Wash Quadrangle (15 Minute)

Mile 20.5, North Canyon

You can take a mile-long hike up the bed of North Canyon through the sand and talus, then along the Supai Sandstone ledges. No water. Great place for a "rock talk."

Mile 22, Left Bank

Widely spaced cairns mark the steep, sometimes exposed route through the Supai Sandstone to a good viewpoint approximately 1 mile out from camp. No water. Escape route: A route has been linked from the Supai through the Coconino Sandstone to reach the rim and Highway 89A. However, this exposed and waterless route should be avoided by inexperienced canyoneers.

Mile 29, Shinumo Wash

More commonly known as Silver Grotto. A short side trip can be taken up this beautiful drainage. But a boat may be needed to ferry people from the pull-in immediately below the mouth of Shinumo to the start of this route. Several boulder moves on polished Muav Limestone may require spotting one another, and several cool plungepools must be swum in order to reach Silver Grotto.

Nankoweap Quadrangle (15 Minute)

Mile 34.8, Nautiloid Canyon

Named after the fossilized Nautiloids found in this canyon. The short side trip up Nautiloid Canyon also involves several boulder moves on polished limestone to reach its terminus at the base of an overhanging section of Redwall Limestone. Depending on river level, a boat may also be required to ferry people to the start of this enchanting route.

Mile 41, Buckfarm Canyon

A mile-long hike can be taken up Buckfarm Canyon, which involves some boulder-hopping and unexposed ledge walking.

Mile 47, Saddle Canyon

This canyon also makes a pleasant 2-mile roundtrip hike from the river. After the initial climb up from the river, the trail levels off, then threads the holly and redbuds before dead-ending in an appealing little waterfall.

Mile 50, Right Bank

A deer trail leads from the lower camp at Mile 50 to the mouth of Little Nankoweap Creek, 2 miles downstream. However, you'll probably cover more like 3 miles en route to Little Nankoweap, because what trail there is undulates through dense stands of tammies where the popular breaststroke is required to make any headway. And when you're not swimming through the tammies, you'll have the opportunity to either boulder-hop or posthole through the mud.

Mile 52.3, Nankoweap Canyon

The steep, three-quarter-mile-long hike to the Anasazi storage bins is unquestionably the most frequently done hike in this area. However, there are several other options in the area worth doing. From the lower camp at the south end of Nankoweap Delta, frustrated distance runners can follow a well-marked 1½-mile lap that climbs over the neck of the delta, drops into Nankoweap Canyon and follows its right side to river level before contouring the eastern base of this delta back to your starting point. From this lower camp, hikers and runners can also follow a faint trail system downstream for approximately 1½ miles.

If all of these hikes fail to get your land legs back, perhaps the Nankoweap/Kwagunt loop hike will do the trick. To start this 10-mile-long trek, you pick up a non-maintained trail on the left (south) side of Nankoweap Creek. For the most part, it stays on the left side of Nankoweap Creek as it weaves and climbs its way over small boulders and through the cottonwood trees for a little over 2 miles to the confluence of the first major drainage coming down off the northwest side of Nankoweap Mesa. This is the beginning of the Butte Fault (see Chapter 9). Scramble up this distinct ridgeline until it forms a near-perfect razorback; it's "six of one, half a dozen of the other" whether you follow its east or west side, though the west side involves less scrambling. Follow this route as it contours around the west side of unnamed Peak 5058 to the Nankoweap Butte/Nankoweap Mesa saddle. From this saddle you have the option of descending into the drainage on the east or west, or continuing down this ridgeline; the drainage on the west sometimes has seasonal water. Continue down to the confluence of Kwagunt Creek, turn left (east), and start boulder-hopping your way back down to the river. Water can frequently be found in Kwagunt Creek, which is somewhat of a narrower drainage in its lower end than Nankoweap Creek. Although it is possible to hike the 4 miles back upstream at river level to the mouth of Nankoweap Creek, most river runners day hiking this loop prefer to be picked up at the camp immediately below Kwagunt Rapids rather than contend with the exotic riparian jungle between the two creeks.

Additional Considerations: The trails in the Nanko-

View of the Colorado River near Kwagunt Creek. *Photo by George H. H. Huey.*

weap Delta area are heavily braided. National Park Service volunteers have been trying to realign them over the last couple of years in order to prevent erosion—please take care to stay on the marked trails.

Vishnu Temple Quadrangle (15 Minute)

Mile 61.5, Little Colorado River Gorge

There are two popular day hikes up the mouth of the Little Colorado River: the obvious short jaunt to Beamer's cabin on the south bank, in the Tapeats Sandstone; and the 4½-mile hike to the Hopi Indians' sacred Sipapu. (Please note: In deference to Hopi religious beliefs, the author agrees the area should not be visited—or photographed—by non-Hopi. If you must pass by *Sipapu* en route to Salt Trail Canyon 6½ miles up from the Colorado River confluence, or coming down the Little Colorado River Gorge from Cameron, please exercise discretion in this area, as the Hopi know and revere it as the opening through which mankind originally emerged.)

Warning: Don't drink the water.

Mile 61.5 to 65.5, Left Side

You can day hike the Beamer Trail from the mouth of the Little Colorado River to Palisades Creek, where you can pick up a boat shuttle (see Chapter 8 for a description of the Beamer Trail). No water en route.

Mile 64.5, Carbon Creek

You can take a mile or mile-and-a-half hike up Carbon Creek to the prominent saddle on the west side of Chuar Lava hill; you can return by the same marked (but trail-less) route, or make your way down to the bed of Lava Canyon and continue to the river and a boat shuttle. No water en route.

Mile 65.5 to 68.5, Left Bank

A river trail and route goes from the mouth of Palisades Creek to the mouth of Tanner Canyon; this can be done as an out-and-back day hike from either of these canyons, or as a point-to-point hike from Palisades Creek to Tanner Canyon using a boat shuttle.

Mile 68.5, Tanner Trail

This trail is sometimes used by private river runners as an interchange to drop off folks who don't have enough time to make a two-week river trip, or to pick up new people who couldn't make it to the Ferry before their party shoved off. Shadeless and no water en route.

Escape Route: People at the Desert View Watch Tower on the South Rim are easily able to see a mirror flash from the mouth of Tanner Canyon; however, if inclement weather precludes emergency mirror signals or hampers radio communication, there's an NPS ranger station at Desert View east of the Tanner trailhead, as well as a public phone (see Chapter 8 for a description of the Tanner Trail).

Mile 68.5 to Mile 71, Left Bank

There's a well-marked river trail that goes from the mouth of Tanner Canyon to the mouth of Cardenas Creek, which can either be hiked as an out-and-back hike from either of these two areas, or as a point-to-point hike from Tanner Canyon to Cardenas Creek using a boat shuttle (see "Tanner Canyon to Red Canyon" in Chapter 8).

Mile 69.5 to Mile 72.5, Right Side

During average river flows, it's possible to walk from the mouth of Basalt Canyon through the tammies along the Dox Sandstone to the mouth of Unkar Creek (see "Tanner Canyon to Unkar Creek" in Chapter 9).

Mile 71, Cardenas Creek

A steep but popular and heavily used trail goes from the mouth of Cardenas Creek a mile or so up to the Unkar Rapids overlook (see "Tanner Canyon to Red Canyon" in Chapter 8). No water en route.

Mile 71 to Mile77, Left Side

A difficult cross-country route goes from the mouth of Cardenas Creek to the Unkar Rapids overlook to the foot of the Tonto Trail at Hance Rapids (see "Tanner Canyon to Red Canyon" in Chapter 8).

Mile 72.5, Unkar Creek

Several trail variations cross the archaeologically significant Unkar Delta, so use care to use the most well-marked of trails in this area. Scientists are still studying this prehistoric Anasazi settlement, the largest in the inner Canyon, and careless foot travel will destroy valuable archaeological data.

Unkar Creek can be used to reach the east end of the north Tonto Plateau (see "Unkar Creek" in Chapter 9) and was used by climber and boatman George Bain to make an epic ascent of 7,529′ Vishnu Temple from the river—and back—in one long day in October 1979.

Mile 77, Escape Route

Two possible escape routes leave the Hance Rapids area on the left bank: the New Hance Trail, which climbs up to the South Rim via Red Canyon; and the Tonto/Grandview trails. If you've not been up the New Hance Trail, use the Tonto/Grandview combination; it's easier to follow, and there's perennial water en route. The Tonto and Grandview trails are described in Chapter 8.

Mile 81.3, Grapevine Creek Camp

From the camp above Grapevine Rapids, you can scramble along the schist on the left bank, gain the mouth of Grapevine Creek, and explore this rugged tributary. This route, which is both exposed and loose in several key sections, is not recommended for inexperienced canyoneers or weak rockclimbers. Also use Bright Angel Quadrangle (15 minute).

Bright Angel Quadrangle (15 Minute)

Mile 84, Clear Creek

From the small camp above Clear Creek on the right, the route into Clear Creek skirts up and around the dark amphibolite before dropping back down into the bed of this heavily visited creek. The first waterfall is located a half mile or so upstream. This waterfall can be passed on the left (west) side in order to continue up Clear Creek for as far as time will permit. Over the years, several boatmen have hiked up Clear Creek to the east end of the Clear Creek Trail, then over to Phantom Ranch, where they were picked up by a boat shuttle the same day.

Mile 87.6, Boat Beach, Right Bank

From Boat Beach you can cross the Kaibab Suspension Bridge and take the River Trail to Pipe Creek and return via the Bright Angel Bridge variant; you can hike upstream a small piece via the Gauging Station Trail, sometimes used by river runners ferrying departing passengers across the river from Last Chance; you can hike the Bright Angel Trail; or you can take the North Kaibab Trail north to the mouth of Phantom Creek, Ribbon Falls, or Roaring Springs. The North Kaibab Trail is described in Chapter 9.

Emergency Help: There's an NPS ranger station near the mouth of Bright Angel Creek, on the west side of the first bridge you approach coming from Boat Beach. There's also a pay phone there, but you have to reverse the charges or use a credit card.

Mile 95 to Mile 96, Left Side

You can hike up Hermit Creek to the Tonto Trail (see Chapter 8), and take the Tonto Trail over to Boucher Creek, which will take you back down to the river and a boat shuttle. This hike is seldom done by river runners, simply because Hermit Rapids is one of the best rides on the river before facing the Jaws of Death 3 miles downstream.

Escape Routes: Hermit and Boucher trails (see Chapter 8).

Mile 98, Crystal Creek

There are two short hikes near the mouth of Crystal Creek, and both have a certain blow-the-heart-right-out-of-your-chest quality to them. The shortest of the two hikes has seldom been missed by river runners since a flash flood formed this frightening rapid in 1966, and it involves a rather straightforward boulder-hop to the head of Crystal Rapid, where airbags are most frequently used on a Colorado River hike. The second hike is a bit longer, requires some rudimentary route-finding ability, and is usually done at a brisk pace by river runners in order to pick up their head boatman before he ends up swimming Tuna Creek Rapid as well.

Havasupai Point Quadrangle (15 Minute)

Mile 107.8, Bass Canyon

From the camp immediately above Bass Rapid on the left, you have to scramble downstream along the schist in order to gain the foot of the South Bass Trail, because the mouth of Bass Canyon cliffs-out right above the river. You can hike up the South Bass Trail to the Tonto Trail junction, and double back due north along the Tonto Trail below Wallace Butte to a second junction northeast of Tyndall Dome. This point makes a fine overlook up canyon or down, before taking the short right (east) fork of the trail back down to the South Bass Trail and camp.

Escape Route: The South Bass Trail is an easy-enough escape route, but unless you hike up it during the summer when the Pasture Wash Ranger Station is usually staffed, its value is questionable; it's some 30-odd miles west of Grand Canyon Village via a seldom-used dirt road (see the South Bass Trail description in Chapter 8).

Mile 108.2, Shinumo Creek Camp

From the Upper Shinumo Creek Camp, the North Bass Trail climbs up over a prominent ridgeline designated BM 2917 before dropping back down to the bed of Shinumo Creek; it follows the right side of Shinumo Creek until Bass's old camp is reached shortly after.

Do not disturb the old tools and relics in this camp!

Escape Route: Assuming you can find your way up the North Bass Trail and reach the trailhead at Swamp Point, it's at least another 20-odd miles via old fire roads to the Kaibab Lodge; so you should weigh all factors carefully before trying to use the North Bass Trail as an escape route (see the North Bass Trail description in Chapter 9).

Mile 114, Right Side

From the camp at Mile 114 you can scramble up a small drainage to the base of the Tapeats and traverse it eastward until you find a break leading up to the Tonto Plateau. Taking a faint burro trail north along this bench for a mile or so will offer good views of 6,275′ Mt. Huethawli on the South Rim and 6,740′ Wheeler Point on the North Rim. It looks like it would be feasible to follow this section of the Tonto Plateau eastward to Burro Canyon and Shinumo Creek. No water en route.

Mile 115.5, Left Side

The route to Upper Elves Chasm and Keyhole Arch leaves the proximity of the second tributary drainage downstream from Garnet Canyon on river left. There used to be a small low-water camp at the foot of this rugged route, since flushed downstream during a flood control exercise by the Bureau of Reclamation in the summer of 1983. The route follows a faint trail up to a break in an obvious travertine deposit; this exposed section is protected somewhat by a rope anchored to a boulder that may or may not be anchored itself. Once atop this section, it's a relatively straightforward trek for a mile or so along this bench to a seven-foot-high stone monument. Turn left (south) and head along the east rim of Royal Arch Creek, where an exposed move or two in the Muav Limestone will take you to the upper floor of this drainage; if you continue downstream, you'll hike under a precarious-looking rock stack and natural arch at the head of a waterfall that feeds Middle Elves Chasm immediately below. From the rock stack, look up to the east and you'll see Keyhole Arch in the Redwall rim above. No water en route.

Mile 116.5, Elves Chasm

The two short jaunts into Lower and Middle Elves are both obvious enough, since the area is so heavily visited; however, the route up to Middle Elves involves several exposed traverses on polished Elves Chasm Gneiss. Warning: Don't drink the water!

Mile 120, Blacktail Canyon

The most frequently done hike in this area is the short hike up the floor of this charming little canyon. However, you can find a route, somewhat exposed, through the Tapeats Sandstone near the mouth of Blacktail Canyon on its east side; this line will provide access to the Tonto Plateau, which you can follow at least as far eastward as the camp at Mile 119. However, the descent off the Tonto Plateau through the Tapeats Sandstone requires careful scouting before you'll be able to eyeball the least-intimidating line back down to river level at Mile 119. (This upper route should not be attempted by weak climbers or inexperienced canyoneers.) From Mile 119, you can scramble back along the river to the mouth of Blacktail. No water on Tonto.

Powell Plateau Quadrangle (15 Minute)

Mile 132, Dubendorff Rapid

From the camp immediately below the mouth of Stone Creek, you can make at least two outstanding hikes in this area. Two to three miles of hiking up the course of Stone Creek will take you to one of the prettiest waterfalls in the Canyon; or you can find the break in the Bass Formation and take a faint trail several miles west along the Hakatai Shale, around Hundred and Thirtythree Mile Creek to the rim overlooking the mouth of Tapeats Creek. From the Tapeats Creek overlook, a more frequently used trail follows the east side of Tapeats Creek and will eventually take you to the floor of the creek itself.

Hikers in Blacktail Canyon. *Photo by George H. H. Huey.*

Mile 133.7, Tapeats Creek

This is one of the must stops for most river runners, and is frequently a layover day for others, because Tapeats Creek provides access to three hikes in this area: the popular, well-marked 4-mile trail to the headwaters of Thunder River, which leaves the west side of Tapeats Creek and climbs immediately through the Diabase and Bass formations before linking up with the well-trod trail to Thunder River (cairns mark several creek crossings); the more arduous trek up from the confluence of Thunder River and Tapeats Creek to Tapeats Cave; and the hike from Thunder River, across Surprise Valley, to Deer Creek Falls and a boat shuttle at the river.

Escape Routes: The Bill Hall Trail is another one of those straightforward but remote escape routes. The trek from Monument to the Kaibab Lodge can be an interminably long one if Big Saddle Camp is unoccupied (see the Thunder River Trail description in Chapter 9).

Kanab Point Quadrangle (15 Minute)

Mile 136, Deer Creek

There are three fairly straightforward day hikes to do in this area. The mile-long romp up through Deer Creek Narrows is the most frequently done hike; the trail up to the Narrows is more obvious than the numerous little white hands that adorn its Tapeats Sandstone walls. The trail up from the Narrows, over Surprise Valley to Thunder River, is far more strenuous but is becoming increasingly popular. One of the most rewarding and least frequently done day hikes in the area, however, is the short, steep trek from Surprise Valley up to the 4,537′ summit of Cogswell Butte. From the Cogswell Butte saddle on the west end of Surprise Valley, take the most prominent north/south ridgeline from the saddle and follow it cross-country toward the summit of Cogswell. En route you'll have to make an eight-foot-long boulder move in the Redwall before zig-zagging your way through the Supai, but the hike presents no real technical difficulties if you use good route-finding judgment. From the summit of Cogswell, you'll have an incredible view of 7,422′ Steamboat Mountain to the east, and neighboring Swamp Point, Muav Saddle, and Powell Plateau; to the south, you can take in virtually all of Great Thumb Mesa—from Apache Point to the mouth of Havasu Creek; to the west, 6,092′ Fishtail Mesa can be readily picked out; and to the north, Indian Hollow and 6,603′ Bridger's Knoll. Allow 25 minutes each way from Surprise Valley. Your escape route from the river via the Bill Hall Trail (described in Chapter 9) should be carefully weighed.

Warning: Watch out for poison ivy on the Deer Creek Trail near river level; it's the only place in the Grand Canyon other than Vasey's Paradise, where the stuff grows.

Mile 143.5, Kanab Creek

It's approximately 4 miles up Kanab Creek to the falls of Whispering Falls Canyon. This is an enjoyable hike through a fairly wide canyon, draped here and there by several travertine falls on its west side; you have to cross Kanab Creek a fair number of times, but you'll also get to skirt across some neat Muav ledges.

From the mouth of Whispering Falls Canyon you can trek Kanab Creek some 50-odd miles to Kanab, Utah, much the way Major John Wesley Powell and his men did in 1872 when he concluded his second voyage down Big Red at the mouth of Kanab Creek. For a more detailed description of that route, see "The Wrinkled Pink Walls of Kanab Canyon" by Rosalie Goldman, *Arizona Highways*, July 1964, pp. 17–18 and 31–35.

Mile 154.5, Olo Canyon

You have to perform two neat tricks in order to get into the mouth of this gem—both of which can be unnerving if someone in your party hasn't been down the 'crik before. The first involves climbing up a dangling rope ladder; the second involves a somewhat slippery and exposed climb up a modern set of "Moki steps" that have been etched into a 20-foot-high travertine falls. Both of these moves are technically easy enough going up them; it's after people have hiked a few miles up this canyon and started rushing back to their boats that problems most commonly occur. So unless everybody in your party is a strong climber, bring a rope to belay one another back down these two abrupt drops. The nearest escape route (if somebody *does* get injured in a fall) is the run to Supai; that usually entails running Upset Rapid with an injured person (which can be a problem for first-time boaters running the Colorado River between 1,000 to 16,000 cfs), making the pull in at Havasu (which can also be a problem for first-time boaters), then running 7½ miles to Havasupai Ranger Station and phone above Mooney Falls (also a problem, since you probably wouldn't start up Havasu until dark). So while this is probably one of the most enticing tributary canyons in the Grand Canyon, just make sure your exits are safely covered.

Mile 148, Matakatamiba

Also known as Matkat, this is another tributary canyon that has been carved and polished through the Muav Limestone; and while it's naturally more heavily visited than Olo, it's also a good alternative to Olo for inexperienced canyoneers simply because it's an easy and enjoyable hike that covers similar terrain as that of Olo. (Please note: In deference to the Havasupai Indians' religious beliefs, the author agrees the area a mile above the mouth of Matakatamiba should not be visited by non-Havasupai; they know and revere this sacred area, and many others around Great Thumb Mesa.)

Tuckup Canyon Quadrangle (15 Minute)

Mile 156.8, Havasu Canyon

The 4-mile hike to Beaver Falls is the most frequently done hike by river runners in Havasu Canyon; the way is obvious, though you will have to look for cairns that mark the five creek crossings you'll make en route to

Beaver Falls. If you're a fair swimmer, and treat your boatman right, maybe he or she will take you into the Green Room. Mooney Falls is certainly the most spectacular falls in Havasu Canyon, and in order to reach it you have to climb up and traverse the travertine deposits on the east side of Beaver Falls, then ford Havasu Creek another three times before reaching the base of Mooney 1½ miles farther. See Chapter 8 for a description of Havasu Trail. You can also use the Kanab Point Quadrangle.

Escape Routes: It's 7½ miles to the Havasupai Ranger Station and private phone above Mooney Falls; Supai is another 1½ miles beyond this ranger station.

Emergency Radio
Frequencies: Lees Ferry to Havasu—122.9.
Havasu to Pierce Ferry—123.05.

Warning: Don't drink the water in Havasu Creek, and if you have any open cuts, don't swim in it.

Mile 164.4, Tuckup Canyon

If you miss the Havasu pull-in, you get to hang out at Tuckup Canyon, in which case you'll have plenty of time to discover the area for yourself.

Beyond Havasu

After the big hiking day in Havasu, folks start getting pumped to run Mile 179.5 rapid. And while there are many hiking opportunities below Havasu Canyon, they don't seem to be hiked as heavily as the areas above Havasu Canyon; then, again maybe Mile 179.5 rapid has a lot to do with this sudden lack of hiker enthusiasm. Here are some areas worth exploring:

Mile 166.5, National Canyon

A half-mile to three-quarter-mile hike can be taken up its bed to an enchanting boulder problem.

Mile 168, Fern Glen

Another short but charming hike. Donald Davis reports in his notes, *A Traverse of the Colorado River From Lee's Ferry to Lake Mead*: "There is a way out as prospectors were here in 1932."

Mile 171.4, Stairway Canyon

In those same notes ex-ranger Davis also poses the possibility that Gateway and Mohawk canyons may have been used together as a cross-Canyon route. This may even have been a cross-Canyon route the Paiute Indians used when, as J. Donald Hughes writes in *The Story of Man at the Grand Canyon*, they "sometimes ventured into the Grand Canyon in search of rock salt and mescal, and sometimes crossed it to contact the Havasupais to the south." Or it could have been the route Mormon pioneer and explorer Jacob Hamblin used when, as author Hughes further notes, he "induced the Kaibab Paiute Chief, Chuar, to locate springs and trails for Powell, including one down to the Colorado River in the Grand Canyon near Toroweap."

Mile 179.1, Lava Falls Trail

With the possible exception of prospector James White, who may have successfully run the steepest drop on the Colorado River on a crude log raft two years prior to Major John Wesley Powell's first successful descent, few river runners have missed this short, usually hot, hike through the black lava to a heart-thumping overlook.

Escape Route: 1½ miles up the Toroweap and 6 miles by dirt road to the seasonally staffed Tuweep Ranger Station; no water en route. Another emergency option is line-of-sight radio contact or mirror flashes with chopper pilots using the helipad on river left at Mile 183 or with the fixed-wing aircraft flying over the area.

Mile 188, Whitmore Wash

In the past, several commercial river outfitters have used this steep, 2-mile-long trail to "interchange" outgoing passengers with incoming passengers, which is worth noting from an emergency standpoint, if not a hiking one. However, a deal may have been struck with the Hualapai Indians to use a helipad on reservation land on the south side of the river (river left), in which case line-of-sight radio contact or mirror flashes may be your best bet.

Mile 225.7, Diamond Creek

Takeout. Peach Springs is located 22 miles up the Diamond Creek Roak. Even during the off-season you should be able to hitch a ride through the Hualapai heartland in the event help is not readily available at Diamond Creek.

Mile 229, Travertine Canyon

It's a half-hour climb past Travertine Falls to the Tonto Plateau; follow the Tonto west for several spectacular miles. Old burro trails frequently skirt the very edge of the Tapeats Sandstone.

Mile 237, Bridge Canyon City

This was yet another dam-threatened area in the Grand Canyon. It's 15 minutes up to the Tonto Plateau, which you can take at least as far west as Separation Canyon several miles distant.

Mile 246, Spencer Canyon

To gain the Tonto Plateau, ascend the first major drainage up from the mouth of Spencer Canyon on the east side; it'll take around 20 minutes to reach this section of Tonto, which, if you proceed eastward, has more difficult footing than either the Travertine or Bridge City sections. It also has one of the densest stands of teddy bear cholla you're likely to encounter on the Tonto Plateau anywhere in Grand Canyon National Park and vicinity.

That's about it for most river runners, who'll motor most of the way out to Pierce Ferry at Mile 279.5.

Emergency considerations below Spencer Canyon: Usually recreational traffic and N.P.S. patrols ply the still waters upstream to Spencer Canyon—and beyond. You shouldn't have much problem hitching a ride back to Pierce's Ferry, or to the phone at Meadview Ranger Station.

CHAPTER 11

Little Colorado River Gorge

First kayaked by Brad Dimock and Tim Cooper in March 1978, the Little Colorado River Gorge is a dark serpentine crevice of Brobdingnagian proportions. Its headwaters begin atop 11,403′ Mt. Baldy—*dzil ligai* ("white mountain"), sacred to the Apache Indians. That's several hundred miles above the confluence of Little Colorado with *the* Colorado in the eastern Grand Canyon. The upper end of the Little Colorado River offers some outstanding backpacking opportunities in the spruce, aspen, and ponderosa forests of the White Mountains. (For trail descriptions and access information on that area, see *Hiking the Southwest*, a Sierra Club Totebook by Dave Ganci.)

The last 57 miles of this gorge are the most appealing from a canyoneering standpoint, a stretch equal to the 35-mile trek down Paria Canyon in charm and difficulty. From Cameron to the Colorado River confluence, the Little Colorado River Gorge barrels its way down what Tim Cooper (who first kayaked it) described as a "gradient more than three times as steep as the river into which it flows." In the process the Little Colorado cuts its way through Permian formations "of resistant sandstones, limestones, and shales that form the upper walls of the Grand Canyon."

To begin this multiday trek, drive to Cameron, which is located 74 miles north of Flagstaff on U.S. 89. The riverbed can be reached by taking the dirt road just south of the Cameron Bridge on its east side. From the Cameron Bridge the way is obvious all the way to the Colorado River confluence 57 miles downstream; there's never really any danger of getting lost. There are two other more important considerations, however: water sources and the season. There is no perennial water between the bridge and the first spring above Blue Springs 35 miles downstream. The water of Blue Springs is high enough in carbonates to render it almost unpalatable unless doctored with ERG or some other powdered drink mix—unless you're in a dire emergency. That fact, perhaps, has more than anything else to do with the season you should undertake this trek. Unless it's a dry year, with little runoff coming off the White Mountains and Colorado Plateau, spring is out of the question; the gorge will either have enough water in it for expert kayakers to boat it (around 750 cfs is considered ideal for this run, assuming you have a Colorado River permit to boat the Colorado River below the confluence), or it will be so muddy that your trek will become a nightmare of postholing through ankle-deep muck from one waterhole to the next. From mid-May to the first week of June—again, depending on the runoff—there is a narrow window during which this gorge can be trekked: when the mud has been sun-baked to near-ideal footing, and when there are plenty of waterholes to preclude the necessity of carrying more than a gallon or gallon and a half of water at a time. However, you must be physiologically adapted to heat stress, as the temperature in the gorge exceeds 105 degrees, and upstream winds blasting across your exit route along the Beamer Trail can make several sections unnerving for non-hang-gliders. The remainder of the summer is out of the question, due either to extreme heat and/or flash-flood dangers during the rains. So, unless you hit that late spring/early summer window, you should plan your trek down this gorge from late October through January, when the temperatures are far cooler and your chances of reaching the first water source (with the water you can carry on your back) are greatest.

The Route: Stay in the riverbed and follow the path of least resistance. The gorge gets exciting when it starts cutting through the Coconino Sandstone, about 8½ miles out; this is the narrowest stretch of the gorge, and you can see how rapidly it drops—an average of 28 feet per mile. There are some test holes in this section, drilled by Bureau of Reclamation engineers as a possible dam site; they also built the footbridge you'll see spanning the Narrows 70 feet above. Like the Narrows in Paria Canyon, this is not the most opportune spot to be hiking during any kind of runoff; it's sheer-walled and a mere 30-odd feet wide.

A half mile or so downstream from the Narrows, the gorge widens again and sluices through broken sections of Coconino. Between approximately Miles 9 and 11, you'll be able to see the first scenic overlook high above on the southern rim. If you get into trouble along this stretch, use your signal mirror to flash for help.

When the author trekked this route from Cameron to the head of the Tanner Trail, May 21–25, 1984, he began seeing water pretty regularly from this point on down.

About 11 miles out, there's a gauging station on the left; from here to the cable crossing another half mile or so downstream there's a section of trail that stays about 50 feet above the bed on its west side and connects the gauging station with the cable crossing and old Green Shack. If you've got plenty of water, there are some nice places to camp in this area, but if you're running low, you'd probably better crank out a few more miles down to Dead Indian Canyon.

From Cameron to Dead Indian Canyon the footing is generally excellent—assuming you hit the right conditions—and is comprised of hard-packed silt or dried mud. It sometimes gets gnarly when the Little C. begins making abrupt descents, however, in which case you'll either be threading or jumping over boulders. About 2 miles down from Dead Indian Canyon, the gorge begins cutting through the Supai Sandstone, and at Mile 23 it makes a dogleg turn through Hellhole Bend. About 7 or 8 miles below Hellhole Bend, the gorge passes through the Redwall Formation.

There are some fine camping areas about a half mile

above Waterhole Canyon; it makes a good objective for day 2 if you're trucking for water but don't quite have enough spit left to make it to Blue Springs. You should encounter your first springs just below Waterhole Canyon, which is about 35 miles downstream from Cameron. Between Waterhole Canyon and Blue Springs, another 5 or so miles downstream, you'll go through a narrow Redwall section that has no less than a half dozen springs gurgling out of the wall on its east side. And if your feet haven't been wet to this point, they soon will be—all the way to the Colorado River.

Approximately 42 miles downstream from Cameron, you'll reach Blue Springs; it bubbles out of the west wall into several travertine pools. While these travertine pools aren't as high as the spectacular big falls in Havasu Canyon, the color of the water is far prettier. This makes an excellent rest and swimming spot. Tough miles lie ahead. From Blue Springs, the roughest hiking you'll encounter on this trek—next to Hell's Half Mile below Waterhole Canyon—will be the 7 or 8 miles down to the mouth of Salt Trail Canyon. An air mattress would come in handy for the numerous deep fords you'll have to make before reaching the first travertine dams, which provide natural footbridges from one side to the other; it's these travertine dams that provide the greatest obstacle to foot travel (and kayak descents), but if you scout the way, you'll usually find passage through along the left bank.

Below the last of these dams, your best course will probably be to stay on the left side of the river all the way to Salt Trail Canyon. There are several dense stands of tammies and arrowweed on the right side that are difficult to get through especially, at the end of a long third day of hiking. Salt Trail Canyon and several other camping areas immediately below.

From Salt Trail Canyon, plan on another day of trekking down to Beamer Trail and on to the foot of the Tanner Trail (described in Chapter 8)—the exit route for this section of the Little Colorado River Gorge. Camping is not allowed within the boundaries of Grand Canyon National Park at the confluence of the Little Colorado and the Colorado River.

Additional Considerations: The 16-mile roundtrip hike from the Cameron Bridge to the Narrows makes a challenging day hike, and the 23-mile roundtrip hike to Cable Crossing is a good overnighter.

PRIMARY ACCESS TRAILS & ROUTES: Cameron Bridge and Tanner Trail. Contact BRO for trail descriptions and access information for Blue Springs and Salt Trail Canyon trails. See "The Lower Gorge of the Little Colorado" by J. H. Butchart, *Arizona Highways*, Sept. 1965, pp. 34–42 for trail descriptions and access information for the following, abandoned rim-

	to-river trails: Horse Trail, Moody Trail, Piute Trail, and Indian Maid Trail.
ELEVATION:	4,218 feet at Cameron Bridge to 2,700 plus or minus feet at Colorado River.
TOTAL ELEVATION LOSS:	1,518 vertical feet.
MILEAGE:	57 miles from Cameron to confluence. Bureau of Reclamation counts miles upstream from confluence, with Colorado River being Mile O and Cameron Mile 57.
WATER:	Blue Springs area.
SEASONS:	Mid-to-late May, and late October through January. Summer can be deadly, and spring walking can be atrocious—depending on runoff.
MAPS:	Cameron, Coconino Point, Blue Springs, and Vishnu Temple quadrangles (all 15 minute).
ESCAPE ROUTES:	Cameron, Colorado River confluence, Beamer/Tanner trails to South Rim.

EMERGENCY SIGNALS: Best spot for mirror flashes to be observed is line of sight from bed of Little Colorado River to Rim vistas between 9–11 miles below Cameron.

NEAREST SUPPLY POINTS: Cameron, Flagstaff, Page, South Rim.

Climbers of Temples and Buttes

(Within and immediately adjacent to old G.C.N.P. boundaries)

Name	Map	Kind of Rock	Elevation	First Known Ascent
Akaba, Mt.,	(K.P./s)	Coconino sandstone & Toroweap	5251′	George Bain, solo, 11-5-80
Alsap Butte,	(Nkwp.)	Supai sandstone	7494′	Donald Davis 6-14-72
Angel's Gate,	(B.T./n)	Coconino sandstone	6400′	Dave Ganci, Chuck Graff 4-72
Apache Point,	(N.P./s)	Kaibab limestone	6000+′	Unknown
Apollo Temple,	(V.T./n)	Supai limestone	6000+′	Butchart 7-17-65 (first ascent unknown)
Awatubi Crest,	(V.T./n)	Supai sandstone	5403′	Grubbs & Haggert 1-8-78
Ayer Point,	(V.T./s)	Redwall & Temple Butte limestones	5200′	Davis 6-26-72
Banta Point,	(V.T./n)	Redwall & Muav limestones	6522′	Ohlman 6-11-78
Barbenceta Butte,	(Nkwp)	Supai limestone	4699′	Harvey Butchart 8-2-63
Battleship, The,	B.A./s)	Hermit Shale	5600′	Unknown
Bourke Point,	(Nkwp)	Redwall limestone	6542′	Jim Ohlman & Richard Dutt 3-22-77
Brady Peak,	(V.T./n)	Coconino sandstone	8107′	Larry Triber, Jim Haggert Chris Beal, June 1975
Brahma Temple,	(B.A./n)	Coconino sandstone & Toroweap	7553′	Donald G. Davis & Clarence "Doc" Ellis 5-15-68

Climbers, continued

Name	Map	Kind of Rock	Elevation	First Known Ascent
Bridgers Knoll,	(P.P./n)	Coconino sandstone & Toroweap	6603′	Butchart, Chuck Johnson 6-3-65
Buddha Temple,	(B.A./n)	Coconino sandstone & Toroweap	7203′	Mark Brown, Chuck Parker, Bruce Grubbs 1973
Burro, Mt.,	(S./s)	Toroweap & Kaibab limestone	5684′	Butchart 4-11-66
Carbon Butte	(Nkwp)		4200+′	Butchart, Dick Springorum 6-12-63
Cardenas Butte,	(V.T./s)	Esplanade sandstone	6269′	Butchart, Nau Hiking Club 3-25-61
Castor Temple,	(H.P./s)	Coconino sandstone & Toroweap	6215′	Davis & Doty 4-19-71
Cheops Plateau,	(B.A./n)	Bright Angel shale	5200+′	Clubb, prior to 1960
Cheops Pyramid,	(B.A./n)	Redwall & Muav limestones	5392′	Clubb, 1960
Chiavria Point,	(V.T./n)	Redwall & Muav limestones	6217′	Butchart 6-8-73
Chuar Butte,	(V.T./n)	Hermit shale, Coconino sandstone, Toroweap and Kaibab limestone	6394′	Grubbs & Haggert 1-9-78 (first recorded ascent)
Chuar Lava Hill,	(V.T./n)	Cardenas lava & basalt	3945′	Butchart 6-10-59

Claude Birdseye Point,	(B.A./n)	Coconino sandstone & Toroweap	6975′	Doty (from Shiva) 6-14-78
Clement Powell Butte,	(B.A./n)	Hermit shale	6400+′	Ohlman, Jim Kirschvink 4-23-78
Cochise Butte,	(V.T./n)	Redwall limestone	6400+′	Butchart 6-7-73
Cogswell Butte,	(K.P./n)	Supai sandstone	4537′	Butchart 8-18-67
Colonade, The,	(B.A./n)	Coconino sandstone & Toroweap	7296′	Doty 9-5-70
Colter Butte,	(V.T./n)	Supai sandstone	7256′	Ohlman (solo) 3-23-77
Comanche Pt. Pinnacle,	(V.T./s)	Toroweap	6800+′	Trieber & Grubbs 4- -75
Confucius Temple,	(B.A./n)	Coconino sandstone & Toroweap	7081′	Butchart 9-3-73
Cope Butte,	(B.A./s)	Redwall limestone	4538′	Chuck Johnson
Coronado Butte,	(V.T./s)	Toroweap & Kaibab limestone	7108′	"Captain" John Hance & tourist before 1900
Dana Butte,	(B.A./s)	Redwall limestone	5030′ (& Pk.5232′)	Walters, Ohlman, Buccello, Martini & Kershflink 5-7-78
Deva Temple,	(B.A./n)	Coconino sandstone & Toroweap	7339′	Butchart 7-18-59
Diana Temple,	(H.P./s)	Toroweap & Kaibab limestone	6400+′	Butchart 7-3-60
Dox Castle,	(H.P./n)	Temple Butte limestone	4404′	Ohlman Party 10-25-80
Dragon, The,	(B.A./n)	Kaibab limestone	8015′	Doty (?)
Dragon Head,	(B.A./n)	Toroweap, & Kaibab limestone	7764′	Butchart 9-1-64 & Dirk Springorum

Climbers, continued

Name	Map	Kind of Rock	Elevation	First Known Ascent
Dunn Butte,	(B.A./n)		5714′	Ohlman party 11-28-80
Duppa Butte,	(V.T./n)	Redwall limestone	6400+′	Butchart, Bob Packard 5-31-73
Ehrenburg Point,	(Nkwp)	Redwall limestone	6800+′	Ken Walters, Ohlman, Kirschwink 5-23-78
Elaine Castle,	(P.P./n)	Coconino sandstone & Toroweap	7420′	Davis 6-27-69
Escalante Butte,	(V.T./s)	Hermit shale & Coconino sandstone	6529′	Sholing & Butchart (?)
Espejo Butte,	(V.T./s)	Coconino sandstone & Toroweap	6000+′	Butchart & Ohlman 9-6-75
Excalibur,			7051′	Bain, Glen Rink June 1981
Fishtail Mesa,	(K.P./n)	Coconino sandstone & Toroweap	6092′	U.S. Forest Service personnel
Fiske Butte,	(H.P./s)	Supai sandstone	4400+′	Doty 10- -74
Fossil Mountain,	(H.P./s)	Kaibab limestone	6400+′	Clubb & Doty
Freya Castle,	(V.T./n)	Coconino sandstone & Toroweap	7299′	Butchart & Cureton 6-24-62
Galeros Butte,	(V.T./n)	Temple Butte limestone	6499′	Haggert 1- -78
Geikie Peak,	(N.P./s)	Redwall limestone	5004′	Walters, Ohlman, Buccello 12-17-77

Guinevere Castle,	(P.P./n)	Coconino sandstone & Toroweap	7257′	Butchart 8-25-65
Gunther Castle,	(V.T./n)	Supai sandstone	7199′	Butchart, Davis, Doty Ellis 6-4-69
Hall Butte,	(V.T./n)	Supai sandstone	5530′	Ellis party, January 1970
Hancock Butte,	(Nkwp)	Esplanade sandstone	8200+′	Al Doty 10-2-76
Hattan Butte,	(B.A./n)	Supai sandstone	5954′	Ohlman, Hartley 12-19-80
Hawkins Butte,	(V.T./n)	Supai sandstone	5200+′	Ohlman, Kirschvink 11-25-77
Hayden, Mt.,	(Nkwp)	Coconino sandstone	8372′	Rick Petrillo & Bob Sigler 10-69
Hillers Butte,	(B.A./n)	Supai sandstone	5600+′	Ohlman, Kirschvink 4-23-78
Holy Grail Temple,	(P.P./n)	Coconino sandstone	6703′	Trieber & Grubbs, 10-23-76
Horseshoe Mesa,	(V.T./s)	Supai sandstone	5238′	Billingsly, Mitchell, Butchart 12-4-66
Horus Temple,	(B.A./n)	Esplanade sandstone & Hermit shale	6000+′	Haggert, Kronberg & Grubbs 1977
Howlands Butte,	(B.A./n)	Supai sandstone	5571′	Ellis 1--70
Hubbell Butte,	(V.T./n)	Esplanade sandstone	6739′	Butchart, Springorum 4-25-63
Huethawali, Mt.,	(H.P./s)	Coconino sandstone & Toroweap	6275′	William Wallace Bass & tourist before 1900
Hutton Butte,	(Nkwp)	Redwall limestone	6709′	Ohlman, Kirschvink, Smith 3-19-81
Isis Temple,	(B.A./n)	Coconino sandstone	7012′	Doty 9-26-70
Juno Temple,	(V.T./n)	Hermit shale	6800+′	Butchart 9-3-61

Climbers, continued

Name	Map	Kind of Rock	Elevation	First Known Ascent
Jupiter Temple,	(V.T./n)	Hermit shale & Coconino sandstone	7081′	Butchart, Springorum 4-26-63
Kibbey Butte,	(V.T./n)	Hermit shale	7600+′	Allyn Cureton, Butchart 5-31-61
King Arthur's Castle,	(P.P./n)	Coconino sandstone & Toroweap	7326′	Clubb 8-17-61
King Crest,	(P.P./n)	Coconino sandstone & Toroweap	6820′	Doty 10-1-71
Krishna Shrine,	(V.T./n)	Esplanade sandstone	6115′	Butchart 9-5-62
Kwagunt Butte,	(V.T./n)	Coconino sandstone, Toroweap, Kaibab limestone	6377′	Larry Trieber, Dennis Abbink, Jim Haggert & Bruce Grubbs 3-24-79
Lava Butte,	(V.T./n)	Tapeats sandstone	4242′	Butchart, Springorum 6-12-63
Little Pup Pinnacle,	(V.T./s)	Toroweap	7200+′	Trieber, Mark Brown, Scott Kronberg March 1974
Lyell Butte,	(B.A./s)	Supai sandstone	5368′	Doty 1-24-70
Malgosa Crest,	(V.T./n)	Coconino sandstone	5584′	Larry Trieber & Bruce Grubbs March 1975
Manu Temple,	(B.A./n)	Coconino sandstone	7181′	Ellis 1--72
Marsh Butte,	(B.A./s)	Redwall limestone	4400+′	Mitch McCombs, Pete Baertlein 10-29-77

Masonic Temple,	(P.P./n)	Hermit shale	6200′	Al Doty 9-25-80
Mencius Temple,	(B.A./n)	Coconino sandstone & Toroweap	6997′	Stevens & Wallquist 9-3-73
Monument Creek Pinnacle,	(B.A./s)	Trinity Gneiss	3200′	Walt Gregs, Spider Herbert, Bill Trevithick 11-6-72
Nankoweap Butte,	(Nkwp)	Sixtymile Formation	6242′	Butchart 8-28-63
Nankoweap Mesa,	(Nkwp)	Coconino sandstone, Toroweap & Kaibab limestone	5430′	Butchart 8-28-63
Newberry Butte,	(V.T./n)	Temple Butte & Redwall limestone	5104′	Butchart 11-10-63
Newton Butte,	(B.A./s)	Esplanade sandstone & Hermit shale	5912′	Doty
Novinger Butte,	(Nkwp)	Supai sandstone	6800+′	Davis, Butchart 6-15-72
Obi Point,	(B.A./n)	Coconino sandstone & Toroweap	7200′	Doty
O'Neil Butte,	(B.A./s)	Hermit shale	6072′	British Columbia climbers 1962
Osiris Temple,	(B.A./n)	Hermit shale & Coconino sandstone	6637′	Davis 3-13-66
Oza Butte,	(B.A./n)	Kaibab limestone	8065′	Unknown
Pattie Butte,	(B.A./s)	Supai sandstone	5306′	Butchart, Jim David 9-19-61
Pollux Temple,	(H.P./s)	Coconino sandstone & Toroweap	6349′	Doty 1970
Poston Butte,	(V.T./n)	Esplanade sandstone	6600+′	Butchart, Springorum 4-25-63

Climbers, continued

Name	Map	Kind of Rock	Elevation	First Known Ascent
Rama Shrine,	(V.T./n)	Hermit shale	6411′	Butchart 9-22-62
Saddle Mountain,	(Nkwp)	Toroweap	8424′	Powell, Walcott 1880
Scylla Butte,	(H.P./s)	Muav limestone	3600+′	Ohlman, Kirschvink 3-18-78
Sheba Temple,	(V.T./n)	Temple Butte & Redwall limestones	4800′	Butchart 6-3-70
Shiva Temple,	(B.A./n)	Hermit shale, Coconino sandstone, Toroweap and Kaibab limestone	7618′	Emory Kolb 1937
Siegfried Pyre,	(V.T./n)	Coconino sandstone & Toroweap	7914′	Davis, Babb 6-7-70
Sinking Ship,	(V.T./s)	Toroweap & Kaibab limestone	7344′	Butchart, Reider Peterson 9-25-65
Sinyala, Mt.,	(K.P./s)	Coconino sandstone & Toroweap	5434′	U.C.L.A. 1958
Solomon Temple,	(V.T./n)	Temple Butte & Redwall limestones	5070′	Butchart 6-3-70
Steamboat Mountain,	(P.P./n)	Coconino sandstone, Toroweap & Kaibab limestone	7422′	Butchart, Marshall Demick 10-17-64
Sullivan Peak,	(Nkwp)	Coconino sandstone	8200+′	Lee Dexter, Steve Studebaker 10-11-75

Sumner Butte,	(B.A./n)	Redwall limestone	5150′	Chuck Johnson
Swilling Butte,	(V.T./n)	Supai sandstone	6400+′	Butchart, Baxter, Dexter, Walquist, Degelleke 10-13-73
Tabernacle, The,	(V.T./n)	Muau limestone	4830′	Butchart 9-2-61
Temple Butte,	(V.T./n)	Supai & Esplanade sandstones	5308′	Grubbs & Haggerty 1-7-78
Thor Temple,	(V.T./n)	Esplanade sandstone & Hermit shale	6719′	Doty 5-14-77
Tower of Ra,	(B.A./n)	Esplanade sandstone & Hermit shale	6076′	Barbara Zinn, Art Christonson and Jim Haggert 1977
Tower of Set,	(B.A./n)	Esplanade sandstone & Hermit shale	6026′	Haggert, Grubbs 11-20-77
Tritle Peak,	(V.T./n)	Toroweap & Keibab limestone	8400′	Al Doty 10-24-70
Tyndall Dome,	(H.P./s)	Redwall & Muav limestones	4800+′	Doty 5-14-72
Venus Temple,	(V.T./n)	Supai sandstone	6257′	Butchart 7-17-65
Vesta Temple,	(H.P./s)	Coconino sandstone & Toroweap	6000+′	Doty 3-21-70
Vishnu Temple,	(V.T./n)	Supai and Espalade sandstones, Hermit shale, Coconino sandstone, Toroweap	7529′	Merrell Clubb & Son 7-13-45
Wallace Butte,	(N.P./s)	Supai sandstone	5204′	Doty 5-14-72
Whites Butte,	(B.A./n)	Supai sandstone	4871′	Butchart, Cureton 1-1-61

Climbers, continued

Name	Map	Kind of Rock	Elevation	First Known Ascent
Wodo, Mt.,	(S./s)	Coconino sandstone & Toroweap	5130′	Butchart, John Ritchey, Mark Price 2-13-71
Wolf Pinnacle, (or Cardenas Pinnacle)	(V.T./s)	Toroweap	7200+′	See Cardenas Pinnacle
Woolsey Butte,	(Nkwp)	Esplanade sandstone	7200+′	Butchart 7-27-62
Wotan's Throne,	(V.T./n)	Coconino sandstone, Toroweap & Kaibab limestone	7633′	Clubb, July 1946
Zoroaster Temple,	(B.A./n)	Coconino sandstone & Toroweap	7128′	Dave Ganci & Rick Tidrick 9-11-59

Abbreviations

Nkwp	Nankoweap Quadrangle	H.P./n	Havasupai Point Quadrangle (North Rim)
V.T./n	Vishnu Temple Quadrangle (North Rim)	H.P./s	Havasupai Point Quadrangle (South Rim)
V.T./s	Vishnu Temple Quadrangle (South Rim)	S./s	Supai Quadrangel (South Rim only)
B.A./n	Bright Angel Quadrangle (North Rim)	K.P./n	Kanab Point (North Rim)
B.A./s	Bright Angel Quadrangle (South Rim)	K.P./n	Kanab Point (South Rim)
P.P./n	Powell Plateau Quadrangle (North Rim only)	Tkp Cyn	Tuckup Canyon

Bibliography

Books to Read First

Babbitt, Bruce. *Grand Canyon: An Anthology.* Flagstaff, Ariz.: Northland Press, 1978. Governor Bruce Babbitt's anthology is an excellent introduction to what early explorers, historians, and naturalists have written about the subject in the past.

Butchart, J. Harvey. *Grand Canyon Treks I, II, & III.* Glendale, Calif.: La Siesta Press, 1976. These three booklets are must reading for experienced canyoneers interested in following in the footsteps of the Grand Canyon's preeminent canyoneer, J. Harvey Butchart. The booklets primarily address trekking the Canyon's remote, trailless nooks and crannies. These invaluable guides were written with the veteran canyoneer in mind; so don't overestimate your abilities or underestimate Butchart's speed, endurance, and steely calm. (Write La Siesta Press, P.O. Box 406, Glendale, CA 91209.)

Collier, Michael. *An Introduction to Grand Canyon Geology.* Grand Canyon, Ariz.: Grand Canyon Natural History Association, 1980.

Collier's concise and readable book explains the Canyon's mind-boggling geology so even a flatlander can understand it. An excellent crash course.

Crumbo, Kim. *A River Runner's Guide to the History of the Grand Canyon*. Boulder, Colo.: Johnson Publishing, 1981.
Crumbo is a Grand Canyon river ranger who's racked up well over 15,000 miles rafting down the Colorado River. His book is a mile-by-mile guide to the mini-dramas played out by scientists, explorers, and adventurers on the banks of the once-wild Colorado River. The book provides the streamside hiker with many thought-provoking and colorful tales. (If the Grand Canyon Natural History Association is out of Crumbo's guide, write: Johnson Publishing Company, 1880 South 57th Court, Boulder, CO 80301.)

Effland, Richard W., A. Trinkle Jones, and Robert C. Euler. *The Archaeology of Powell Plateau: Regional Interaction at Grand Canyon*. Grand Canyon, Ariz.: Grand Canyon Natural History Association, Monograph No. 3, 1981.
This is a more scientific discussion of the Canyon's archaeology.

Hamblin, W. Kenneth, and Joseph R. Murphy. *Grand Canyon Perspectives: A Guide to the Canyon Scenery by Means of Interpretive Panoramas*. Provo, Utah: Brigham Young University Geology Studies, Special Publications No. 1, 1969.

This informative text will help you plot your course both above and below the rim, and the superb line drawings add visual perspective to both Hughes's and Collier's books.

Hughes, J. Donald. *In the House of Stone and Light.* Grand Canyon, Ariz.: Grand Canyon Natural History Association, 1978.
This is an updated and retitled version of former park ranger-naturalist Hughes's *The Story of Man at the Grand Canyon*. Hughes's colorful tales and annotated text provide without question the best all-around history of man and the Grand Canyon.

Jones, Anne Trinkle, and Robert C. Euler. *A Sketch of Grand Canyon Prehistory*. Grand Canyon, Ariz.: Grand Canyon Natural History Association, 1979.
If you're fascinated by the Canyon's prehistoric settlement, this informative, easily read overview of Grand Canyon anthropology and archaeology is not to be missed.

Mitchell, Rodger. *Grand Canyon Jeep Trails I*. Glendale, Calif.: La Siesta Press, 1977.
This is the only guide that describes access points into the remote Shivwits Plateau country of the western Grand Canyon, on that Australian-style frontier known as the Arizona Strip. (Write: La Siesta Press, P.O. Box 406, Glendale, CA 91209.)

Spanner, Earle E., ed. *Bibliography of the Grand Canyon and the Lower Colorado River*. Grand Canyon,

Ariz.: Grand Canyon Natural History Association, Monograph No. 2, 1981.
This is *the* Grand Canyon bibliography—covering periodicals, series, theses, dissertations, popular works, geography, geology, hydrology, ecology, archaeology, history, maps and charts, and miscellaneous entries.

Stevens, Larry. *The Colorado River in Grand Canyon: A Guide*. Flagstaff, Ariz.: Red Lake Books, 1983.
While this is actually a river guide, written, illustrated, and produced for river runners, it is also the best field guide to the riparian habitat of the inner Canyon. (If the Grand Canyon Natural History Association is out of Stevens's guide, write: Red Lake Books, P.O. Box 1315, Flagstaff, AZ 86002.)

Whitney, Stephen. *A Field Guide to the Grand Canyon*. New York: William Morrow, 1982.
Whitney offers a comprehensive overview of the Canyon's natural history. The book has a wealth of color illustrations, black-and-white drawings, and detailed (though capsulized) descriptions that will help you identify nearly every species of bird, wildflower, cactus, mammal, reptile, amphibian, butterfly, tree and shrub, fern, rock, and fish.

The Grand Canyon Natural History Association is a nonprofit corporation whose primary goal is to assist the National Park Service at the Grand Canyon in programs of interpretation, education, and research. By becoming a member, you can support these goals, obtain a 20 percent discount on all interpretive items purchased from the association, and receive its biweekly newsletter. Annual membership is only $3 for individuals and $10 for organizations, and if that's not the best deal going, I don't know what is.

For a complete list of books and pamphlets available through the Grand Canyon Natural History Association, send a self-addressed stamped envelope to: Grand Canyon Natural History Association, P.O. Box 399, Grand Canyon, AZ 86023. Or browse through their well-stocked bookstore, located at the Visitor Center on the South Rim. Hours are 7:15 A.M. to 6:30 P.M. daily.

Supplemental Reading

Annerino, John. "Climbing in the Grand Canyon: A Historical Introduction Combined with a Personal Account of the Climbing Possibilities in the Grand Canyon of the Colorado River, Arizona. With an Appended Table of Summits within the Canyon Confines." *Mountain* 77 (January/February 1981): 15, 25–35.

Baars, Donald L. *The Colorado Plateau: A Geologic History*. Albuquerque: University of New Mexico Press, 1983.

Bartlett, K. "How Don Pedro de Tovar Discovered the Hopi and Garcia Lopez de Cardenas Saw the Grand

Canyon, with Notes upon Probable Route." *Plateau* 12 (1940): 37–45.

Breed, William J., and Evelyn Roat, eds. *The Geology of the Grand Canyon*, 2nd ed. Flagstaff: Museum of Northern Arizona and the Grand Canyon Natural History Association, 1976.

Brown, B. T., S. W. Carothers, and R. Roy Johnson. *Birds of the Grand Canyon Region*. Tucson: University of Arizona Press, in press.

Casanova, Frank E. "Trails to Supai in Cataract Canyon." *Plateau* 39 (1967): 124–130.

Colton, Harold S. *Black Sand*. Flagstaff, Ariz.: Northland Press.

——. "Prehisoric Trade in the Southwest." *Plateau*

——. "Principal Hopi Trails." *Plateau* 32 (1959): 91–94.

Coues, Elliott. *On the Trail of the Spanish Pioneers: The Diary and Itinerary of the Francisco Garces*. New York: Harper, 1900.

Cushing, F. H. "The Nation of Willows." *Atlantic Monthly* 50 (1882): 362–374, 541–549.

Dobyns, Henry F., and Robert C. Euler. "A Brief History of the Northeastern Pai." *Plateau* 32 (1959): 49–57.

Eiseman, F. B. "The Hopi Salt Trail." *Plateau* 32 (1959): 25–32.

Euler, Robert C. "The Canyon Dwellers." *American West* 4 (1967): 2.

———. "Future Archaeological Research in the Grand Canyon." *Plateau* 46 (1974): 4.

———. "Willow Figurines from Arizona." *Natural History* 75 (1966): 3.

———, and Susan M. Chandler. "Aspects of Prehistoric Settlement Patterns at Grand Canyon." In Robert C. Euler and George J. Gummerman, eds., *Investigations of the Southwestern Anthropological Research Group*. Flagstaff: Museum of Northern Arizona, 1978, pp. 73–86.

———, George J. Gummerman, et al. "The Colorado Plateaus: Cultural Dynamics and Paleoenvironment." *Science* 205 (1979): 1089–1101.

———, and Alan P. Olsen. "Split-Twig Figurines from Northern Arizona: New Radio-Carbon Dates." *Science* 148 (1965): 3669.

———, and Frank Tikalsky, et al. *The Grand Canyon: Up Close & Personal*. Dillon: Western Montana College Foundation, 1980.

Farguhar, Francis. *The Books of the Colorado River and the Grand Canyon*. Los Angeles: Glen Dawson, 1953.

Farmer, Malcolm F. "The Mojave Trade Route." *Masterkey* 9 (1935): 155–157.

Fowler, Don D., Robert C. Euler, and Catherine S. Fowler. *John Wesley Powell and the Anthropology of the Canyon Country*. U.S. Geological Survey Professional Paper 670. Washington, D.C.: U.S. Government Printing Office, 1969.

Fradkin, Philip L. *A River No More*. New York: Knopf, 1981.

Garrett, W. E. "The Grand Canyon." *National Geographic* 154 (1978): 2–15.

———. "Grand Canyon, Are We Loving It to Death?" *National Geographic* 154 (1978): 16–51.

Garth, J. S. *Butterflies of Grand Canyon National Park*. Grand Canyon, Ariz.: Grand Canyon Natural History Association, 1950.

Granger, Byrd H. *Grand Canyon Place Names*. Tucson: University of Arizona Press, 1960.

Hamblin, W. Kenneth, and J. Keith Rigby. *Guidebook to the Colorado River: Parts 1 and 2*. Provo, Utah: Brigham Young University, Department of Geology, 1968–69.

Heald, W. F., and R. Patties. *Inverted Mountains*. New York: Vanguard, 1948.

Hoffmeister, D. F. *Mammals of the Grand Canyon*. Urbana: University of Illinois Press, 1971.

James, G. Wharton. *In and Around the Grand Canyon: The Grand Canyon of the Colorado River in Arizona*. Boston: Little, Brown, 1901.

Jones, A. Trinkle. "Agricultural Systems at Grand Canyon: Walhalla Glades." Masters thesis, Arizona State University, 1983.

____. "Excavation of Five Sites Along the Colorado River in Grand Canyon." Tucson, Ariz.: Western Archaeological and Conservation Center, Publications in Anthropology No. 28, 1985.

Karlstrom, Thor N. V., Gordon A. Swann, and Raymond L. Eastwood, eds. *Geology of Northern Arizona with Notes on Archaeology and Paleoclimate*. Flagstaff: Northern Arizona University and Geological Society of America, Rocky Mountain Section, Part I, Regional Studies, 1974.

Lavender, David. *Colorado River Country*. New York: Dutton, 1982.

____. *River Runners of the Grand Canyon*. Grand Canyon, Ariz.: Grand Canyon Natural History Association, 1985.

Maurer, Stephen G. *Solitude and Sunshine*. Boulder, Colo.: Pruett, 1983.

McDougall, W. B. *Seed Plants of Northern Arizona*. Flagstaff: Museum of Northern Arizona, 1973.

McKee, Edwin. "On Canyon Trails." *Grand Canyon Nature Notes* 8 (1933): 173–177, 191–194.

McPhee, J. *Encounters with the Archdruid*. New York: Farrar, Straus, and Giroux, 1971.

Mead, J. I. "The Last 30,000 Years of Faunal History Within the Grand Canyon, Arizona." *Quaternary Research* 15 (1981): 311–326.

Miller, D. M., et al. *Amphibians and Reptiles of the Grand Canyon Region*. Grand Canyon, Ariz.: Grand Canyon Natural History Association, Monograph No. 4, 1982.

Minckley, W. *Fishes of Arizona*. Phoenix: Arizona Game and Fish Commission, 1973.

Morris, Larry A. *Hiking the Grand Canyon and Havasupai*. Tucson, Ariz.: AZTEX, 1981.

Nutt, Katherine F. *Grand Canyon and the Colorado Plateau: A Bibliography of Selected Titles in the NAU Libraries*. Flagstaff: Northern Arizona University Libraries, Discovery Series No. 14, 1978.

Ortiz, Alfonso, ed. *Handbook of North American Indians, Southwest, Vol. 10*. Washington, D.C.: Smithsonian Institution, 1983.

Powell, J. W. *The Exploration of the Colorado River and Its Canyons*. New York: Dover, 1961.

Rahm, David A. *Reading the Rocks*. San Francisco: Sierra Club Books, 1974.

Rusho, W. L., and C. G. Crampton. *Desert River Crossing*. Salt Lake City, Utah: Peregrine Smith, 1975.

Schwartz, Douglas W. "The Havasupai 600 A.D.—1955 A.D.: A Short Culture History." *Plateau* 28 (1956): 77–85.

———, Jane Kepp, and Richard C. Chapman. *Archaeology of the Grand Canyon: The Walhalla Plateau*. Grand Canyon Archaeological Series, Vol. 3. Santa Fe, N. Mex.: School of American Research Press, 1981.

Sierra Club Guides to the National Parks. *Desert Southwest*. New York: Stewart, Tabori, & Chang, 1984.

Simmons, Leo W. *Sun Chief*. New Haven, Conn.: Yale University Press, 1942.

Stanton, Robert Brewster. *Colorado River Controversies*. Boulder City, Nev.: Westwater Books, 1982.

Thomson, Barry. *The Enchanted Light*. Flagstaff: Museum of Northern Arizona, 1979.

Thybony, Scott. *A Guide to Hiking the Inner Canyon*. Grand Canyon, Ariz.: Grand Canyon Natural History Association, 1980.

Tillotson, M. R., and F. J. Taylor. *Grand Canyon Country*. Stanford, Calif.: Stanford University Press, 1929.

Titiev, M. "A Hopi Salt Expedition." *American Anthropologist* 39 (1937): 244–258.

Tower, Donald B. "The Use of Marine Mollusca and Their Value in Reconstructing Prehistoric Trade Routes in the American Southwest." *Papers of the Excavator's Club* 2 (1945).

Turner, R. M., and M. M. Karpiscak. *Recent Vegetation Changes Along the Colorado River between Glen Canyon Dam and Lake Mead, Arizona*. U.S. Geological Survey Professional Paper 1132. Washington, D.C.: U.S. Government Printing Office, 1980.

Utah Historical Quarterly 37 (Spring 1969).

VanMatre, Steve, and Bill Weiler, eds. *The Earth Speaks: An Acclimatization Journal*. Warrenville, Ill.: Institute for Earth Education, 1983.

Walker, Herb. *Butch Cassidy: The Congenial Desperado*. Amarillo, Tex.: Baxter Lane, 1975.

Wampler, Joseph. *Havasupai, A Canyon Home*. Berkeley, Calif.: Wampler, 1981.

Index